THE MADHOUSE OF LANGUAGE

Writing and reading madness in the eighteenth century

Allan Ingram

London and New York

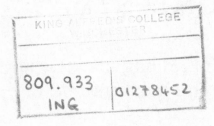
First published 1991
by Routledge
11 New Fetter Lane, London EC4P 4EE

Simultaneously published in the USA and Canada
by Routledge
a division of Routledge, Chapman and Hall, Inc.
29 West 35th Street, New York, NY 10001

© 1991, Allan Ingram

Set in 10/12 pt Bembo by Selectmove
Printed and bound in Great Britain by
TJ Press (Padstow) Ltd, Padstow, Cornwall

British Library Cataloguing in Publication Data
Ingram, Allan
The madhouse of language: writing and
reading madness in the eighteenth century.
1. Linguistics
I. Title
410

Library of Congress Cataloging in Publication Data
also available

ISBN 0–415–03190–7

CONTENTS

ACKNOWLEDGEMENTS

I have been fortunate during the writing of this book to receive help from generous friends and colleagues who have read and advised, have introduced me to material of which I was unaware, and have generally been unstinting in their encouragement. I should particularly like to thank Jane Armstrong, Jill Fenwick and Jan Hewitt for their respective parts in helping the work to a conclusion, and also Lesley Gordon and Robert Firth of Newcastle University Library for access to and assistance with the Pybus Collection. I am most grateful, finally, to Roy Porter, who read my chapters in manuscript. His interest and expert response were invaluable supports in seeing my way to the end. Where I have drifted into waywardness, however, I have only myself to blame.

Newcastle upon Tyne   Allan Ingram

1

INTRODUCTION: TO BUILD A HOUSE FOR FOOLS AND MAD

In the early hours of the morning of Friday, 7 November 1788, after two days of delirium, George III arose from his bed and walked into the next room to find a conference of his sons, his physicians, his equerries and his pages. He expressed amazement and consternation. He demanded to know the meaning of the gathering. He grew angry, and publicly berated his personal physician, Sir George Baker, penning him into a corner and calling him an old woman whose advice he never should have followed. No one had the temerity to intervene until at last one of those present, a Mr Fairly, took him by the arm and got him back to bed.[1]

There was no escaping the magnitude of the disaster.

> Here, then, was the turning point. This was the precise moment when ceased the dominion of a Sovereign over his subjects, and when began, on the contrary, the dominion of sound minds over an unsound one. Here, then, let History pause.[2]

Before his recovery, many more violent means were to be adopted in order to keep him in his bed, or to subdue his agitations, including medicines, blisters, the strait-waistcoat and the restraining-chair.

George's first bout of serious mental illness began properly in October 1788, at Windsor, and lasted through a winter of confinement at Kew until March 1789. The acknowledgement of a mad king on the throne of England brought many issues into play, and there were many other 'pauses' during the crisis. Not least, the government of the country was thrown into a state of perpetual pause, with the Prince of Wales and Opposition figures like Burke, Fox and Sheridan intriguing for a Regency, while the Prime Minister, Pitt, and other ministry figures waited in the hope

1

of a complete recovery. Yet recourse to a regency itself suffered from pause, as William Grenville noted:

> No Regent can be appointed or authorized to exercise acts of royal authority but by Act of Parliament; nor can any such Act be valid and binding in law without the King's consent. . . . It is a heavy calamity that is inflicted upon us in any case except that of his perfect recovery; but in the event which there seems most ground to fear, it may give rise to serious and difficult questions, such as cannot even be discussed without shaking the security and tranquillity of the country.[3]

At least one of the royal physicians, Dr Richard Warren, was known to support the Prince of Wales and to have, therefore, an interest in the king's continuing insanity, though Baker and others were simply at a loss as to how to diagnose or treat the illness, or even how to approach their patient. The constitutional pause was mirrored by a professional and medical one, which was itself complicated by a pause in propriety. Accustomed to receive orders when called in to a royal consultation, physicians had no precedent for prescribing, still less for enforcing instructions of their own. Warren had to form his first opinion of the royal state of mind by listening at a keyhole when George refused to see him. Early in the crisis, Fanny Burney, then a lady-in-waiting to the queen, recorded: 'It seems, but Heaven, avert it! a threat of a total breaking up of the constitution.'[4] Her concern is for the king's health, but she automatically expresses it in terms that reflect the threat to the political sanity of the entire nation.

One of the earliest signs of the impending collapse was George's 'incessant loquaciousness'.[5] Fanny Burney reported on Saturday, 25 October, that 'He spoke, with a manner so uncommon, that a high fever alone could account for it; a rapidity, a hoarseness of voice, a volubility, an earnestness – a vehemence, rather – it startled me inexpressibly.'[6] Ironically (and the crisis is as full of ironies as of pauses), while Grenville refrained from even discussing the madness issue for fear of 'shaking the security and tranquillity of the country', and the royal physicians struggled to discover the proper address to an unsound royal mind, the king talked himself into hoarseness. His 'ramblings', records Robert Fulke Greville, a royal equerry, 'continued, and were more wild than before, amounting alas to an almost total suspension of reason – No sleep this Night –

The Talking incessant throughout'.[7] At times the king spoke with an almost Shakespearian sense of enigma:

> I am not ill, but I am nervous: if you would know what is the matter with me, I am nervous. But I love you both very well; if you would tell me the truth: I love Dr Heberden best, for he has not told me a lie: Sir George has told me a lie – a white lie, he says, but I hate a white lie! If you will tell me a lie, let it be a black lie![8]

As his illness progressed, the ramblings became more indecent, with constant allusion to Lady Elizabeth, Countess of Pembroke. He worried, too, about the imminent flooding of London, and he called upon his youngest daughter (then aged 5) to save him from his tormentors.

As the king's language became wilder and less restrained, those around him, and those at the head of the nation, became more and more cautious over every word they let out. 'Rex noster insanit', wrote Warren, confidentially, to Lady Spencer.[9] Sheridan, in a letter to J.W. Payne concerning a proposed statement from the Prince of Wales, pointed out: 'Every syllable of *the Declaration* will be canvass'd and all sort of *meaning* discovered in every syllable.'[10] The *Morning Post* reported on an attempt by 'one of the leaders of Opposition . . . to induce the Conductors of the Public Prints not to mention the illness of the KING'.[11] Dr John Willis, in attendance day and night, maintained discretion even in his private journal, reducing his record of the application of the strait-waistcoat to the decency of '&c'.[12] But it is in the daily health bulletins, released by the physicians from Kew, that the delicacy of the language issue is most sharply focused. On the state of the king's health depended not only the professional reputations of the physicians, but the prospects for a regency. Each word, then, was weighed in the scales of professional and political rivalry. On the morning of 16 December, for example, Francis Willis (father to John) proposed the wording 'a very good night' after the king had slept for six hours. However,

> The 6 hours sleep was composed of 3 different sleeps. Upon which Sir L. Pepys said, 'you see Dr Willis, do what you will, you cannot make it a good night without splicing'. Dr Willis would only sign to very good night. Sir G. Baker would not sign to the word *very*.

The bulletin, signed by all three men, eventually read: 'His Majesty had a very good night having had six hours sleep.'[13] Willis's reputation moved up a couple of syllables, Baker's down, and a regency became a fraction less likely.

The whole crisis was complicated still further by the compelling figure of Francis Willis. When the royal physicians failed to make any progress, despite frequent additions to their number, desperate measures were recognised as necessary. Willis was not a regular doctor, not orthodox, hardly respectable. He was a clergyman turned madhouse keeper from Lincolnshire, already in his seventies, with a reputation for 'breaking in' patients. When proper professional address failed, the professionals agreed to try someone they did not even regard as a medical man. And Willis's approach was quite different from Warren taking notes through the keyhole, or Baker suffering ignominious verbal abuse from an unsettled sovereign.

> His usually friendly and smiling expression changed its char-
> acter when he first met a patient. He suddenly became a
> different figure commanding the respect even of maniacs.
> His piercing eye seemed to read their hearts and divine their
> thoughts as they formed. In this way he gained control over
> them which he used as a means of cure.[14]

Language, in Willis's approach, was secondary. The eye was the medium of address, not the voice, though the eye achieved its supremacy by seeming to 'read' the patient himself. Willis was quite capable, however, of utilising language as part of his treatment.

> Dr Willis had the King confined to his Chair this Morning for
> a short time, & gave Him a severe lecture on his improper
> conversation, Eliza, &c.; H. My. becoming more loud &
> impatient under this Lecture, Dr Willis ordered a Handkerchief
> to be held before his Mouth, & He then continued & finished
> his Lecture.[15]

Language, though, is made to support an entire regimen in which subordination of the patient is paramount – physical confinement, mental surveillance, linguistic restraint. Willis *lectures* the king on his conversation. Language is used to subdue language, but depends for its efficacy both on Willis's insight into the patient's mind and on his employment of the restraining-chair and the gag.

When Willis and his team of sons and keepers entered the corridors of the royal mind, they brought the management of madness to the very centre of national consciousness. Private madhouses had been in existence since at least the seventeenth century, and had developed throughout the eighteenth, unregulated until the Act of 1774 (which related only to houses within a seven-mile radius of London). They offered confinement for usually only a few patients whose family could afford to be relieved of a public embarrassment. James Boswell's elder brother John spent most of his life in a private madhouse in Newcastle, paid for by his father, the Scottish law lord, Lord Auchinleck. Medical, or semi-medical, treatment was also provided.[16] Suddenly, in December 1788, the private world of discreetly concealed lunacy was in the public domain. The royal palace at Kew had itself become a house of madness, complete with mad-doctor, strong attendants, restraining apparatus, and a raving madman who really was king of England.

The crisis of 1788-9 was a personal one, for the king apparently came close to death during the early part of his illness, and, once recovered, never forgot the treatment to which he had been subjected. It was a political crisis, and also a medical one. It raised issues of power and authority. What happens to constitutional power when the head is deranged? How should the balance of power between physician and patient be understood, between mad-doctor and madman, now that psychiatry had been invited in from the cold? But it also brought into focus an issue which will be the subject of this book: the relationship between the power of insanity and the authority of language.

One of the most influential books to be written this century on the subject of madness is Foucault's *Madness and Civilization: A History of Insanity in the Age of Reason*.[17] Foucault argues two major theses: that madness during the age of reason was subjected to an increasingly rigorous physical confinement, and that what madness had to say for itself was effectively reduced to silence. The first of these claims has been largely invalidated by the researches of more recent historians of madness: with only around 5,000 people estimated as inmates of asylums by 1800, the eighteenth century in England cannot properly be regarded as the age of 'The Great Confinement'.[18] But confinement does not need to be physical to be effective. For Foucault, madness in the eighteenth century was permitted no language because it had nothing to say. It was heard to be speaking only its own 'scandal' and to the ears of reason had therefore no special truth to communicate. While the religiously inspired madman or woman, or the witty fool, of earlier periods was granted a privileged role within the social framework, and thereby retained a voice in the acknowledged discourse of sanity, a more rational age heard nothing but the threat of impending 'unreason' in the unrecognised logic of the mad. Foucault's exploration of the discourse of madness, its structures and imperatives, its parody of the forms of reason in the face of reason's obstinate inattentiveness, is the history of a resolute linguistic repression.

Foucault regarded discourse as historically located, and insisted on dealing with discursive practices rather than with general descriptions of discourse. We are enabled to speak of certain subjects at certain times because certain discursive practices allow us the language and freedom to do so.[19] I propose to examine the language of the mad between the late seventeenth and the early nineteenth centuries, both the accounts of madness produced by madmen and former madmen like Alexander Cruden and Urbane Metcalf, and the poetry and more acknowledged literary productions of, for example, Cowper and Smart. In order to do so, however, I shall spend some time in providing a linguistic and medical context for the discursive practices of the eighteenth-century mad. George Rosen, in 1967, argued for the importance of context in conducting medical history:

> to view health and its problems within a societal context rather than as defined by the professional interests of physicians, it becomes necessary to learn about people with whom the healers at any given period are concerned. This involves the ascertainment as far as feasible of population structure and change, modes of life, occupations, social organization, including such matters as the social position of women.[20]

Such a broad context is beyond my reach. But no less demanding is the context provided by contemporary linguistic practice. The editors of *The Anatomy of Madness* argue that

> the recognition and interpretation of mental illness, indeed its whole meaning, are culture-bound, and change profoundly from epoch to epoch, in ways inexplicable unless viewed within wider contexts of shifting power relations, social pressures, and ideological interests.[21]

Language, above all, remains from earlier periods as a measure of social, ideological and psychological contexts for the exploration of madness. Ways of being mad are held 'to show most clearly the cultural, social, and ideological factors which influence definitions and perceptions of disease and constrain the behaviour of both patients and their doctors'.[22] The language in which madness is discussed – its structures, its devices, its silences – is a key to such factors.

The first part of this study will concern itself with the question: what forms of expression already existed for talking and thinking about madness? In Chapters 2 and 3 I shall give a survey of attitudes to the causes and cure of madness in the works of some of the more significant theoreticians and practitioners of the period, and in Chapter 4 will turn to closer analysis of the expression of attitudes towards the mad in literary and semi-literary works. This will involve looking beyond medical books and pamphlets to a range of contemporary writing – essays, journals, correspondence, conversation, legal opinion, and also the works of recognised writers, including satirists like Swift and Pope and novelists like Smollett and Godwin. These chapters will provide a linguistic context for the subsequent discussion of mad writing. In understanding something of the models, the forms and rhetoric of seeing madness in the eighteenth century, in listening to what can be said about it, and to what is avoided, we shall find one edge of what it was possible to say when attempting to give voice to the actual experience of madness.

To take just one example, Thomas Willis's *Cerebri Anatome*, published in 1665, began to develop our ideas about the workings of the nervous system, and in doing so influenced not only Locke's theories of perception as propounded in *An Essay Concerning Human Understanding*, but also successive generations of doctors and patients over the next century for whom 'nerves' became available for suffering and cure.[23] Willis also replaced the older language of humours and balances with a new rhetoric. He developed, along with the system that was to become neurology, images of motion, excitement, distillation, flowing and radiance, and thus sanctioned an idiom as well as a medical condition. Here, then, is one framework in place for talking about madness, and it is exploited for satiric purposes by Swift and Sterne, just as it is picked up by writers searching for ways to express genuine derangement.

So James Boswell can speak of his mind being in 'high and fine flow of thought', of its capacity to 'melt and refine', but also of its tendency to take on opposite qualities, to be 'smoky', to 'blacken', to present gloomy and stagnant views, to show 'a cloud as far as he can perceive' which 'will be charged with thicker vapour, the longer it continues'.[24]

Foucault and Locke work over similar ground in exploring the relation between madness and the formal and rational aspects of language. Foucault wrote that 'Language is the first and last structure of madness, its constituent form; on language are based all the cycles in which madness articulates its nature.'[25] In assenting to this we should not deny the existence of madness as something that is also beyond the framework of a linguistic construct. The experience of pain and of mental suffering must always proceed in a region that is remote from language, even if the sufferer attempts to retrieve that experience through the medium of language. It is at the point of expression that the critic or historian is entitled to take an interest. Locke, too, in distinguishing between madmen and idiots, put 'idiots' beyond the reach of language by grouping them with 'brutes': they 'make very few or no propositions, and reason scarce at all'. Madmen, however, 'put wrong ideas together, and so make wrong propositions, but argue and reason right from them'. In this they 'suffer by the other extreme' from idiots.[26] Once the power of reason is granted, the articulations of madness can no longer be regarded as ravings or rambling, but become available as linguistic acts to be read and understood within a system of grammar, and within a social system, just like any other.

Basil Bernstein, in taking Chomsky to task, refuses to sever 'the relationship between the formal properties of the grammar and the meanings which are realized in its use'. This is because in studying 'la parole' we are inevitably 'involved in a study of rules, formal and informal, which regulate the options we take up in various contexts in which we find ourselves'. And he goes on to discuss the relationship between the 'linguistic rule system' and the 'culture system'. Language, he suggests,

> is a set of rules to which all speech codes must comply, but which speech codes are realized is a function of the culture acting through social relationships in specific contexts. Different speech forms or codes symbolize the form of the social relationship, regulate the nature of the speech

encounters, and create for the speakers different orders of relevance and relation. The experience of the speakers is then transformed by what is made significant or relevant by the speech form.

At the same time, there will be conditions under which a given speech form will be able to

> free itself sufficiently from its embodiment in the social structure so that the system of meanings it realizes points to alternative realities, alternative arrangements in the affairs of men. Here we become concerned immediately with the antecedents and consequences of the boundary maintaining principles of a culture or subculture.[27]

The linguistic acts of the mad depend, on one side, on the specific context of a social system, and on another on the linguistic rule system to which speech in that social system must comply. Where they are unique is in the imperatives for expression being themselves unacknowledged by that social system, even if language should prove to be capable of accommodating their utterances without infringement of the rules of grammar. To this extent, Bernstein's 'alternative realities' both govern the formation of the speech acts and are disturbingly liberated in their production.

This is illustrated in the writing of a patient of the early nineteenth century, James Tilley Matthews. Confined in Bethlem Hospital, Matthews, according to John Haslam, the Bethlem apothecary, who reported the case in *Illustrations of Madness*, began a 'decree' to the world by asserting his own authority: 'James, Absolute, Sole, & Supreme Sacred Omni Imperious . . . Arch Sovereign . . . Arch-Emperor . . .'. The resources of language and language structure are being stretched in order to give some degree of satisfactory expression to the writer's sense of his own worth, and subsequently, of the outrageous injustices he has undergone. The same kind of stretching is there in his description of suffering and torture: 'foot-curving, lethargy-making, spark-exploding, knee-nailing, burning out, eye-screwing, sight-screwing, roof-stringing, vital-tearing, fibre-ripping'.[28] This is language used at a high level of inventiveness, and achieving a distinctive yet compelling expressiveness. An alternative reality, based in strongly felt and deeply resented personal suffering, impels the construction of this writing yet finds no necessity to depart from what is grammatically possible in the search for ways to express itself.

The strength of language of the mad, the success with which it is able to liberate 'alternative arrangements in the affairs of men', is one decisive reason for Foucault's conspiracy of inattention imposed by reason on the discourse of unreason. But for Foucault, 'expressiveness' is not itself a meaningful term. The writings and speech of the mad no more express what is within them than the works of the canonised writers are acts of conscious self-realisation raised to the level of art in, for example, the Romantic lyric. The discourses of the mad, like the discourses of a Wordsworth or a Browning, are made possible by the 'discursive practices' within that society, and as individuals they are neither expressed by them nor, ultimately, responsible for them. Indeed, in *Madness and Civilization*, the instilling into the mad of a sense of responsibility for their own madness is seen as yet another stratagem deployed by reason to silence the discourse of the unreasonable.

Here, Foucault is sharply at odds with Locke, who devotes a long section of the *Essay Concerning Human Understanding* to a consideration of personal identity and selfhood. For Locke, 'consciousness' is the crucial quality. A *'person'*, he argues,

is a thinking intelligent being that has reason and reflection and can consider itself as itself, the same thinking thing in different times and places; which it does only by that consciousness which is inseparable from thinking and, as it seems to me, essential to it: it being impossible for anyone to perceive without perceiving that he does perceive.

This fundamental sense of personality, of individuality, carries with it inevitable implications for the self's responsibility for the self.

In this *personal identity* is founded all the right and justice of reward and punishment: happiness and misery being that for which everyone is concerned for *himself*, not mattering what becomes of any substance not joined to or affected with that consciousness.[29]

Locke develops the view that as individuals we are responsible for our own identities: we become ourselves through the perceptions and experiences we as individuals undergo. To this extent, madness is caused not, say, by an imbalance in the humours of the body, but by some delusion that arises within the bounds of our own identities. It is all that we are that makes us mad, and all that we have been.

This is particularly the case with our capacity for rational thought, and consequently for the expression of our ideas. Beasts, for example, may have 'fit organs to frame articulate sounds' and can 'pronounce words distinctly enough' but do so without 'application'. Men that are dumb, on the other hand, find ways of expressing ideas 'by signs which serve them instead of general words'. Madmen are mad, for Locke, because 'the violence of their imaginations' makes them take 'their fancies for realities'. They have not 'lost the faculty of reasoning', but rather they 'err as men do that argue right from wrong principles'.[30] Not only, therefore, are madmen responsible for their own error, but they are also as capable as any sane man of expressing the ideas that are operating powerfully upon them.

The differences between Locke and Foucault are, of course, manifold, and my purpose is not to adjudicate between two intellectual giants. Rather, I wish to take from Locke the principle that for the eighteenth century the articulations of the mad could be regarded as an expression of that madness, albeit dismissible as meaningless because based entirely on error, and from Foucault the insistence on understanding the discourse of the mad within the context of current discursive practices. Foucault, in fact, broadens discourse from the linguistic to include the language of the body: such discourse, he says, 'is both the silent language by which the mind speaks to itself in the truth proper to it, and the visible articulation in the movements of the body.'[31]

Here we encounter a problem about the recovery of mad discourse. If we are unable to recover 'the movements of the body' that are, if not part of the discourse of madness, then at least part of the context for that discourse, are we ever likely to understand the language as spoken by the mad? Of course, the language to be dealt with is for the most part in the form of written productions, and when it is spoken (like George III's remarks about white and black lies) it is available only because it has been committed to writing, usually by a third person. This in itself presents problems. If we are dealing with third-person reports, as we are with John Haslam's account of James Tilley Matthews, can we properly claim to be in touch with the discourse of the mad? Even when using the texts of madmen, we frequently find that their accounts were produced after the event, and were written with a specific purpose, often to protest at wrongful confinement (such is Alexander Cruden's *The London-Citizen Exceedingly Injured*), or else to expose the conditions prevailing within madhouses (as Urbane Metcalf's *The Interior of Bethlehem Hospital*). Do we regard these as sane accounts recollecting madness, or as madness still in progress?

Perhaps mad poems, like those of James Carkesse, best represent the authentic voice of the mad. Here, though, we come across a particular problem of mad writing: how far does the order of written English (at its most demanding in the forms and requirements of poetry) actually order madness into prearranged patterns that violate the primal experience of madness? If the forms of poetry, even for the eighteenth century, have the tendency to render ordered the experience of vision, inspiration, passion, is it in fact possible to write a mad poem? Conversely, if, as Foucault claims, the patterns of mad discourse share the logical ordering of so-called reasonable discourse,[32] is it possible to regard any writing at all as convincingly sane? Must we not know the context of any man's writing – his personality, the movements of his body, what his neighbours think and say about him – before we can be satisfied that his writing is not that of a madman? Or, is it possible to pronounce our neighbour convincingly sane until we have read what he has committed to paper? Roy Porter recounts the history of Goodwin Wharton, who died in 1704, an MP for fourteen years, JP, a Lord of the Admiralty and Knight of the Shire, but also a man who for nearly twenty years kept up an autobiographical account of his courtship by Queen Penelope, queen of the fairies, and of his protracted dealings with rival fairy dukes and the fairy Pope. He also received messages through angelic presences, and was to be guided to the hiding places of vast hordes of treasure by the spirit of Cardinal Wolsey.[33]

The eighteenth century's obsession with madness was not, in fact, simply the desire to silence the alternative discourses of unreason. Behind the impulse to restrain was a very real fear of the terrifying proximity of insanity. The satirists' preoccupation with the difference between outside and inside easily translates into the pressing need to distinguish between sane and insane. The novelists' interests in narrative and character are attempts to find meaning and consistency in human consciousness and identity. Swift's concern for establishing the English language upon firm principles was a first line of defence against an anarchy that would threaten the very means whereby the mind was able to convince itself that it exerted control over its own ends.

Language has been described as a prison house.[34] One of the purposes of this book will be to explore the extent to which it is, rather, a madhouse. Queen Charlotte, in the midst of her husband's madness, complained of the disagreements between his physicians that they were 'sufficient to disturb the whole house, & the world too'.[35] The discourses of the so-called sane are experienced by her as part of the same structure of disturbance, torment, suffering, madness, as the so-called insane. The discourse of the sane is as much a construction of individual self-interest, narrowness, blindness and error as the thoughtless loquacity of the king. The Palace of Kew has become the meeting-place for sanity and insanity, a model of the intertextuality that is the world's reading of madness, that is madness's writing of the world. The language that is the natural medium for the one offers itself, the promise and security of its structures, the shape and colour of its richness, equally to the other. 'Meaningless disorder as madness is,' says Foucault, 'it reveals, when we examine it, only ordered classifications, rigorous mechanisms in soul and body, language articulated according to a visible logic.'[36] The 'house' of madness is the structure afforded by language, and especially by the language of literary form, in which madness can retrieve itself, or retrieve something that is nearly itself, for, as John Perceval, who spent several years in asylums in the 1830s, remarked, words acquire slightly different meanings in madness.[37]

By a supreme irony, legal history was made when Thomas Erskine, the future Lord Chancellor, defending James Hadfield after his attempt on the life of George III in 1800, so eloquently expounded on the nature of madness (it has been called 'one of the ablest and most lucid pleadings of all time')[38] that Hadfield's trial was halted and the jury directed to find him 'Not Guilty; he being under the influence of Insanity at the time the act was committed', in spite of all the appearance of rationality in Hadfield's bearing and conversation. Legal language was capable of proving mad the man who tried to murder the king who had himself been mad, and who would end his life in madness. Hadfield was sent to Bethlem Hospital, after the passing of an Act for the Safe Custody of Insane Persons charged with Offences. There he joined Margaret Nicholson, imprisoned during the king's pleasure for an attempt upon George's life made in 1786 with a kitchen knife. Margaret, unlike James, was never charged with her offence. Her insanity was as apparent as the king's in 1788–9, and was proven for Doctors John and James Monro (the physicians to Bethlem Hospital), giving evidence before the Privy Council, because 'her language was perfectly unintelligible and it was impossible to relate it'.[39] Like George, her language was enough to show her as mad. A fellow inmate of Nicholson and Hadfield was James Tilley Matthews, confined since 1797. Matthews entered drawings for the design of the new Bethlem Hospital which was built in St George's Fields in 1815. The man who, for John Haslam, was the absolute illustration of madness because of the delusions he expressed in such compelling language, participated in building a house for the mad while still an inmate himself.

When Swift concluded his 'Verses on the Death of Dr Swift,'

> He gave the little Wealth he had,
> To build a House for Fools and Mad:
> And shew'd by one satyric Touch,
> No Nation wanted it so much:[40]

he was saying no more than the plain truth. Swift did found St Patrick's asylum, Dublin, in his will, but in expressing the fact in this poem he is also performing the 'satyric Touch' that confounds what is with what is read. We should not be misled by the philanthropy of the deed into overlooking the characteristic devices of Swift the satirist at work throughout the poem – the mock throwaway tone, the self-effacement, the generous quotation from other kinds of discourse like that of the royal world, the commercial world, the world of the club. In particular, in spite of the easy acquiescence in the fact of his death, we must remember, now that the Dean *is* dead, that he was *not* dead when he wrote this poem. Its subject is not Swift's death and legacy, but the faults of mankind,[41] and the overt intertextuality with his own satiric work places it firmly alongside *A Tale of a Tub* and *Gulliver's Travels* as writing that develops a thoroughly ambiguous relationship with the reader. Swift may have founded a madhouse, but it was his writing that so shook the sanity of his readers that a madhouse was found to be wanting. Readers cannot help but read, once the doors of language are opened. When they read Swift, they are building for themselves a 'House for Fools and Mad'. Moreover, as Swift also pointed out when considering the likely patrons for his asylum, readers would not be the only inmates from the house of language to require hospitalisation.

What a mixed multitude of ballad-writers, ode-makers, translators, farce-compounders, opera-mongers, biographers, pamphleteers, and journalists, would appear crowding to the hospital.[42]

In the following chapters I shall be looking over some of the productions of the candidates for admission.

2

THE HISTORY OF SILENCE

In the serene world of mental illness, modern man no longer communicates with the madman. . . . As for a common language, there is no such thing; or rather, there is no such thing any longer; the constitution of madness as a mental illness, at the end of the eighteenth century, affords the evidence of a broken dialogue, posits the separation as already effected, and thrusts into oblivion all those stammered, imperfect words without fixed syntax in which the exchange between madness and reason was made. The language of psychiatry, which is a monologue of reason *about* madness, has been established only on the basis of such a silence.

I have not tried to write the history of that language, but rather the archaeology of that silence.[1]

The language of psychiatry, of talking '*about* madness', was a field of discourse that expanded more and more rapidly during the course of the eighteenth century. Madness in all its manifestations – mania, melancholy, hysteria, religious enthusiasm, hypochondria, vapours – engaged some of the leading medical and philosphical minds of the period, and publications on the causes, symptoms and treatment of different shades of insanity were legion.[2] Many writers addressed themselves to specific conditions: Edward Synge's *The Cure of Melancholy* (London, 1742), Benjamin Fawcet's *Observations on the Causes and Cure of Melancholy, especially of that which is called Religious Melancholy* (Shrewsbury, 1780), or Andrew Wilson's *Nature and Origin of Hysteria* (London, 1776). Others attempted to cover a wider range of types: Bernard Mandeville's *A Treatise of the Hypochondriack and Hysterick Passions, Vulgarly call'd Hypo in Men and Vapours in Women . . . In Three Dialogues* (London, 1711),

16

or Nicholas Robinson's *A New System of the Spleen, Vapours, and Hypochondriack Melancholy: Wherein all the Decays of the Nerves, and Lownesses of the Spirits are Mechanically Accounted for* (London, 1729). More ambitious works dealt with insanity as a specialised branch of medicine, and discussed its classification and pathology as well as kinds of cure: Alexander Crichton's *An Inquiry into the Nature and Origin of Mental Derangement. Comprehending a Concise System of the Physiology and Pathology of the Human Mind and a History of the Passions and their Effects* (London, 1798), Thomas Arnold's *Observations on the Nature, Kinds, Causes, and Prevention of Insanity, lunacy, or madness* (Leicester, 1782–6). Increasingly, towards the end of the century, works based on observations of specific cases also became popular: William Perfect's *Annals of Insanity, Comprising a Selection of Curious and Interesting Cases in the Different Species of Lunacy, Melancholy, or Madness, with the Modes of Practice in the Medical and Moral Treatment as Adopted in the Cure of Each* (London, 1794) and William Pargeter's *Observations on Maniacal Disorders* (Reading, 1792). Letters and pamphlets advocating specific treatments were also published: David Bayne Kinneir on camphor (1727), George Young on opium (1753), George Adams on electricity (1792). The self-confidence of the professionals generated a new rhetoric for the expounding of theories about madness and its cure, but, in doing so, also helped to silence the spoken evidence of what the mad could have to say for themselves.

The history of silence can be registered through the succession of published statements made by those who were in a position to speak not on behalf of the mad but as the voices of a new authority formulating and overseeing society's concern for mental abnormality. As such, they were early members of an emerging and increasingly powerful profession. In their attitudes towards the causes and cures of insanity, towards case histories, and towards the thoughts and particularly the language of madness, we begin to hear the resonance of the silence of the mad. The silence takes different forms as the period advances. It is occasionally and significantly broken. But the pauses in the history of silence are not always easy to hear, and even when heard are frequently shouted down by the enthusiasm of medical opinion talking against or 'about' them.

Fundamentally, the opposition between the professionals in the debate about madness comes down to the difference between two attitudes: suppression, and endorsement. A suppressive stance at its most extreme regarded madness as incurable and mad patients as therefore not worth the trouble of treating. So, inmates of the lunatic ward of Guy's Hospital were 'left to themselves without medical attention until 1783 when some unexpectedly and spontaneously recovered, a possibility not visualised'.[3] Ironically, at the other extreme, an attitude of endorsement held that madness, left to itself, would dispel, and should therefore as a matter of sound medical practice not be treated. Most theoreticians and practitioners found themselves somewhere in between these extremes. Those of suppressive tendencies looked upon madness as a departure from the norm of a healthy mind, though they might well differ as to what in the mind was responsible for that departure – impaired judgement, for example, or a diseased imagination. Those more inclined to endorsement saw in the particular form of madness a response to a set of circumstances, a way of life, or a social system. Suppression treated the bodies of the mad, as would happen in any physical disease. Endorsement, while not eschewing physical remedies, also paid attention to what the mad had to report regarding their own condition, believing that being mad in an individual way meant that some degree of individual treatment was necessary. At bottom, suppression and endorsement differed over whether the experience of madness contained any kind of truth. If, like whooping-cough or gout, it was simply something to get through or die of, the experience itself was worthless, a hiatus in a normal life. If, however, madness was saying something *about* normal life, and was also a commentary upon itself, then the mad could offer important clues for the understanding both of themselves and of the world of the sane. These opposing attitudes, which will be the subjects of this and the next chapter, carried implications for the explanation of madness, its treatment, and the handling of and provision for lunatic patients.

Thomas Willis, whose works were first published in Latin in the 1660s and 1670s, and in translation in the 1680s, was one of the most influential of all medical writers for those who practised or theorised about madness during the eighteenth century, for Willis not only authorised standard treatments for both the melancholy and the maniacal forms of insanity (indeed, he was the first to identify the mania–melancholy alternation), but he also propounded a theory to explain the workings of the brain and the nervous system. In particular, Willis described the function of the 'Animal Spirits' as conducting agents 'flowing from the Brain and Cerebel . . . as it

were from a double Luminary' to 'irradiate the nervous System'.[4]
The disordering of the animal spirits produced either melancholic
or manic symptoms through unusual relaxation or tension of the
system. Of hysterical fits, for example, he concludes:

> the Passions commonly called Hysterical . . . arise most often,
> from that the animal spirits, possessing the beginning of the
> Nerves within the head, are infected with some taint, to
> wit, they being either acted or brought into Confusion, or
> being tincted with vitious humours, get to themselves an
> heterogeneous and explosive *Copula*, which they carry away
> with themselves, into the Channells of the nerves: and when
> the same spirits are filled to a plenitude . . . they enter into
> explosions, and so stir up Convulsive motions.[5]

While the model of relaxation and tension is a version of the
'humours' theory of excess and depletion, its dynamics provided
a much more satisfying explanation for unusual inertia or frenetic
activity, and was based, moreover, partly upon anatomy and
dissection, thus adding a practical authority to Willis's ideas.

Already, however, it is apparent that the possibility of a meaning
in madness is being overlooked as explanations for its occurrence
become more scientifically based. The body is the battlefield for
'Troops' of 'animal Spirits',[6] which in madness are subject to
'explosions' or invasions. The post-mortem examination of the
madman's brain completes a process by which his madness is
wholly objectified by the physician. What the patient has to say
for himself is summarily dismissed: 'Melancholick people talk idly',
while the furiously mad, even during their calm intervals, still
'continue amiss, as to their imagination and judgment, and speak
and do many absurd or incongruous things'.[7]

As to treatment, for Willis this must be determined by the
degree of relaxation or tension that is responsible for the kind of
madness displayed. The melancholy patient is to be 'roused up'
by 'light business' such as 'Mathematical or Chymical Studies, also
Travelling', and 'withdrawn from all troublesome and restraining
passion' through 'pleasant talk, or jesting, Singing, Musick, Pic-
tures, Dancing, Hunting, Fishing'. That this palatable regime is
not based on any regard for the convenience or personality of the
patient is clear when we look at what Willis recommends, on the
same theory, for the maniac (and we should remember that for

Willis this may well be the same patient, for 'these Distempers often change, and pass from one into the other'):

> The first Indication, *viz*. Curatory, requires threatnings, bonds, or strokes, as well as Physick. For the Mad-man being placed in a House for the business, must be so handled both by the Physician, and also by the Servants that are prudent, that he may be in some manner kept in, either by warnings, chiding, or punishments inflicted on him, to his duty, or his behaviour, or manners. And indeed for the curing of Mad people, there is nothing more effectual or necessary than their reverence or standing in awe of such as they think their Tormentors. For by this means, the Corporeal Soul being in some measure depressed and restrained, is compell'd to remit its pride and fierceness; and so afterwards by degrees grows more mild, and returns in order: Wherefore, Furious Mad-men are sooner, and more certainly cured by punishments, and hard usage, in a strait room, than by Physick or Medicines.

It is interesting that Willis expects the patient to 'think' of the physician and servants as 'Tormentors': the delusions already present are to be supplemented by fresh ones regarding the role of those who are supposedly attending in a curative capacity. Such 'Physick' as is to be used is equally harsh, for it should

> suppress or cast down Elation of the Corporeal Soul. Wherefore in this Disease, Bloodletting, Vomits, or very strong Purges, and boldly and rashly given, are most often convenient; which indeed appears manifest, because Empiricks only with this kind of Physick, together with a more severe government and discipline do not seldom most happily cure Mad folks.

(The awkwardness of the final clause is an attempt to render the original Latin construction, but Willis's 'happily' in the context of the prescribed treatments should be noted, as should 'convenient'.) 'Chirurgical Remedies' are also recommended, for 'besides, opening a Vein, many other helps are wont to be had for the curing of this Disease. Cupping-glasses with Scarification, often help. Blisterings, Cauteries both actual and potential are praised of many. Others commend cutting an Artery, others Trepanning, or opening the Skull, others Salivation.'

None of these treatments is without a basis in theory. Blood-letting with leeches or cups, together with vomits and purges, was inherited from the humoral view of health and sickness and was designed to correct a constitutional imbalance due to excess. Such treatment would deplete the system and so weaken the raging of the madness. Similarly, trepanning (the removal of a small section of bone from the skull) and 'opening the Skull' were expected to relieve pressure, while blistering (the raising of artificial blisters through the application of an irritant such as cantharides, mustard or antimony), and cupping and scarification (the inflicting of scratches from which blood was then drawn by means of a cupping-glass) were intended to produce inflammation and suppuration, and thereby divert the mind from its own derangement with a greater pain. Willis's recommendations for the general management and keeping of the mad are also based upon the belief that depletion of bodily and mental vigour will produce a cure.

> The vital Indication institutes how mad people ought to be handled, concerning their government, dyet, and sleep. In this Disease there is no need of keeping up the flesh, as in most other Diseases: For the spirits ought not to be refreshed with Cordials, nor strength to be restored with Medicines; but on the contrary, both being too raging of themselves, things are to be administer'd as it were for the suppression or extinction of a flame raging above measure. Therefore let the diet be slender and not delicate, their cloathing course, their beds hard, and their handling severe and rigid. But sleep, for that it is very necessary, ought to be caused sometimes by Anodynes; for which end, Hypnotick Remedies or Medicines above prescribed for Melancholy, are also convenient in this Disease. In inveterate and habitual Madness, the sick seldom submit to any medical Cure; but such being placed in Bedlam, or an Hospital for Mad people, by the ordinary discipline of the place, either at length return to themselves, or else they are kept from doing hurt, either to themselves or to others.[8]

Willis thus endorses and sanctifies a regimen for the treatment of the mad that, while founded upon a legitimate understanding of the systems of the body, permitted both cruelty and economy on the grounds of approved practice. The common beliefs that

21

the mad felt no pain, and did not suffer from extreme cold, also had a kind of medical authority, even though explicitly denied by many professionals over the course of the eighteenth century. Poor food, scant clothing, sleeping on boards or straw, little provision of heating, together with harsh discipline and restraint were all allowable when the testimony of the mad was regarded as being without meaning.

Few of the great medical writers of the late seventeenth or early eighteenth centuries had any serious disagreement with Willis, or with the standard attitudes towards and treatment of the mad. Thomas Sydenham, for example, a significant figure in the history of medicine and an almost exact contemporary of Willis, though more a practising physician and less of an academic, recommends treatment for 'ideotism' and for hysteric diseases, but in doing so displays an interesting combination of the kinds of remedies that Willis might also have prescribed. For Sydenham, 'common madness' proceeds from 'the over-richness and spirituousness of the blood', while 'ideotism' arises from the opposite state. In the latter case, therefore, part of the treatment is designed to strengthen the blood.

> There is also another kind of madness, that succeeds an intermittent of long standing, and at length degenerates into ideotism, which arises from the depressed state of the blood, occasioned by its long fermentation. In this case therefore strong cordials are to be prescribed, such as *Venice* treacle, the electuary of the egg, the countess of *Kent*'s powder, Sir *Walter Raleigh*'s cordial, in plague water, or any similar vehicle along with a restorative diet.

An electuary is made by mixing the active ingredient (usually in powder form) with honey or syrup. Venice treacle was an electuary in which many ingredients were combined, and supposedly possessed preventative and preservative qualities, and was thought to be effective as an antidote to poison. But Sydenham also prescribes as a necessary accompaniment to restorative measures what is standard treatment for the excesses of 'common madness' – bleeding and purging. The physician is instructed to take 'eight or nine ounces of blood from the arm in young subjects', which is to be repeated 'twice or thrice, at the distance of three days between each bleeding', and then should 'bleed once in the jugular'. He should then administer a purgative ('white briony-root in powder' and 'syrup of violets' are recommended) 'every third or fourth day, till the patient recovers', though leaving a gap of a week or even a fortnight 'after the patient has been purged eight or ten times'.[9]

The reasoning behind this application of the same treatment for conditions that were supposed to arise from opposite causes becomes apparent when Sydenham writes about hysteric diseases, in which he had a special interest. While hysteria requires 'strengthening the blood, which is the source and origin of the spirits', nevertheless

> as this disorder of the spirits may by its long duration have vitiated the juices, it will be proper first to lessen their quantity by bleeding and purging, if the patient be not too weak, before we proceed to strengthen the blood; which can scarce be done, so long as we are obstructed by the abundance of foul humours lying in the way.

Bleeding and purging, in fact, are used to relieve or remove any kind of excess, from over-richness of the blood itself to the presence of vicious humours. After bleeding, Sydenham prescribes 'some chalybeate medicine' (that is, one containing iron or steel) in order to strengthen the now depleted blood and spirits.[10]

As for the language of those affected, Sydenham reports that a woman suffering from 'the hysteric passion' 'talks wildly and unintelligibly, and beats her breast', she experiences 'so violent a palpitation of the Heart' that she 'is persuaded, those about her must needs hear the heart strike against the ribs'. And while the body is indeed indisposed, 'the mind is still more disordered; it being the nature of this disease to be attended with an incurable despair; so that they cannot bear with patience to be told that there is hopes of their recovery, easily imagining that they are liable to all the miseries that can befall mankind; and presaging the worst evils to themselves'. So, they 'indulge terror, anger, distrust, and other hateful passions; and are enemies to joy and hope'. They 'love the same persons extravagantly at one time, and soon after hate them without a cause'. They 'propose doing one thing, and the next change their minds, and enter upon something contrary to it, but without finishing it'. In short, 'they observe no mean in any thing, and are only settled in inconstancy'.

During consultation, however, Sydenham, like all physicians, is obliged to rely on the word of those whose minds and speech cannot be trusted to remain the same from one moment to the next:

> when ever I am consulted by women concerning any particular
> disorder, which cannot be accounted for on the common
> principles of investigating diseases, I always enquire, whether
> they are not chiefly attack'd with it after fretting, or any
> disturbance of mind; and if they acknowledge this, I am
> well assured that the disease is to be ascrib'd to the tribe
> of disorders under consideration, especially if the diagnostic
> appears more evident by a copious discharge of limpid urine
> at certain times.[11]

The remarks neatly illustrate one major dilemma facing traditional
physicians investigating mental disorders: how can disturbances of
the mind be accounted for and treated if the only evidence to be
obtained is from observation of bodily, or somatic, symptoms?
If what the patient has to say cannot be trusted (unless, as here,
it happens to confirm a prejudice of the physician), then it is no
surprise to find a largely mechanistic explanation for all kinds of
madness, and preponderantly suppressive treatments recommended
by orthodox medical practice.

The patterns of explanation and management exhibited in the
writings of Willis and Sydenham recur throughout the eighteenth
century, though with increasing sophistication, increasing personal
fixation upon certain conditions or treatments, and increasing
reliance upon technological innovation. Nicholas Robinson, for
example, who published his *New System of the Spleen, Vapours, and
Hypochondriack Melancholy* in 1729, and was heavily influenced by
Willis, saw madness as arising from changes in the '*Machinulae* of the
Nerves and Fibres' of the brain. Denying that any form of madness
could arise from 'a wrong Turn of the Fancy', Robinson attributed
all mental disorder to 'Change in the Motions of the Animal Fibres'.
So, no mind can fall 'from a chearful, gay Disposition' into 'a sad
and disconsolate State, without some Alterations in the Fibres',
and 'neither the Fancy, nor Imagination, nor even Reason itself
. . . can feign a Perception, or a Disease that has no Foundation
in Nature'. Inevitably, Robinson, in advocating treatment for
madness, sought to cure the body rather than the mind, for 'it
will be absolutely impossible to give any considerable Turn to the
Disease . . . without instituting a Course of Medicine of the most
violent Operation': only thus can be made 'those Alterations in the
Fibres of the Brain, necessary to procure a Freedom from those
Affections, the Mind labours under during the Continuance of this

Disease'. A horrendous regimen is then recommended, as being in the best interests of the mad patient.

> Give me leave to say, that no Man can have a tenderer, or more compassionate Concern for the Misery of Mankind than my self; yet it is Cruelty in the highest Degree, not to be bold in the Administration of Medicines, when the Nature of the Disease absolutely demands the Assistance of a powerful Remedy. . . . It is owing to these safe Men . . . that chronick Diseases are so rife now-a-days, and so generally incurable; not that they are so in themselves, but only render'd so by those, that are afraid to proceed in a Way only capable of curing them. In this Case, therefore, the most violent Vomits, the strongest purging Medicines, and large Bleeding, are to be often repeated. While the Madness holds on, a spare, thin, attenuating Diet is known to be of singular Service, which, in conjunction with the foregoing Remedies, I believe will be able to relieve any Degree of Lunacy, capable of a Cure.

Ironically, Robinson endorses the 'real Affections of the Mind', which are 'no imaginary Whims or Fancies', but views them as 'arising from the real, mechanical Affections of Matter and Motion' rather than as indicating anything to be taken seriously about the experience or personality of the sufferer. Nor, therefore, does speech or language have any part in his treatment. Indeed, 'you may as soon attempt to counsel a Man out of the most violent Fever, as endeavour to work any Alteration in their Faculties by the Impressions of Sound, tho' never so eloquently apply'd'.[12]

Robinson's theories place him near the extreme in terms of attitudes towards the validation of his patients' feelings, individuality or speech, but he was not at all unusual in his methods of treatment. John Monro, who was physician to Bethlem for most of the latter half of the century, and can therefore be taken to speak of what was common practice, asserts 'that the most adequate and constant cure' for madness is 'by evacuation', of which 'evacuation by *vomiting* is infinitely preferable to any other'. Monro claims that 'I never saw or heard of the bad effect of vomits, in my practice; nor can I suppose any mischief to happen, but from their being injudiciously administered; or when they are given too strong, or the person who orders them is too much *afraid of the lancet*'. He also recommends purging, emetics and bleeding:

The prodigious quantity of phlegm, with which those abound who are troubled with this complaint, is not to be got the better of but by repeated *vomits*; and we very often find, that *purges* have not their right effect, or do not operate to so good purpose, until the phlegm is broken and attenuated by frequent *emeticks*. . . . *Bleeding* and *purging* are both requisite in the cure of madness.

Monro cites the experience of 'Dr *Bryan Robinson*', who has applied such remedies 'for a whole year together, sometimes once a day, sometimes twice, and that with the greatest success'. 'Issues between the shoulders' are also 'of great service', while 'cold bathing likewise has in general an excellent effect, but as it is sometimes apt to hurry the spirits, it is not to be prescribed indiscriminately to every one'.[13]

Away from the hospital, the attempts at classification of mental illness undertaken by William Cullen, professor first at Glasgow and then at Edinburgh universities between 1751 and 1790, influenced a generation of medical students who were to become prominent in less suppressive attitudes towards the insane, including Thomas Arnold and Alexander Crichton. Ironically, though, Cullen's own attitude towards treatment was harshly repressive. Because he attributed madness to impaired judgement, treatment was to aim at making the patient think correctly. So, while 'Restraining the anger and violence of madmen is always necessary for preventing their hurting themselves or others', restraint should also 'be considered as a remedy'. 'Angry passions' would grow worse by 'indulgence', but fear would diminish the 'angry and irascible excitement of maniacs' who should be under 'a very constant impression of fear' and inspired 'with the awe and dread of some particular persons, especially of those who are to be constantly near them'. Whatever means that are necessary should be employed in order to acquire 'awe and dread', 'in the first place, by their being the authors of all restraints' and 'sometimes . . . even by stripes and blows'. Cullen therefore relied on and endorsed traditional cures and handling: thin diet, purges, bleedings, vomits and emetics.[14]

John Haslam, as apothecary to Bethlem between 1795 and 1816, was one of those medical men who followed John Monro into print. His *Observations on Insanity*, published in 1798, was based on close contact with a variety of mad patients. (The central section of the work details over twenty brief case histories, each of which ends with a post-mortem examination.) Haslam, like Robinson, regarded mental illness as arising from somatic causes: it was a disease of the brain, not of the mind, and certainly not '*a disease of ideas*'.[15] Here again is justification for harsh management and strong medicines, though Haslam also advocates restraint in the application of both. Those in attendance should gain ascendancy over their charges, but also their respect. Confinement should be used as a punishment rather than indiscriminately, but the offender should know why he is being punished, otherwise such a recourse would be 'absurd', and it is more effective if carried out in view of other patients, for 'As madmen frequently entertain very high, and even romantic notions of honour, they are rendered much more tractable by wounding their pride, than by severity of discipline.' Regularity of conduct is important in order to divert the mind 'from the favourite and accustomed train of ideas'.[16] Attendants are warned never to deceive a madman, for this will be found hurtful, and 'confidence and respect' will thereby be sacrificed. Bleeding and purging, inevitably, are favoured, upon the foundation of experience: 'it is concluded, from very ample experience, that cathartic medicines are of the greatest service, and ought to be considered as an indispensable remedy in cases of insanity'. Indeed, Haslam denies the common supposition that the mad are invariably constipated, for their ordinary complaints are 'diarrhoea and dysentery', the first of which 'often proves a natural cure of insanity'. Yet he rejects vomiting, camphor (then in use to produce sweating, vomiting and diarrhoea, and to both stimulate and depress the nervous system), 'Cold Bathing', blisters to the head, setons (a thread used to keep open an issue) and opium, which he found to increase the violence and fury of madness. (We should, however, note that in spite of some apparently enlightened attitudes, Haslam was dismissed from his post in 1816 for his involvement in the malpractices uncovered by the 1815 parliamentary investigation of Bethlem.)[17]

Haslam, then, while retaining many of the orthodox attitudes towards the treatment of insanity, does show some interest in the patient as an individual, and as having a mind capable of being reached in some way, though not necessarily as a sane mind is reached. He realises, for example, that patients are at times able to see the 'folly' and 'incongruity' of their own ideas, but that 'they complain that they cannot prevent their intrusion'. He also obviously regards them as sufficiently rational to understand the concept of punishment. He observes, too, that 'insane people easily detect the nonsense of other madmen without being able to discover, or even to be made sensible of the incorrect associations of their own ideas'.[18] He does not, however, believe in attempting to reason a man out of his madness, and reserves particular scorn for the notion of the *disease of ideas*.

> In what manner are we to effect a cure? To this subtle spirit the doctor can apply no medicines. But though so refined as to exclude the force of material remedies, some may however think that it may be reasoned with. The good effects which have resulted from exhibiting logic as a remedy for madness, must be sufficiently known to every one who has conversed with insane persons, and must be considered as time very judiciously employed: speaking more gravely, it will readily be acknowledged, by persons acquainted with this disease, that if insanity be a disease of ideas, we possess no corporeal remedies for it: and that to endeavour to convince madmen of their errors, by reasoning, is folly in those who attempt it, since there is always in madness the firmest conviction of the truth of what is false, and which the clearest and most circumstantial evidence cannot remove.[19]

Language, exchange of ideas of any kind, engagement with the personality of the patient, is finally irrelevant to the treatment of madness.

Many of the principal remedies that were advocated during the course of the century also leave no room for engagement with the madness of the madman. Quite apart from the application of drastic purges, the administering of a ferocious range of medicinal substances including mercury, hellebore, tin, sagapenum and steel, and the ever-present bleeding by various methods, ingenious practitioners invented or developed ways of attempting to shock their charges into their senses. The shock theory held that an artificially induced crisis could restore the mind, as the crisis in a fever was observed to precede recovery. Bleedings and purgings could also achieve this, but mechanical means, especially the relatively simple mechanics of water therapy, were widely practised. Water was traditionally supposed to be antagonistic to hydrophobia and therefore to madness, a view that validated ducking as a treatment. This involved holding the patient under water, often by means of suspension, until unconscious. Such treatment would be particularly efficacious if the patient could be taken by surprise, for example by being dragged out of bed, or blindfolded.[20] The instigator of the treatment was the seventeenth-century Dutch physician, Jean Baptiste van Helmont. Later practitioners, however, improved and refined van Helmont's basic ideas. Patrick Blair, in the early part of the eighteenth century, was particularly convinced of the reliability of shock by water. He describes his treatment of a madman suffering from 'a fiery zeal for Religion', who could not be held in his bed by eight men, 'but they were forc'd to make use of ropes and fetter his hands and feet with Iron':

> Next day I attempted the Cold Bath and ordered him to be plung'd thus bound into an hogshead of water all of a sudden, and throwing 8 or 10 palefulls of water by the force of so many people upon his head all at once, but this had scarce any effect because I neglected to blindfold him, but though he was somewhat calm'd a little after.

Undeterred, Blair 'contriv'd a byspout from a Current of water (for a Cornmill) which had a 20 foot fall'. The patient was placed in a cart under this fall:

> Thus I kept him under this vast pressure of water for 15 minutes untill his spirits were fully dissipated and his strength quite exhausted, and it is to be observ'd that he who being blindfolded and led by 2 persons came whistling singing dancing and merrily leaping along about ½ mile to the fall of the mill was fain to be carried home in a Litter.

A complete cure followed, with the patient subsequently apprenticed to a brewer, 'where he has led a very sober life'. Blair later improved his own methods by utilising a '35 foot high' water tower near Boston, Lincs. A pipe from 'a cistern on the top of the Tower which will contain about 80 Tun of water' was taken to a room below where 'a bathing Tub 6 foot long' with a chair was provided, to which the patient was tied. The flow of water could be regulated by a cock.[21]

Nicholas Robinson also favoured water treatment, but felt that the patient should be thrown 'from a considerable Height into the Water'.[22] Others recommended ice (William Cullen, for example), or unexpected loud noises, while later in the century, with advances in science and mechanics, the employment of violent movement or electric shocks became possible. James Smyth is credited with the reintroduction of the swinging chair as a form of therapy in the 1790s, but the method was developed by Erasmus Darwin and Joseph Mason Cox. Cox in particular believed that, as madness was supposedly incompatible with other forms of severe illness, the body should be rendered as if diseased. The patient would be rotated until 'vertigo, vomiting and circulatory collapse to the point of unconsciousness'[23] was achieved. The perfected machine, with the patient 'secured in a strait waistcoat' and strapped and buckled into 'a common Windsor chair', allowed 'oscillatory' or 'circulating' motion at varying speeds, and in 'either the horizontal or perpendicular position'. The effects, according to Cox, were dramatic:

> I have sometimes seen a patient almost deprived of his loco-motive powers, by the protracted action of this remedy, who required the combined strength and address of several experienced attendants to place him in the swing, from whence he has been easily carried by a single person. . . . One of the most constant effects of swinging is a greater or lesser degree of vertigo, attended by pallor, nausea, vomiting, and frequently by the evacuation of the contents of the bladder.

Cox recommends swinging in hopeless cases 'in the dark' and accompanied by 'unusual noises, smells, or other powerful agents, acting forcibly on the senses' whereby 'its efficacy might be amazingly increased'. He reports the most beneficial consequences:

> After a very few circumvolutions, I have witnessed its soothing lulling effects, tranquillizing the mind and rendering the body quiescent; a degree of vertigo has often followed, which has been succeeded by the most refreshing slumbers; an object this the most desirable in every case of madness . . . but though it can be employed so as to occasion the mildest and most gentle effects, yet its action can be so regulated as to excite the most violent convulsions of the stomach, with the agitation and concussion of every part of the animal frame; thus rendering the finest system of vessels pervious, or, in other words, removing obstructions, and altering the very nature and quality of the secretions.[24]

Machinery captured the imaginations of the professionals in the mad business, and none more, or more enduringly, than electrical apparatus. While electrical shocks obtained from natural objects had long been used in medical treatments, it was not until the middle years of the eighteenth century that generating machines and the Leyden jar allowed widespread enthusiasm among all classes of practitioner, amateur as well as professional.[25] John Wesley was an early advocate only some ten years after Benjamin Franklin's first experiments, and a utiliser of electrical apparatus, carrying a machine on many of his travels around the country from the mid-1750s in order to treat, free of charge, a whole range of conditions, including convulsions, paralysis and rheumatism. He published *The Desideratum: or, Electricity Made Plain and Useful* in 1760 from fear that the therapy would sink out of fashion and use through the 'Vehemence' of opposition to it. Unlike many advocates for favourite remedies, however, Wesley confesses an ignorance as to why his treatment is so successful:

> And yet there is something peculiarly unaccountable, with regard to its Operation. In some Cases, where there was no Hope of Help, it will succeed beyond all Expectation. In others, where we had the greatest Hope, it will have no Effect at all. Again, in some Experiments, it helps at the very first, and promises a speedy Cure: But presently the good Effect ceases, and the Patient is as he was before. On the contrary, in others it has no Effect at first: It does no good; perhaps seems to do hurt. Yet all this Time it is striking at the Root of the Disease, which in a while it totally removes.[26]

Nor does his advocacy of what with hindsight can be judged as a suppressive measure mean that Wesley lines up with Nicholas Robinson or John Monro, for he elsewhere remarks against physicians who 'prescribe drug upon drug, without knowing a jot of the matter concerning the root of the disorder. And without knowing this they cannot cure, though they can murder, the patient.' Indeed, in the case of the woman whose stomach pain gave rise to these remarks, Wesley specifically recommends *asking* the patient: 'Whence came this woman's pain (which she would never have told had she never been questioned about it)? From fretting for the death of her son. And what availed medicines while that fretting continued?' Wesley draws the conclusion: 'Why, then, do not all physicians consider how far bodily disorders are caused or influenced by the mind?'[27]

If Wesley allows language a primacy over technology and drugs, he is unusual among his contemporaries. As a man for whom the spoken word had a particular significance, we might expect equal respect for the words of those in need of spiritual or of bodily cure. To this extent, Wesley's amateur status in the world of medicine was no doubt beneficial and made him untypical amongst the proponents of the scientific treatment of madness. Roy Porter reminds us that the techniques of 'early psychotechnology' did at least 'represent attempts to break free of the hidebound depletive therapeutics of blood-letting, vomits and purges . . . hindsight can oversimplify'.[28] In the story of the progress of medicine, the steps taken by the early psychotechnologists are undoubtedly significant, even if the end of the story is not an unambiguously happy one. In the history of silence, however, few enthusiasts showed Wesley's regard for what could be spoken by those about to swing, drown or jolt.

John Birch, surgeon to St Thomas's Hospital in London in the closing years of the century, documented his experiments with electrical treatment of his patients, especially of those suffering from melancholy, or any kind of lowness of spirits. What is characteristic of Birch's treatments is that, as with any more standard drug or therapy of the time, little distinction is made between the possible causes of the illness. Where a traditional physician would have prescribed bleeding and purging for most of a wide range of mental (and indeed physical) conditions, and more bleeding and longer purging when the condition proved stubborn, and Blair greater quantities of water more forcefully directed, Birch increases the voltage, or applies it more frequently. One man, first seen in November 1787, 'in a state of melancholy, induced by the death of one of his children' a few months earlier, is successfully treated.

> I covered his head with a flannel, and rubbed the electric sparks all over the cranium; he seemed to feel it disagreeable, but said nothing. On the second visit, finding no inconvenience had ensued, I passed six small shocks through the brain in different directions. As soon as he got into an adjoining room, and saw his wife, he spoke to her, and in the evening was cheerful, expressing himself, as if he thought he should soon go to work again. I repeated the shocks in the like manner on the third and the fourth day, after which he went to work: I desired to see him every Sunday, which I did for three months after, and he remained perfectly well. I then dismissed him.

By August 1791, the patient is melancholy again, upon which Birch advises him 'to apply for medical aid, and to the hospital, if he grew worse, as I was leaving town'. Birch knew at the outset, however, that 'Seven years before, he had been seized in the same manner from a similar event', and that in 1783 'he was a second time seized, and remained in this melancholy state upwards of twelve months'. This pattern of periodic depression seems little different from that which gave rise to Wesley's question: 'what availed medicines while that fretting continued?'

A second case is that of a professional singer who was 'extremely melancholy . . . from a variety of distressing causes'. Birch does not specify these, though his use of the word 'distressing' clearly endorses them, while the earlier expressions, 'the death of one of his children' and 'a similar event' remain more clinically detached. This patient is given the same treatment: 'Considering this in the same light as the former case, I began with passing shocks through the head, about six in number.' This is repeated daily, and, after a fortnight, every other day. The singer is then dismissed to pursue (apparently with success) his career. Interestingly, in this case the patient finds through the beneficial effects of electrical treatment the capability to reveal to Birch the true story of his mental state. He had several times contemplated suicide prior to the initial consultation, though was prevented by accidents from actually making the attempt.

> He had resolved however to effect it, and was in the most distressful agitations about it, the morning he first applied to me. In the evening of that day, he declared he was sensible of the divine intervention in preventing his wicked design; that he found himself able to return thanks; and this relief of his mind was followed by a refreshing sleep, from which he awoke a new being: that he felt sensible of the powers of electricity every day after it's application, being capable of mental exertions immediately. He could not be satisfied, he said, without making this declaration to me, as no one but himself could have an adequate idea of the sudden change the first electric shocks wrought in his mind.

Here, apparently, the therapy, far from repressing linguistic expression, provides the stimulus that allows the patient fully to acknowledge his own derangement and to present it as a tribute to his therapist. His words are to provide an 'adequate' understanding of the impact of the electricity, though both Birch and the patient seem unaware of the irony of his recognising 'divine intervention' only after the receipt of six 'shocks through the head'.

Birch's third case, however, demonstrates how completely experimental this therapy was, how little adapted to the individuality of the condition or its causes, and how accidental the instances of successful treatment were. A young gentleman 'with a moping melancholy' of many years continuance 'was brought to me . . . for experiment'. Birch judges 'this a proper case to carry the experiment as far as prudence would direct'. Using 'a Leyden bottle', he passes 'two strong shocks from it, in directions from the frontal to the occipital bone, and from one temporal bone to the other'. The consequences, as described by Birch, show both a chillingly serene progress through the experiment and a remarkable degree of complicity in a patient apparently indifferent to bodily pain.

> The patient was at first surprised, not stunned with the shock, and in a few minutes desired me to repeat it if I pleased. The next day, he sat down with firmness, and as no inconvenience had occurred from the shocks, I increased the strength, and passed two shocks in the same direction as before. On the third day, he was reported to have found no sort of inconvenience or alteration from the experiments; so I ventured to pass the full force of the bottle; this likewise produced no other effect than a slight head-ach, which lasted for an hour. I chose to omit two days, and then repeated the experiment; the patient strongly expressing himself satisfied, that this was the most likely means to do him service. I was, myself, most surprised that I could practise so boldly, without any serious inconvenience to the brain; and having carried the experiments as far as I wished, I dismissed the patient, in the same unhappy state he had so long suffered.[29]

The suppressive attitude finds one edge here, in that cure is not actually intended. The word of the patient is registered in so far as he testifies to the effects of the treatment, but what prevents this from in any way endorsing the patient's experience is that the shocks being administered are not treatment at all. The melancholy man is a subject in an experiment, and what he is asked to report is only important in that it allows the experiment to proceed. Birch's own attitude, far from showing an interest in the patient's state of mind, in the personality that persists in his 'moping', is one of eager surprise in being able to carry the experiment so boldly and so far. The dismissal of the gentleman 'in the same unhappy state' is an apt conclusion to a procedure that was never intended to help him.

What is common to all the therapies so far discussed is the presence of madness not in the person of a man or a woman but as an object. The lunatic under the knife, undergoing the insertion of setons, the application of cups or blistering compounds, swallowing purges, strapped into the revolving chair or under the fall of water, or submitting to a charge of electricity – all are *done to* the patient. Every remedy, by being imposed on the authority of the physician, surgeon or apothecary, is something from without, an invasion upon individual experience, albeit perhaps performed with the patient's consent. But when medical authority can call, as it certainly could in the context of the madhouse, upon whips, chains and confinement, consent is hardly a matter of interest. The suppressive attitude seems to rest finally on this assumption: the madman is not a person, he is out of himself, absent from his own normality. Even in terms of his illness he is not ill as normal patients are ill. When and if cured he will be returned to himself, and will then become a person again. Meanwhile, all his behaviour, feelings, speech are those of a madman, and therefore of no account.

This relation between doctor and patient, between authority and its object, finds its most potent symbolic expression not in any act of linguistic origin, but in the strait-waistcoat. This device, which was in use early in the century, renders complete the status of the madman as object, for it prevents all of the functions by which an individual may express individuality with the single exception of language: but the peculiar irony of the strait-waistcoat is that its application transforms the individual into an object-person for whom language is an absurdity.

> These waistcoats are made of ticken, or some such strong stuff; are open at the back, and laced on like a pair of stays; the sleeves are made tight, and so long as to cover the ends of the fingers, and are there drawn close with a string, like a purse, by which contrivance the patient has no power of using his fingers; and, when he is laid on his back in bed, and the arms brought across the chest, and fastened

in that position, by tying the sleeve-strings fast round the waist, he has no power of his hands. A broad strap of girth-web is then carried across the breast, and fastened to the bedstead, by which means the patient is confined on his back; and if he should be so outrageous as to require further restraint, the legs are secured by ligatures to the foot of the bed.[30]

The strait-waistcoat was justified by the need to restrain dangerous patients from doing hurt to themselves or to others, but theorists also decided that such restraint was capable of rendering serene the passions of the mad, and was therefore actually of benefit to them. As Hunter and Macalpine observe, 'The history and use of the strait-waistcoat and its justification exemplifies how tenuous may be the dividing line in psychiatry between treatment and restraint.'[31]

If the history of silence can be heard through the overt statements of those taking responsibility for keeping down the noise of the mad, it can also be detected in less overt remarks made by those same professionals regarding what the mad actually said. Few record lengthy conversations with insane patients, for there would be no point, it would be nonsense. But there are tantalising snatches of dialogue, or of monologue, as well as plentiful generalisations about what the mad customarily have to say. Some of the evidence reinforces the suppressive views already illustrated, while other items begin to give some hints of what other history might have been told, had silence not reigned so implacably and for so long.

An interested amateur, Thomas Tryon, writing at the end of the seventeenth century, gives a humane and critical view of the conditions and treatment of madness, and questions in particular the efficacy of the traditional 'cures', which he regards as mistaking 'the Cause' of madness and treating 'the Effect'. However, he also gives a fairly standard account of the language of the mad.

> Now when the five inward senses of the Soul are weakened or destroyed, then they can no longer present before the Judge the Thoughts, Imaginations or Conceptions, but they are all formed into words as fast as they are generated, there being no controul or room for Judgment to censure what are fit, and what unfit to be coyn'd into Expressions: For this cause Mad People, and innocent Children, do speak forth whatever ariseth in their Phantasies.[32]

For Tryon, mad discourse was 'unfit', and insane speech was indecent speech, unrestrained, unfinished, incoherent, little better than the sounds of animals. John Monro, arguing against the 'deluded imagination' theory of madness, spoke of cases where 'every . . . quality, which distinguishes a man from a brute, except a few unconnected incohaerent words, seems totally obliterated'.[33] For David Kinneir, who practised in Edinburgh and Bath during the first part of the eighteenth century, and who particularly espoused the use of camphor, it was the same story. He records treating a melancholy 'Gentlewoman of Nineteen Years of Age' who had suddenly fallen 'a starting and laughing . . . then began to talk wildly, and continu'd so all that Night, She became next Morning very furious'. Another patient, 'A Mercer's Wife of Thirty Six Years of Age, having born Four Children . . . fell so ill, all of a sudden, One Day at Sermon, that with much ado they could get her out of Church with common Decency. She tore every thing about her, talk'd much, and utter'd horrid Oaths.'[34] George Young, also of Edinburgh, and a contemporary of Kinneir, treated with opium a 'gentlewoman who lost the use of her reason on a sudden, by the barbarous treatment of her husband', successfully effacing 'the incoherent set of ideas which possessed her mind'. Another patient 'labouring under a religious melancholy', had been driven mad by 'despair' and 'talked of nothing but the unpardonable sin'.[35] Nicholas Robinson designated 'that kind of melancholy Madness, where Men rave in an extravagant Manner, Lunacy', while John Haslam described one of his inmates as 'constantly muttering to himself, of which scarcely one word in a sentence was intelligible. When an audible expression escaped him it was commonly an imprecation.'[36] Interestingly, this patient is described as speaking in sentences, even though his words are unintelligible. What we cannot of course say is whether the division into sentences was an actual feature of this man's language, or, more likely, simply imposed by the auditor upon an undistinguishable set of ramblings.

Language misuse is a feature of madness, it is one means whereby madness may be recognised as madness, but it cannot apparently be attended to as a means of treating the mad. Dr Johnson defined 'rave' as: '1. To be deluded; to talk irrationally. 2. To burst out into furious exclamations as if mad.' The language of the raving madman is simply an extension of his physical fury or agitation. The same passion that drives his unpredictable bodily contortions is responsible for the equally contorted nature of his speech. He would clearly be unreceptive to rational argument, nor would he say anything coherent or to the point. Robinson, as we have seen, would tolerate no role for 'the Impressions of Sound' in the cure of insanity. Even when not actually raving, one prime feature of the madman's discourse is obsession, the returning always to one subject of conversation, such as 'the unpardonable sin', or lewdness, or religious rapture. John Haslam wrote about the 'lucid interval' during which the patient 'in a short conversation will appear sensible and coherent'. However, while unknowing persons will be taken in by this, the professional man will remain cautious:

> insane people will often, for a short time, conduct themselves, both in conversation and behaviour, with such propriety, that they appear to have the just exercise and direction of their faculties; but let the examiner protract the discourse, until the favourite subject shall have got afloat in the madman's brain, and he will be convinced of the hastiness of his decision. . . . He who is in possession of the peculiar turn of the patient's thoughts, might lead him to disclose them, or by a continuance of the conversation they would spontaneously break forth.[37]

In the first of Haslam's case histories, the patient 'JH' simply and continually 'said he was resolved to die', while in Case VII, 'AM', a woman of 27, believing 'her inside full of the most loathsome vermin', attributed the condition to divine retribution, and 'said, that God had inflicted this punishment on her, from having (at some former part of her life) said the Lord's Prayer backwards'.[38]

Haslam had greater opportunities than theorists or physicians for the close scrutiny of patients over long periods, and his *Observations on Insanity* is full of reported speech, either in exchanges with attendants or with Haslam himself, or else in solitary discourse. One man, a violent inmate of 42,

> when unoccupied, would walk about in a hurried and distracted manner, throwing out the most horrid threats and imprecations. He would often appear to be holding conversations: but these conferences always terminated in a violent quarrel between the imaginary being and himself.[39]

Another, 'JC', who had been a publican for thirty years, was obsessed with the fear that 'different people had gone off without paying him', but also refused all food, saying 'it was ridiculous to offer it to him, as he had no mouth to eat it'. When forced to eat, he 'insisted that a wound had been made in his throat, in order to force it into his stomach'.[40] A woman of 44, 'MW', had suffered the loss of some property: 'The constant tenor of her discourse was, that she should live but a short time.' She lived in fear of poisoning by 'some malevolent person', and, in proof of her assertions of this, was 'constantly shewing her teeth, which had decayed naturally, as if this effect had been produced by that medicine'.[41] Yet another 'believed himself a child, called upon the people about him as his playfellows, and appeared to recall the scenes of early life with facility and correctness'.[42]

This kind of recollection was not unusual in Haslam's experience: 'To many conversations of the old incurable patients to which I have listened, the topic has always turned upon the scenes of early days.' Yet along with this recollection, he suggests, there is also a forgetfulness, which partly accounts for the problems mad patients commonly suffer with language.

> If in a chain of ideas, a number of the links are broken, the mind cannot possess any accurate information. When patients of this description are asked a question, they appear as if awakened from a sound sleep; they are searching, they know not where, for the proper materials of an answer, and, in the painful, and fruitless efforts of recollection, generally lose sight of the question itself.[43]

What Haslam does not say, of course, is that patients 'of this description' are capable of recognising the structure and intonation of a question as opposed, say, to that of a command, and can remember that a question requires an answer, even though in attempting to supply it they may forget what the question was. He also testifies, albeit unwittingly, to the efforts his patients exert in struggling to remain in touch with the conventions of conversational exchange. Language, here, if anything, is an intrusion on the serenity of madness, and obliges the stirrings of a return to some of the social mechanisms used by other men, even though to the medical mind it is the patient's inability to respond adequately that is a confirmation of his madness. Haslam gives a further convincing reason, again apparently unwittingly, for the difficulty the mad experience in conversation. Some, he observes, develop an 'ideotism' from being 'for some years . . . the silent and gloomy inhabitants of the Hospital, who have avoided conversation, and sought solitude; consequently have acquired no new ideas'. Written language, in those capable of writing, is also perceived to decay, for even 'Insane people who have been good scholars, after a long confinement lose, in a wonderful degree, the correctness of orthography; when they write, above half the words are generally mis-spelt – they are written according to the pronunciation'.[44]

Haslam's work provides illuminating material on attitudes to-wards the mad and their language, and will be discussed again in later sections. But he also demonstrates convincingly that the discourse of the mad, when conducted in the context of other mad discourse, will increasingly 'lose sight' of the structures and coherence of 'sane' discourse, and, when attended to only by those convinced of the patient's madness, will be regarded as further evidence of insanity.

The most extreme version of the line of thought represented in such detail by Haslam is found in the practice of Patrick Blair, whose water treatment has already been described. One particular case dramatically brings together a therapy and an attitude towards mad language. Here what the patient has to say, and what she chooses not to say, are the major symptoms of derangement, and her ability, or willingness, to say the right thing is, for Blair, the sure sign that she is cured. The signs of madness are that the woman

> neglected every thing, would not own her husband nor any of the Family, kept her room, would converse with nobody but kept spitting continually, turning from any that turn'd from her and chiding any who put their hand in their sides, telling them she was not a whore.[45]

Blair straight away recognises the seriousness of the case, and begins the 'great preparation' of treating 'the vitiated humours' in order to render the patient well enough to undergo the water therapy. This necessitates 'frequent bleedings, violent Emeticks, strong purgatives and potent Sudorificks and Narcoticks' as well as 'sutable and specifick Alteratives'. (A 'Sudorifick' was given to encourage perspiration.) No change is apparent, however, even after a month of such treatment. The 'second course of physick', which continues for five weeks, is 'a salivation which I usually have recourse in such cases'. (Salivation depended upon the administration of a substance such as mercury in order to produce excessive saliva.) This proves more successful, and the patient begins 'to enquire more seriously into the state of domestic affairs . . . shew'd a desire to be at home, quitted much of her former gestures speech and behaviour' and 'was obedient when reprov'd because of them'. Yet she retains 'the dislike of her husband', even though 'she would sometimes allow her self to be called by his name which she could not endure before'.

In the encounter between linguistic and behavioural independence and the physical violence of orthodox medicines, a kind of truce has been achieved. The patient has modified the offending habits of speech and has returned to her normal character in being concerned for the house and family. Thus far she has shown herself willing to readopt the role expected of her by husband, physician and society. She will not, however, reassume the role of wife. Having denied the name of 'whore' at the beginning of her 'illness', she will not now automatically accept her husband's name. Her linguistic and sexual rebellion is not wholly subdued in this most significant of points. She has ceased to be her husband's object, and in so doing has become the object of medical practice. But she is apparently prepared, even after more than two months of treatment, to stand out for her individual rights – to an existence as an individual, to a language of her own, to a name of her own.

Blair has recourse to the ultimate solution.

I train'd her into the Engine house putting her in hopes of getting home from thence that night but when she went into the Room in which she was to Lay I ordered her to be blindfolded. Her nurse and other women stript her. She was lifted up by force, plac'd in and fixt to the Chair in the bathing Tub. All this put her in an unexpressable terrour especially when the water was let down. I kept her under the fall 30 minutes, stopping the pipe now and then and enquiring whether she would take to her husband but she still obstinately deny'd till at last being much fatigu'd with the pressure of the water she promised she would do what I desired.

Next day, however, she remains 'obstinate', so Blair resumes the treatment a week later, this time with an extra means of assault at his disposal.

I gave her another Tryal by adding a smaller pipe so that when the one let the water fall on the top of her head the other squirted it in her face or any other part of her head neck or breast I thought proper. Being still very strong I gave her 60 minutes at this time when she still kept so obstinate that she would not promise to take to her husband till her spirits being allmost dissipated she promised to Love him as before.

The secondary attack with the 'smaller pipe' on the 'stript' woman's blindfolded 'head neck or breast' brings home the strongly sexual nature the encounter has now assumed, with the physician taking on the role of substitute husband and conducting an assault every bit as shocking as anything the patient might previously have suffered in her former existence as a 'whore'. Ironically, the 'unfit' or improper speech that was the first sign of this woman's 'illness' has been succeeded by a chain of reactions and therapies in which the medical man finally carries out a species of rape which, in a crazy overturning of all sense of propriety and linguistic decency, he 'thought proper'.

Still the woman will not keep to the word she has given under the duress of Blair's treatment, and after 'Evacuations . . . for 2 or 3 dayes more' she is brought once again to the water. 'I gave her the 3d Tryal of the fall and continued her 90 minutes under it, promised obedience as before but she was as sullen and obstinate as ever the next day.' A sort of dialogue then ensues, which proves to be one-sided when Blair gives not answers to what seem quite reasonable questions, but threats. These do seem to have the required effect.

Being upon resentment why I should treat her so, after 2 or 3 dayes I threatned her with the fourth Tryal, took her out of bed, had her stript, blindfolded and ready to be put in the Chair, when being terrify'd with what she was to undergo she kneeld submissively that I would spare her and she would become a Loving obedient and dutiful Wife for ever thereafter. I granted her request provided she would go to bed with her husband that night, which she did with great chearfullness.

Blair, curious about such things, calculates 'that in 90 minutes there was 15 Ton of water let fall upon her'.

The physician's success, based on becoming himself a more terrifying threat to sanity and selfhood than the husband, is a curious victory, for his patient is simply required to speak the sentences he wishes to hear. The madness that found expression in her uncharacteristic language will only be regarded as dispelled when her words prove that she has returned to an acceptable norm of linguistic capability. Mad language is attended to, but only in so far as it demonstrates the madness. What is not attended to is what the mad language is saying. Similarly, sane language is listened for, and sane behaviour is required to follow, but provided words and deeds match then neither physician nor husband are concerned at what such lip-service has cost in terms of real sanity. The madness and its successful cure are both measured on the same register, but it is a register against which anything the profession does not wish to hear will be ruled out of order, 'unfit', obsessive, or raving. Blair, visiting his former patient after a month, 'saw everything in good order'.[46] He 'saw' that which proved the success of his treatment. He could not hear anything that might have made him think again: he would not have been listening, and it could not have been spoken. Mad language, if it has any sense, goes into retreat in the face of sane treatment.

3

CRACKS IN THE WALLS

One of the most significant documents in the history of madness in the eighteenth century was William Battie's *Treatise on Madness*, published in 1758. Battie was both a classical scholar and a medical man. He became a governor of Bethlem Hospital and, in 1750–1, participated in the founding of St Luke's Hospital for Lunaticks where he was its first physician. He also ran, as many mad-doctors did, his own private madhouse. In 1764 he was elected president of the College of Physicians, the same year as his retirement from St Luke's.[1]

If Bethlem Hospital stood for all that was traditional in attitudes towards the treatment of the insane – restraint, confinement, evacuative remedies and a dynasty of secretive physicians in the Monro family – St Luke's was founded with innovative intentions. One area of innovation was expertise. Among the 'Principal' ends for founding the hospital, as set out in the appeal for funds made in 1750 (which was written by Battie), were the need to attract the best minds to 'this Branch of Physick', and thus to stimulate improvements in the understanding and treatment of the mentally ill, and the necessity for training qualified attendants. As Hunter and Macalpine point out, 'The reference to "Servants peculiarly qualified" was perhaps the first printed statement that mental nursing requires special training.' Care for the patients' well-being was also to be particularly looked to: 'every Patient must have a separate Room, and Diet, most of them, equal to Persons in Health'. After a few years of operation, the hospital, unlike Bethlem, resolved to take in pupils, which was itself a remarkable opening up of the silent world of the confined mad, for it meant that future specialist physicians (including Sir George Baker) were trained through actual observation of patients, and under the instruction of Battie, who thus became 'the first teacher of psychiatry in England if not the world'.[2]

The *Treatise on Madness* was based, therefore, on an attitude towards madness that embraced both openness and a humane concern for the welfare of patients. Battie attacked, for example, the traditional remedies prescribed indiscriminately for all kinds of madness: 'e.g. bleeding, blisters, caustics, rough cathartics, the gumms and faetid anti-hysterics, opium, mineral waters, cold bathing, and vomits'. Bleeding, for Battie, was 'no more the adequate and constant cure of Madness, than it is of fever', while 'the lancet, when applied to a feeble and convulsed Lunatic' was no 'less destructive than a sword'. In fact, fundamental to his approach was the conviction that madness, which 'is frequently taken for one species of disorder, nevertheless, when thoroughly examined, . . . discovers as much variety with respect to its causes and circumstances as any distemper whatever'.[3] For this reason, 'all general methods' should be avoided in the treatment of mad patients, quite apart from the observed inutility of most of them. Indeed, not only does Battie recommend the laying aside of treatments when they are clearly achieving nothing, but he also goes so far as to recommend no treatment at all.

> Nor let us immediately despair at being obliged to withhold that assistance which seemed the most effectual, or conclude that, because the patient cannot be relieved by art, he therefore cannot be relieved at all. For Madness, like several other animal distempers, oftentimes ceases spontaneously, that is without our being able to assign a sufficient reason; and many a Lunatic, who by the repetition of vomits and other convulsive stimuli would have been strained into downright Idiotism, has when given over as incurable recovered his understanding.[4]

Instead of the previous names and species of disorder, however – '*Lunacy, Spleen, Melancholy, Hurry of the Spirits, & c*'[5] – Battie prefers a simple division into two: '*Original*' and '*Consequential*'. 'Original' madness 'neither follows nor accompanies any accident', is often hereditary, and gives rise to the fear 'that the nerves or instruments of Sensation in such persons are not originally formed perfect and like the nerves of other men'. Such madness 'is not removable by any method, which the science of Physick in its present imperfect state is able to suggest', though patients may of themselves make a 'perfect recovery'. 'Consequential' madness does follow upon 'other disorders or external causes', both physical and emotional, including injuries, concussions, inflammations, the operation of poisons, various diseases such as venereal, the experience of violent passions, concentration of the mind into an obsession, different kinds of overindulgence, and inactivity. One distinction of Battie's attitude towards this species of madness is that he regards relief as possible not by purges or vomits or any other medicinal application, but simply 'by the removal or correction of such disorders or causes'. This must be speedily effected, however, for 'the force and continued action of such causes' will render habitual the deranged operations of the mind.[6]

What is apparent in Battie's attitudes, and especially with regard to 'Consequential Madness', is that becoming mad was an outcome of some distinctive experience or accident in the patient's former life. Battie, differing from the suppressive line of theorists and practitioners discussed in the previous chapter, attributes madness to 'deluded imagination':

> Deluded imagination, which is not only an indisputable but an essential character of Madness . . . precisely discriminates this from all other animal disorders: or that man and that man alone is properly mad, who is fully and unalterably persuaded of the Existence or of the appearance of any thing, which either does not exist or does not actually appear to him, and who behaves according to such erroneous persuasion.[7]

Of particular significance in Battie's departure, as Klaus Doerner points out, is that his ideas involved 'taking the perceptions of the insane seriously'.[8] No longer was madness something to be coerced into conformity, for the judgement was not the faculty suffering from vitiation. Rather, the judgement remained unimpaired but judged upon the basis of wrongly perceived or mistakenly believed evidence: 'erroneous persuasion'. Moreover, instead of madness being the obstinate refusal of the madman to accept what other men took as rationally true, each lunatic could now be regarded as mad in his own distinctive manner, depending upon the individual delusions of his imaginative faculty. Disorder, as Doerner adds, 'is recognized as more profound and more real, as a new, autonomous reality – precisely in its fictitiousness'.[9]

To endorse the 'fictitiousness', as Battie's attitude implies, is not to give up hopes of effecting a cure. Instead of 'treatment', however,

Battie preferred to speak of 'management'. Along with his dismissal of the efficacy of traditional 'general' medicines, he endorses 'the saying of a very eminent practitioner in such cases *that management did much more than medicine*'. Management necessitates confinement, but in conditions that are comparable to those provided for the sufferers from any other illness, for

> Madness is, contrary to the opinion of some unthinking persons, as manageable as many other distempers, which are equally dreadful and obstinate, and yet are not looked upon as incurable: and that such unhappy objects ought by no means to be abandoned, much less shut up in loathsome prisons as criminals or nusances to the society.

That John Haslam was still wondering, in 1798, how far the decay of his patients' faculties was owing to 'long confinement' with other 'silent and gloomy inhabitants' is a measure of how far Bethlem and the traditionalists lagged behind Battie and St Luke's. For Battie, confinement is not the removal of the madman in order to prevent him from becoming a social nuisance, but a positive prerequisite for a cure, sometimes even the means of cure itself: 'repeated experience has convinced me that confinement alone is sometimes sufficient, but always so necessary, that without it every method hitherto devised for the cure of Madness would be ineffectual'.[10]

Positive confinement gave prominence to the notion of the 'asylum'. Confinement no longer meant shutting in, but rather the exclusion of all those pressures and pleasures that could be seen as contributing to the madness. If a patient had become mad through the influence of his or her whole way of life, then the first steps towards cure had to be removal from home, family, friends, business, habits and indulgences, and immersion in the regimen of the asylum. Thus was governed the patient's waking and sleeping hours, his company, servants, diet, exercise and daily activities. Within this temperate and ordered mode of living, the appetites would become accustomed to moderation, the imagination turned to new channels, while the nerves were protected from excitement or harassment. The patient, with or without the application of medicinal remedies, would be managed back to health.

Battie's significance is threefold. Most immediately, he brought about a reply to his *Treatise* from John Monro, the second member of the family to reign as physician to Bethlem Hospital. After two hundred years of silence from Bethlem, Monro's publication seems to be a genuine crack in the walls of psychiatric reticence, a professional of the old school speaking out on the secrets of his profession. Monro had been implicitly charged by Battie with keeping treatment of the insane to a select group of physicians, with relying on a set of useless medicines and treatments, and with retarding the knowledge and cure of madness. Monro published his *Remarks on Dr Battie's Treatise on Madness* only a few months later, in 1758, but it is a document full of ironies, for Monro finds himself talking about that which, as he says, he sees no point in discussing. Madness, for Monro, is 'of such a nature, that very little of real use can be said concerning it', nor would 'My own inclination . . . have led me to appear in print' but for the necessity of answering Battie's 'undeserved censures'.[11]

Monro's *Remarks*, then, is a document that should never have been, the manifestation in print of a silence that resents in every word the instigation that has compelled it to exist. The pamphlet is a mere sixty pages long, and depends largely upon answering the *Treatise*, though with occasional reference to Monro's own cases in order to prove a point. The very typography of the text, with italicisation or capitalisation of Battie's words at every opportunity, and its litter of footnotes citing the page references in Battie, displays its unwillingness to come forth in its own right.

> The author's definition of madness, as well as I can recollect it, is this; *the perception of objects not really existing, or not really corresponding to the senses*, is a *certain sign of madness; therefore* DELUDED IMAGINATION *precisely discriminates this, from all other animal disorders*. Definitions are of no use, unless they convey precise and determinate ideas; and if this be one of the right kind, I am very unfortunate in not being able to comprehend it.

It is a quandary of all 'answerers' that their work would not exist had it not been for the existence of a previous document. Monro not only confesses that he has nothing to say for himself: in scorning Battie's arguments he also attempts to negate the force of that publication, to render it as futile as he acknowledges his own to be. If Battie, from the unorthodox wing of the psychiatric profession, broke a silence, and thereby led the orthodox Monro to speak out, what Monro actually produced came as close as any publication could to consigning the entire exchange to the void. Monro's own definition of madness is 'a *vitiated judgement*', to which he adds, 'though I cannot take upon me to say that even this definition is absolute and perfect'.[12] Attempting to define true madness may not quite be nothing but mad, but the implication of Monro's remarks is that the whole discussion is simply spinning out language to no useful purpose. Silence, apparently, is preferable to wasted words.

From the historian's point of view, Battie has a further significance in that he gives focus and authority to an undercurrent of medical thought and practice that had existed throughout the eighteenth century. Not all writers on madness were committed to the suppressive stance, though it is often difficult to disentangle suppressive and endorsive strands within individual authorities. But a distinctive line does emerge of medical and semi-medical men who expressed marked interest in the mad as individual cases, as personalities to be attended to, and as capable of speaking a language that could be recorded, understood and responded to.

Richard Baxter, for example, the seventeenth-century divine whose *Signs and Causes of Melancholy* was posthumously collected from his works in 1716 by Samuel Clifford, saw dialogue with melancholy persons as part of a group activity that would ease them back into health.

> As much as you can, divert them from the Thoughts which are their Trouble; keep them on some other Talk or Business; break in upon them, and interrupt their Musings; raise them out of it, but with loving Importunity: Suffer them not to be long alone, get fit Company to them, or them to it. . . . It's an useful way if you can, to engage them in comforting others, that are in deeper Distresses than themselves: For this will tell them, that their Case is not singular, and they will speak to themselves, while they speak to others.[13]

Timothy Rogers, like Baxter and Clifford a Nonconformist minister, not only recommends sympathy and engaging in discourse with melancholy patients, but even advises having 'recourse to such Doctors as have themselves felt it; for it is impossible fully to understand the nature of it any other way than by Experience'. Talking, for Rogers, can effect a great deal, and his readers are warned not to 'think it altogether needless to talk with them'. And in particular the speech of melancholiacs should be taken seriously:

You must be so kind to your Friends under this Disease, as to believe what they say. Or however, that their apprehensions are such as they tell you they are; do not you think that they are at ease when they say they are in pain. It is a foolish course which some take with their Melancholly Friends, to answer all their Complaints and Moans with this, That its nothing but Fancy; nothing but Imagination and Whimsey. It is a Real Disease, a Real Misery that they are tormented with: and if it be Fancy, yet a diseased Fancy is as great a Disease as any other.[14]

As Nonconformist divines, Baxter and Rogers were within a tradition in which prayer, talk with God, and community were significant features of everyday life. Rogers's insistence on the validation of suffering, whatever its cause, reflects a reliance on the strength of communal support for individual weakness.[15] Sir Richard Blackmore, who became physician to William and to Anne, made a similar assertion to Rogers's in writing in 1725 about the 'hypocondriacal and hysterical affections':

It is certain, that Hypocondriacal Men, as well as Hysterick Women, are often afflicted with various Pains and great Disorders; and could it be supposed that this was nothing but the Effect of Fancy, and a delusive Imagination, yet it must be allowed, that let the Cause of such Symptoms be never so chimerical and fantastick, the consequent Sufferings are without doubt real and unfeigned. Terrible Ideas, formed only in the Imagination, will affect the Brain and the Body with painful Sensations.[16]

Other writers close to practical medicine also showed themselves capable of responding effectively to the personalities and speech of their patients without recourse to the suppressive therapies of more orthodox practitioners. Peter Shaw, who attended at various times both George II and George III, published his pamphlet *The Juice of the Grape; or, Wine Preferable to Water. A Treatise Wherein Wine is Shewn to be a Grand Preserver of Health, with a Word of Advice to the Vintners* in 1724, and a much longer work, *The Reflector: Representing Human Affairs as they Are; and may be Improved* in 1750. In the latter he cites approvingly a 'certain Author' who 'defines a Doctor to be a Man who writes Prescriptions, till the

Patient either dies, or is cured by Nature',[17] a sentiment shared with Sir George Baker, Battie's pupil and physician to George III. Baker's argument, however, is made at greater length, and is particularly concerned with the role of the mind in illness: it is, he says,

> impossible for the mind to suffer without the body becoming sick also or the body to be ill without the mind being associated with it in the distemper. From ignorance of this fact it comes about that in curing diseases there is often a great deal of confused meddling which is entirely vain and achieves nothing for all its untimely intervention. In how many cases is the mind at fault when a hodge-podge of medicines composed of almost all the elements collected from every source is applied to the stomach. It will exhaust the patient's purse a good deal sooner than it will get rid of the trouble. Surely here the best medicine is no medicine.[18]

Shaw, anticipating Battie's *Treatise* by some eight years, places the emphasis in both the cause and the cure of mental diseases upon the imagination: 'Many Diseases arise from a perverted Imagination: and some of them are cured by affecting the Imagination only. It appears almost incredible, what great Effects the Imagination has upon Patients; but especially those of a particular Turn and Make'.[19] The skill requisite in a good physician, particularly in cases of mental derangement, for Shaw, is that which will attune him to his patient's frame of mind, to his or her 'Turn and Make'.

In *The Juice of the Grape*, Shaw gives examples of such attunement, and the effectiveness of the 'cures' he is thereby able to induce. He instances the case of a 'Maiden Gentlewoman of a considerable Fortune' who has suffered 'for many years' from 'the hysterical Disease (which is the same in Females as the Hippo in Men)'. She consults Shaw after a long period on orthodox medicines – 'such Quantities of Cathartick, Antihysterick, Bezoartick and Chalybeate Medicines, as for several succeeding Years cost her Eighty Pounds per Annum' – by which time she has been 'reduced to a very low State indeed, and worn almost to a Skeleton, and appearing with a very meagre Look, and wanting all manner of Appetite'. Her mental symptoms include being 'full of Whimsies and strange Fancies' and 'daily foretelling at what Minute of Time she shou'd expire the next Day'.

I said to her with an Air of Chearfulness, Madam, your several Physicians were very ingenious Gentlemen, and have perform'd all within the Compass of Art, so that I find nothing left for me to do in the ordinary Road, suffer me therefore to put you into a new Method, and to shew you how you may become your own Physician. Be pleas'd, Madam, said I, in the Presence of her Sister, to slice the Rind of two *Sevil Oranges*, and set it to steep, for a Day or two, in a Quart Bottle of Sherry; and of this Liquor, when strain'd, take half a Wine-Glass every Morning, fasting; as much an Hour before Dinner, and again the like when you go to Bed.

To the patient's protests, 'But, Sir . . . will you prescribe me nothing to take? I must have Physick, some Bolusses, and a Cordial, or I shall never live till Morning', Shaw replies that he intends 'to make you your own Physician, and wou'd have you take to your self the Care and Honour of the Cure'. 'At least, Madam,' he continues, 'for one Day let alone all Physick except that of your own preparing'. This patient, adds Shaw, 'in her Health had a great Inclination to Physick, and was never better pleas'd than in preparing some cordial Water or Conserve'. Now she takes equal pleasure in 'making her own Wine' and on the next visit she 'propos'd to improve my Medicine, by an Addition of some Spices'. Gradually, as 'her Appetite and Strength began to return' so 'her Fits of crying and other Symptoms left her' and she completely recovered 'without any other Remedy'.[20]

What is distinctive in Shaw's presentation of the case is, first and foremost, that he is actually perceived in dialogue with the patient. Shaw's own words during consultation are set down in a scene of some liveliness (the 'Chearfulness' of his address, the interjected 'Madam', the presence of the sister, the alarm of the patient), and the patient is allowed the comparative privilege of speaking for herself, rather than being simply the reported set of symptoms so common in medical case histories. She is taken at her own valuation, what she has to say is responded to directly, and her treatment is made to suit the style and distinctiveness of her personality. The physician in fact depends upon linguistic exchange for the initiation of his prescription, and the more genuine that exchange is the better chance his prescription has of success. Shaw's effectiveness with words is evident both in the consultation and in his reporting of it. A convincing encounter is described, and the fact that the participants carry conviction also acts as an endorsement of Shaw's approach to mental disturbance. The efficacy of his treatment, of his whole attitude towards patients and prescribing, is conveyed by his capacity in rendering the scene as much as by our knowledge of the successful outcome.

George Cheyne provides an interesting variation among physicians whose explanation and treatment for mental illnesses endorse rather than suppress the experience and individuality of the patient. Cheyne, above all eighteenth-century medical men, exemplifies Rogers's insistence that the doctor should himself have experienced the melancholy for which he treats his patients, for not only had he been a chronic hypochondriac but had also cured himself of his condition, and alleviated the obesity that accompanied it (he reported himself as weighing over 32 stones) by diet alone. Cheyne's own case is included in his book *The English Malady: or, a Treatise of Nervous Diseases of all Kinds*, published in 1733. Cheyne does endorse the experience that has led to the individual's condition, but does so with a rigour and disapprobation that puts the blame for illness firmly with the patient, with his life style, and with his engagement in the luxuries and idlenesses of contemporary society. One *is* ill distinctively for Cheyne, but that means facing, as he had himself done, the responsibility for having brought about one's own mental and physical downfall. The English malady is our badge of shame, and is caused by

> intemperance, want of due Exercise, rioting in sensual Pleasures, casual excessive Evacuations of any Kind, Fevers and other acute Diseases not duly manag'd, by which the Juices have been made sizy or corrosive, and the due Tone, Spring and Elasticity of the Nerves or Solids relax'd and broken, whereby the true acquir'd Nervous Disorders are produc'd.[21]

There is, certainly, a mechanical reason for falling ill, and in this Cheyne is a follower of Thomas Willis (though he does overtly dismiss Willis's 'animal spirits'), but his writing has a peculiarly moral slant when he points solely to the way the individual lives his life in accounting for the onset of mental illness. He is especially harsh on 'the present Custom of Living, so much in great, populous, and over-grown Cities', not least in '*London* (where nervous Distempers are most frequent, outrageous, and unnatural)', for in cities one finds

> the infinite Number of Fires, Sulphureous and Bituminous, the vast expence of Tallow and foetid Oil in Candles and Lamps, under and above Ground, the Clouds of stinking Breaths, and Perspiration, not to mention the Ordure of so many diseas'd, both intelligent and unintelligent Animals.[22]

Illness, for Cheyne, is punishment inflicted by nature for the life one has lived.

> In itself this Law and Establishment of Nature has infinite Beauty, Wisdom, and Goodness: *viz.* by this progressive and continual Succession from one Root, that the Healthy and Virtuous should thereby be growing continually healthier, and the Bad continually becoming more miserable and unhealthy, till their Punishment forced them upon Virtue and Temperance; for Virtue and Happiness are literally and really Cause and Effect.[23]

At least this even-handedness by nature allows the prospect of redemption, and indeed the unhealthy vicious individual has it in his power to enage actively in the pursuit of health and virtue. This involves, not unexpectedly, choosing to turn aside from the ways of excess to a plainer, more sparing mode of living. First, however, the help of the physician is needed in order to restore the body's tone in preparation for the radical change in diet upon which Cheyne insists. This help comes in the achievement of three 'Intentions'. Initially, treatment must be prescribed in order 'to thin, dilute, and sweeten the whole Mass of the Fluids, to destroy their Viscidity and Glewiness' and to make their 'Circulation full and free'.[24] This is to be achieved by the traditional methods of '*Bleeding, Purging, Vomiting*', and includes recommendation of mercury and '*Wild Valerian*'.[25] The next 'Intention' is to 'divide, break and dissolve the saline, acrid and hard *Concretions*, generated in the small Vessels, and to destroy all *Sharpness* and *Acrimony* lodged in the Habit, and to make the Juices soft, sweet, and balsamick'.[26] For this, those medicines that are 'of the most *active* and *volatile* Kind' are required for their '*penetrating* Steam or Vapour . . . like that of Fire or Light'. These will 'most readily pervade the Solids, and get into the most inmost Recesses of the Habit'. '*Assa foetida*' is recommended here, along with 'The Product of our own

Country, *Garlick* and *Horse-Radish'*. The *'Bath* Waters' can be taken, 'because of their *Sulphur'*, and also *'Steel'*.[27] Cheyne's *'third* and last *Intention'* is to 'restore the *Tone* and *elastick* Force, to crisp, wind up, and contract the *Fibres* of the whole *System'*, which is something that can be very imperfectly achieved by the 'Power of *Art'*.[28] Yet the physician should try medicines of 'the Strengthening and Astringent Kind', those 'which *contract, corrugate,* wind up and give Firmness and Force to the weak and relaxed Solids, Fibres and Nerves', for example *'Jesuit's Bark, Steel, Gentian . . . Wormwood . . . Mistletoe . . . Acorns'*.[29]

So far Cheyne's recommendations do not differ markedly from, say, Sydenham's. There is the same model of illness and the same range of prescriptions for cure. Where Cheyne is unusual, however, and what distinguishes him from the suppressive line of prescribing, is in the responsibility he now places on the patient for completing and consolidating his own restoration. Where the 'Power of *Art'* can cure but imperfectly, the patient is obliged to take over and accomplish an entire change through the *'Milk* and *Vegetable Diet'*. This consists of 'Milk, with *Tea, Coffee, Bread* and *Butter, mild Cheese, Salladin, Fruits,* and *Seeds* of all Kinds, with tender *Roots* (as *Potatoes, Turnips, Carrots*) and, in short, every Thing that has not *Life'*.[30] This, he declares in 'The Author's Case', is his own regimen 'at present', arrived at after a long course of suffering and self-help.

The moral and spiritual dimensions to Cheyne's analysis of the English malady and his recommendations for its cure gain particular force from his account of his own illness and recovery. Repeatedly, his descriptions of his own physical symptoms are elaborated upon in terms of spiritual analogy. He suffers from vertigo and apoplexy:

> I found after this, some small Returns of my *Vertigo* (in Bed especially) on lying on a particular Side, or pressing upon a particular Part of my Head; but by degrees it turned to a constant violent *Head-ach, Giddiness, Lowness, Anxiety* and *Terror,* so that I went about like a *Malefactor* condemn'd, or one who expected every *Moment* to be crushed by a *ponderous* Instrument of death, hanging over his Head.[31]

Similarly, a turning-point in his cure is not when he recognises himself as physically ill, but when the force of his spiritual desolation impresses itself upon him.

I began to reflect and consider seriously, whether I might not (through *Carelessness* and *Self-sufficiency*, *Voluptuousness* and Love of *Sensuality*, which might have impaired my *Spiritual* Nature) have neglected to examine with sufficient Care . . . *if* there might not . . . be higher more noble, and more enlightening *Principles* revealed to Mankind *somewhere*.[32]

Physical cure and moral awakening go hand in hand in Cheyne's medical universe, and the patient who can put his own spiritual house in order will inevitably be rewarded with a healthy body.

The nature of individual responsibility for illness and health is constantly impressed by Cheyne upon his readers, in spite of the parade of traditional medicines and treatments he also feels obliged to recommend. His own case, however, brings a uniquely personal focus to his work. Here is a physician whose prescriptions are not delivered from a stance of detachment, an aloof commentator on the bodies he is called upon to treat. Instead, medical language is being adapted to accommodate part of the life story of the man who is to be taken by the reader as living proof of the efficacy of his own maxims. This emphasis on 'I', on personal emotion and sensation, on the individual working his way towards the vision of moral and physical health, gives a reassuringly human, even a confessional, tone to his writing. Language is capable, in Cheyne's work, of recovering the testimony of the mentally afflicted in order to enforce the authority of medical knowledge. Personal experience, publicly recalled, gives direction and force to *The English Malady*, but is also the context for Cheyne's professional account of mental illness. In his description of the second stage of 'Vapours', for example, there is the feeling of felt affliction in what could have been simply a list of symptoms. This stage is marked by

a deep and fixed *Melancholy*, *wandering* and *delusory Images* on the Brain, and *Instability* and *Unsettledness* in all the intellectual Operations, *Loss of Memory*, *Despondency*, *Horror* and *Despair*, a *Vertigo*, *Giddiness* or *Staggering*, *Vomittings* of *Yellow*, *Green*, or *Black Choler*: sometimes unaccountable Fits of *Laughing*, apparent *Joy*, *Leaping* and *Dancing*; at other Times, of *Crying*, *Grief*, and *Anguish*; and these generally terminate in *Hypochondriacal* or *Hysterical Fits* (I mean *Convulsive* ones) and *Faintings*, which leave a Drowsiness, *Lethargy*, and extreme

Lowness of Spirits for some Time afterwards.[33]

There were physicians, then, such as Cheyne, who placed a value on the testimony of the mentally ill. In Cheyne's case, he turned that testimony to system in working out and advocating his own regimen. The strength of Cheyne's moral analysis of madness, however, and of the moral nature of the individual's responsibility for its cure, does not achieve its full force until the moral management movement towards the end of the century, and its institutionalisation in the York Retreat for Quaker insane, founded by William Tuke in 1792. Meanwhile, away from the clinic, there was a strong line of philosophical discourse on the nature of the mind and of our understanding of mental processes that provides another strand in the thought and practice that preceded and accompanied the work of Battie at St Luke's. Moral philosophers such as Frances Hutcheson in the first half of the century, and later Thomas Reid and John Gregory, who were part of the movement known as the Scottish 'Common Sense' school of philosophy, developed modes of enquiry into our capacity for feeling and thinking, and into the interrelations of body and mind, passions and thoughts, that, in the work of Gregory in particular, have a direct bearing on attitudes towards the mentally ill.

Hutcheson, who was Professor of Moral Philosophy in the University of Glasgow, and founder of the 'Common Sense' line, argued that 'our Passions are not so much in our Power, as some seem to imagine, from the topicks used either to raise or allay them'. On the contrary,

> We are so constituted by Nature, that, as soon as we form the Idea of certain Objects or Events, our Desire or Aversion will arise toward them; and consequently our Affections must very much depend upon the Opinions we form, concerning any thing which occurs to our Mind, its Qualities, Tendencies, or Effects.

Such is our lack of control of our passions that 'a certain Temperament may be brought upon the Body, by its being frequently put into Motion by the Passions of Anger, Joy, Love, or Sorrow', while 'the Continuance of this Temperament shall make Men prone to the severall Passions for the future'. Crucially, therefore, for Hutcheson, 'we see how impossible it is for one to judge of the

57

Degrees of Happiness or Misery in others, unless he knows their Opinions, their Associations of Ideas, and the Degrees of their Desires and Aversions'. 'Common Sense' leads to this conclusion: that individual states of mind, of pleasure and misery, are far from common, and that assessment of the individual mind requires an ability to put aside one's own 'Opinions . . . Associations of Ideas . . . Desires and Aversions' in order to engage with those of another.

Hutcheson's discussion of the passions and associated emotions allows a considerable measure of proximity to the central issues of madness, particularly in terms of the strengthening or weighting of the fundamental appetites by mental or emotional pressure. Our 'bodily Appetites', says Hutcheson, are 'easily satisfied':

> Nature has put it in almost every one's power, so far to gratify them, as to support the Body, and remove Pain. But when Opinion, and confused Ideas, or Fancy comes in, and represents some particular kinds of Gratifications, or great Variety of them, as of great Importance; when Ideas of Dignity, Grandure, Magnificence, Generosity, or any other moral Species, are joined to the Objects of Appetites, they may furnish us with endless Labour, Vexation, and Misery of every kind.

The consequence of these 'Associations of Ideas' is

> that they raise the Passions into an extravagant Degree, beyond the proportion of the real Good in the Object: And commonly beget some secret Opinions to justify the Passions. But then the Confutation of these false Opinions is not sufficient to break the Association, so that the Desire or Passion shall continue, even when our Understanding has suggested to us, that the Object is not good, or not proportioned to the Strength of the Desire.

If this suggests an agreement with Nicholas Robinson on the inutility of attempting to reason a man out of his madness, Hutcheson's position is in reality diametrically opposed to Robinson's. For Robinson, the madman's madness is the culmination of a set of mechanical events. For Hutcheson, not only are we all potentially not under the control of our own understanding, but we can only begin to appreciate the behaviour of ourselves and our fellows when we have given due weight to the hidden compulsion exerted by 'Associations'. That we are so often unable to achieve this understanding is, in part, owing to the contagious nature of extravagant passions:

> the constant Indulgence of any Desire, the frequent Repetition of it, the diverting our Minds from all other Pursuits, the Strain of Conversation among Men of the same Temper, who often haunt together, the Contagion in the very Air and Countenance of the passionate, beget such wild Associations of Ideas, that a sudden Conviction of Reason, will not stop the Desire or Aversion.[34]

This interrelatedness of mind and body, an interrelatedness that includes the modes of mental agility that can reconcile a desire or aversion with an understanding that has weighed and justly assessed the object of passion, was further explored by Hutcheson's successors. Thomas Reid, who also became Professor of Moral Philosophy at Glasgow, placed his emphasis upon the necessity of exploring in the finest detail the human mind. His *Inquiry into the Human Mind, on the Principles of Common Sense* was published in 1764. Reid lamented the advantage of the anatomist, who could examine 'with equal accuracy, bodies of all different ages, sexes, and conditions', over the 'anatomist of the mind'. For the latter, while he could 'collect the operations of other minds' from 'outward signs', had to rely on 'what he perceives within himself' in order to interpret this evidence. Ideally, says Reid, we should wish to see a whole history of an individual mind from its earliest infancy.

> Could we obtain a distinct and full history of all that hath passed in the mind of a child from the beginning of life and sensation, till it grows up to the use of reason; how its infant faculties began to work, and how they brought forth and ripened all the various notions, opinions, and sentiments, which we find in ourselves when we come to be capable of reflection; this would be a treasure of natural history, which would probably give more light into the human faculties, than all the systems of philosophers about them since the beginning of the world.

'Reflection', however, which is 'the only instrument by which we can discern the powers of the mind', is a faculty that 'comes too late to observe the progress of nature in raising them from their infancy to perfection'. It therefore depends upon the individual enquirer to 'unravel' his own 'notions and opinions, till he finds out the simple and original principles of his constitution', allowing due weight to 'all the prejudices of education, fashion, and philosophy' under which he has 'grown up'.[35]

Reid's approach, while it has obvious implications for the writing and reading of autobiography and fiction, is also of marked significance to the attempt to understand the onset and progress of mental illness. How can we possibly begin to treat the deranged mind when we have so limited an access to the normal one? Indeed, when Hutcheson's arguments are also taken into account, how can we tell what is normal, or where a 'normal' measure of uncontrol begins to shade into derangement? These aspects of the enquiry find a specifically medical focus in the writing of John Gregory, for Gregory was not only a professor of philosophy, but subsequently of medicine and of the practice of physic, and also became Scottish physician to George III. Like many of his predecessors, Gregory saw the mind–body relation as fundamental to an understanding of man and his illnesses.

> It has been the misfortune of most of those who have study'd the Philosophy of the Human Mind, that they have been little acquainted with the structure of the Human Body, and the laws of the Animal Oeconomy; and yet the Mind and Body are so intimately connected, and have such a mutual influence on one another, that the constitution of either, examined apart, can never be thoroughly understood. For the same reason it has been an unspeakable loss to Physicians, that they have been so generally inattentive to the peculiar laws of the Mind and their influence on the Body.

For Gregory, the physician may therefore as properly be called upon to treat the imagination as the body. But in the understanding of the disordered imagination he is hampered by the variety and complexity of theories and facts available to him. The physician who treats bodily disease requires nothing 'but assiduous and accurate observation, and a good Understanding to direct the proper application of such observation'. The mental physician, however, finds that his observation must encompass human nature itself in all its forms and idiosyncrasies, and the application of it depends as much upon instinct as upon formal understanding.

To cure the diseases of the Mind, there is required that intimate knowledge of the Human Heart, which must be drawn from life itself, and which books can never teach, of the various disguises, under which Vice recommends herself to the Imagination, the artful association of Ideas which she forms there, the many nameless circumstances that soften the Heart and render it accessible, the Arts of insinuation and persuasion, the Art of breaking false associations of Ideas, or inducing counter associations, and employing one Passion against another; and when such a knowledge is acquired, the successful application of it to practice depends in a considerable degree on powers which no extent of Understanding can confer.[36]

The physician of mental disorders must therefore have acquired an intimate understanding of a wide range of human minds if he is to achieve anything by his art. The implications of this requirement are daunting. Far from regarding his patient as a set of observable symptoms, to be categorised in traditional ways and treated by means of traditional remedies, each patient is now a unique case, mad in a way that comprehends the entirety of his or her past, personality and unconscious habits of mind. The physician is to attempt to enter those mental processes, to pass through the cracks in the walls of madness in order to test and survey the structure and texture of the mad mind. At the same time, however, there is also the implication that the madman does not constitute a separate category from the sane individual. His mind, rather, stands towards one end of a spectrum of human minds, sharing many of the mental features and processes of other minds, and sharing, too, their uniqueness. The physician is not to consider him in isolation, but as one variation in the multiplicity of forms available for human mental existence.

One of the most forbidding challenges to the acquisition and communication of this understanding is identified by Reid. It is the problem of language itself. What he has to say about the language of philosophers is equally applicable to the language of medical enquirers into the same field of investigation: the human mind.

The language of philosophers with regard to the original faculties of the mind, is so adapted to the prevailing system, that it cannot fit any other; like a coat that fits the man for whom it was made, and shows him to advantage, which yet will fit very awkward upon one of a different make, although perhaps as handsome and as well proportioned.

Language is here a barrier to understanding and to acceptance of new observations and ideas. But language must inevitably be refashioned if new processes are to be made available for discussion. Gregory is reduced to speaking to those 'nameless' emotional circumstances that influence the workings of the 'Human Heart'. Reid regards prejudice and misunderstanding as unavoidable, and expects a gradual process of familiarisation before the acceptance of new ideas about the mind. But the problem of how to describe the mind itself, of how to gain entry to the 'nameless' regions of mental isolation remains, for Reid, a problem of how language can be appropriated to enable the advance of philosophical knowledge.

It is hardly possible to make any innovation in our philosophy concerning the mind and its operations, without using new words and phrases, or giving a different meaning to those that are received; a liberty which, even when necessary, creates prejudice and misconstruction, and which must wait the sanction of time to authorise it. For innovations in language, like those in religion and government, are always suspected and disliked by the many, till use hath made them familiar, and prescription hath given them a title.[37]

One practical way in which language was used by medical practitioners in opening new frontiers into mental illness was through the medium of the case history. Physicians had not uncommonly recorded in their published works instances of treatment and cure in order to provide evidence of the efficacy of whatever remedy or theory they happened to be advocating. Such is the 'History of Four Cases' given in 1727 by David Kinneir, who wrote to espouse the use of 'Camphire'.

I. A Gentlewoman of Nineteen Years of Age, from an obstinate Fasting for Two Days, and Aversion to see Company, in a religious Turn before Easter, fell into a deep Melancholy, would not talk, nor answer any Questions for some Time, but moan'd and sigh'd continually; slept very little for Ten Days . . . whereupon a Physician was call'd, who bled her Four Times a Week . . . vomited her, purg'd her, us'd the Cold Bath, and many other Methods common in such Cases, all to no Purpose. . . .

I first began her with an Antimonial Vomit, which had no other Effect than that of setting her fast asleep for Twelve Hours. Next Day I gave her half a Dram of Camphire in a Bolus, and as much at Night. She continu'd to rest well all that Night, and had a great Moistness all over her Body, and in the Day-time a plentiful Discharge of Urine. Thus for Four Days I ply'd her, and afterwards, in the Day-time, I order'd her Pills of Æthiops, Gum-guaiac. Cinnab. Antim. & pulv. de Gutteta; and at Night, the Dose of Camphire. Sensible Alterations every Day for the better, and in Three Weeks Time she enjoy'd the full Use of her Reason.[38]

The status of this patient as object of the physician's treatment and theories is reinforced here by the linguistic patterns of the 'History'. The economy of the first paragraph derives from the writer's need to hasten to the details of his own treatment, which is the reason for writing at all. The cursory listing of the supposed causes of the condition, awkwardly crowding into the sentence before the main verb, and the sequence of main clauses in which the observable symptoms are each given a brief prominence, inevitably detract from the personality of the patient herself while throwing the weight of her identity on to the outward signs of her illness. By the time the list of prior treatment is presented, she has become completely absorbed into the remorseless grammar of traditional medical practice: 'bled her . . . vomited her, purg'd her, us'd the Cold Bath, and many other Methods common in such Cases'. When Kinneir turns in the second paragraph to his own proceeding, his writing becomes a little more leisurely, but this does not alter the patient's status as a personal pronoun and object to the main verbs of the physician's actions. In fact some of the verbs which replace 'vomited' and 'purg'd' are notable for being medically vague and indeed unusual in any form of relation between two people: he 'began her', he 'ply'd her'. Finally, as the terms employed become increasingly abbreviated and exclusively pharmaceutical, the syntax ceases to comply with the norms of English writing ('Alterations every day for the better'), doing so, ironically, as the patient herself begins to enjoy 'the full Use of her Reason'. Far from adapting language as a means of advancing the physician's understanding of the uniqueness of his patient's mental processes, this is language in the process of falling apart as the writer advances the claims of a pre-selected treatment.

Kinneir's patient is reported as talking 'wildly', and even as calling 'for some Water to drink', but nowhere is she granted the privilege of having her actual words set down. The fact that this 'History' is given in *'a letter from Dr David Kinneir . . . to Dr Campbell'*, and begins by referring to their recent 'conversation' on the use of 'Camphire in Maniac Disorders', makes explicit the assumption that meaningful speech is something that goes on between professionals apart from and about patients, while the patient herself has nothing to contribute to the dialogue.

Others, such as John Haslam, presented case histories not in order to advocate a therapy, for the cases recorded by Haslam are not those of cured patients, but as preliminaries to autopsy. Haslam in fact gives no details of treatment, concentrating instead on the behaviour of his cases, and sometimes on their supposed motives. There is never any question but that this patient is mad: beyond that Haslam his little interest. One man

> was a very violent and mischievous patient, and possessed of great bodily strength and activity. Although confined, he contrived several times during the night to tear up the flooring of his cell; and had also detached the wainscoat to a considerable extent, and loosened a number of bricks in the wall. When a new patient was admitted, he generally enticed him into his room, on pretence of being an old acquaintance, and, as soon as he came within his reach, immediately tore his clothes to pieces. He was extremely dexterous with his feet, and frequently took off the hats of those who were near him with his toes, and destroyed them with his teeth. After he had dined he generally bit to pieces a thick wooden bowl, in which his food was served, on the principle of sharpening his teeth against the next meal.[39]

This is the prose equivalent of the by then discontinued practice of visiting 'Bedlam', lunacy as entertainment. Haslam has mixed mad slapstick, described in strong simple overstatements ('tore his clothes to pieces') with a sly vein of insinuating superiority that suggests an ironic complicity between a detached writer and an entertained reader. This shows through in the more civilised diction of words and phrases like 'to a considerable extent', 'enticed', 'dexterous with his feet', and the Swiftian inaptness of 'After he had dined'.

Another of Haslam's cases is rendered more purely in terms of intentions:

> He was an artful and designing man, and with great ingenuity once affected his escape from the hospital. His time was mostly passed in childish amusements, such as tearing pieces of paper and sticking them on the walls of his room, collecting rubbish and assorting it. However, when he conceived himself unobserved, he was intriguing with other patients, and instructing them in the means, by which, they might escape. Of his disorder he seemed highly sensible, and appeared to approve so much of his confinement, that when his friends wished to have him released, he opposed it, except it should meet with my approbation; telling them, in my presence, that although, he might appear well to them, the medical people of the house, were alone capable at judging of the actual state of his mind; yet I afterwards discovered, that he had instigated them to procure his enlargement, by a relation of the grossest falsehoods and unjust complaints.[40]

What Haslam seems to resent about this patient is his capacity for turning the tables on the observer, of undermining and arrogating to himself the medical privilege of detached manipulation. If Haslam observes him 'unobserved', the apothecary, it emerges, has also been studied and practised upon in so far as the patient has contrived a display with his 'friends' in order to further an alternative truth, another way of describing ('a relation of the grossest falsehoods and unjust complaints') to the authorised version.

All of Haslam's case histories end the same way:

> The head was opened twenty hours after death. There was a greater quantity of water between the different membranes of the brain than has ever occurred to me. The tunica arachnoidea was generally opake and very much thickened: the pia mater was loaded with blood, and the veins of that membrane were particularly enlarged.[41]

The status of the patient as object of the physician's treatment, his observation, his syntax, is fully and finally confirmed when his scalpel enters the brain in order to measure and weigh it, to drain it of its fluids, to compare it with 'normal' brains, and to close the account by setting down its texture, colour and dimensions.

Getting the measure of madness for Haslam was the extent to which the opened brain confirmed the observations made while the patient was alive. For Kinneir it was the quantities of camphor required to produce a cure, while for Blair it was how much water from what height and for how long. But the creative and innovative potential of language as envisaged by Reid had also been developed by physicians more attentive to the inner case histories of their patients. John Woodward, for example, who practised in London during the early years of the century, and whose *Select Cases, and Consultations, in Physick* was published posthumously in 1757, far from hastening over the early details in order to concentrate on the cure, begins his case histories with the patient's birth and childhood:

> *Mrs* HOLMES, *London Bridge* was born March 3, 1689–90, being one of two Girls at that Birth; the other died seven Weeks after. This was puny, and ailing, till she was seven Years old; when she had a very dangerous Fever. But recovering, she had her Health thenceforward somewhat better.

He proceeds through known illnesses and significant events until the present crisis is reached.

> In May 1716, looking out of a Window, she observed a large Porpoise, in the Thames; and was much delighted with the viewing of it. About a Fortnight after, when she was gone about twenty Weeks with Child, and just quickned, she was suddenly invaded by a very great gnawing Pain at the Pit of her Stomach, passing thence directly across to the opposite Part of her Back; and at the very Moment something rose thence up to the Mold of her Head, and the Top of her Forehead, attended with a Heat and Agitation, like that of Water boiling, and with a Sense of Fullness, as if some new Fluid was actually poured in. This Disorder of her Head was followed, instantly, with a strong perplexing Thought of the Porpoise; and a Fright, lest that should mark her Child; which yet did not happen.

The precision with which Woodward records the types and locations of the pains attests to a real ability to listen to what his patient has told him, and an anxiety to draw from her ways of describing pain in her own terms – the 'very great gnawing Pain', the 'something' that 'rose' in her head, the 'Heat and Agitation, like . . . Water boiling', and the 'Sense of Fullness' like a 'Fluid' being 'poured' into her. Here is straightforward, domestic language being utilised, under the encouragement of an interested listener, in the unusual function of describing the inner disorders of the body, of giving an account of what a very individual sensation actually felt like. The linguistic creativity is not, from the textual evidence, that of the physician himself, but nevertheless depends upon his skill as midwife to his patient's imaginative resources.

The same reliance on close attention to the patient's descriptive capacity is evident when Woodward records her increasingly distressing mental experiences, which apparently become ineradicably associated with the porpoise that she originally 'saw with Pleasure'.

> But the Thought was now attended with Dread, Fright, and Melancholy; and obtruded itself upon her, much to her Surprize, and without any Reason that she could conceive. But it molested, teized, and put her into a Disorder, so great as almost to distract her. . . . She was persecuted almost incessantly with this Thought of the Porpoise Day and Night. . . . She frequently endeavoured to cast that Thought out; and to introduce another, that might be more pleasing to her; in which she sometimes succeeded; but the new Thought, however pleasant at first, became, in a little time, as troublesome and disturbing as that of the Porpoise. . . . Amongst others, she had Thoughts of the Devil, as tempting and vehemently urging her to ill; particularly to fling her Child into the Fire, beat its Brains out, and the like; to which she had the Utmost Horror and Aversion; being naturally mild, good natured, and very virtuous. . . . She had frequently Temptations to lay violent Hands on herself. . . . She never saw anything; but seemed to hear a Voice, which she apprehended was of the Devil; calling her into the next Room; she constantly refusing, praying &c.

The pace and patterns of the prose are those of an agitated mind recapturing the stages through which it has passed to its present distress. The build-up is enacted through co-ordinating sets of key nouns or of verbs and verbal phrases. Any one of 'Dread, Fright, and Melancholy' would have been sufficient to complete the clause grammatically, but together they present an account of the swift succession of the patient's emotions and of her inability to predict or control what has been happening to her. With 'molested, teized, and put her into a Disorder', something of the force of the experience is conveyed through making one personal pronoun, 'her', act as the object of three co-ordinating verbs. Significantly, the patient here is the object of the condition from which she is suffering, while in Kinneir's prose she was grammatically the object of the physician's treatment.

What Woodward's account captures is the woman's experience of the illness as being at the mercy of a force that not only takes over sensation and emotion, but also inhabits and corrupts the very language in which she thinks and speaks. Whole phrases, eventually, come to her in co-ordinating structures – 'to fling her Child into the Fire, beat its Brains out, and the like' – which are now identified as 'Thoughts' sent to her by the Devil and presented in the guise of her own language. The final stage is her hearing the 'Voice' of the Devil himself, no longer emanating from within her own mind, but apart from her, at loose in her own house, and apparently able to assert an identity of its own. The linguistic identity of the Devil, however, is constructed from the range and register of the woman's normal domestic parameters: what it says is not now to do with burning or flinging, but is the sinister, everyday act of 'calling her into the next Room'. Her only resistance to this annexation of her language is the resort to a linguistic formula that has been sanctioned by faith and tradition, the impersonality of repeated prayer.

Unlike Kinneir, Woodward's description of his own treatment for this patient is brief and to the point: she is given a purge and a 'Clyster', which ease the pain in her stomach. This relief is accompanied by her thoughts becoming 'free' while 'what she calls the Suggestions of the Devil' wholly cease. With her body and her language restored to her, she has 'been lightsome, cheerful, easy, and well, ever since'.[42]

Many medical men recorded case histories in substantial detail during the course of the eighteenth and early nineteenth centuries, and while the treatments administered between them are not necessarily very different, the patterns of the linguistic habits of their writing betray a marked range of attitudes towards patients and patient suffering. Some clearly allow their accounts to follow the personality and experience of the patient, while for others the only angle that matters is the medical one. Some, like Erasmus Darwin, are particularly accommodating to the language of their patients, and present actual dialogues that have taken place between sufferer and physician.

> Miss G—— . . . said as I once sat by her, 'My head is fallen off, see it is rolled to that corner of the room, and the little black dog is nibbling the nose off.' On my walking to the place which she looked at, and returning, and assuring her that her nose was unhurt, she became pacified, though I was doubtful whether she attended to me.

> Master——, a school-boy about twelve years old, after he came out of a convulsive fit and sat up in bed, said to me, 'Don't you see my father standing at the foot of the bed, he is come a long way on foot to see me.' I answered, no: 'What colour is his coat?' He replied, 'A drab colour.' 'And what buttons?' 'Metal ones,' he answered, and added, 'how sadly his legs are swelled.' In a few minutes he said, with apparent surprise, 'He is gone,' and returned to his perfect mind.[43]

Others, like William Perfect, record cases that afford, through the detail picked up, insight into the peculiar consequences of mental derangement for language and linguistic creativity. Perfect owned a madhouse in West Malling, in Kent, and published his *Select Cases* in 1787 (in fact a later edition of a work first published in 1778). His 'Case XIII' was of 'Miss A.C. a young lady of delicate habit' placed under Perfect's care in March 1776.

> She was naturally of a lively, active disposition, and remarkable for quickness of parts; under the influence of her delirium, she shewed great vivacity of imagination, and would very often express herself in well-adapted metre; though, when in her right senses, she was never known to have any particular propensity to it.[44]

Many of the fullest case histories are characterised by close attention to the patient's own experience of his or her state of mind, and a readiness to suspend medical language in deference to a register and structure that is dictated by the nature of the individual illness. A case reported by John Hunter in the 1780s (his 'Lectures on the Principles of Surgery' were taken down 'in short-hand by Mr Nathaniel

Rumsey of Chesham . . . in the years 1786 and 1787')[45] demonstrates this physician's care in unravelling the intricacies of the
patient's understanding through following the curious paths of his
mental idiosyncrasies. Hunter describes a 'gentleman' whose 'delirium'
led him to be 'constantly talking of former circumstances of his life,
but referring them to the present moment and to some other person'.
The mind in this case, thought Hunter, was not 'itself hurt', but 'it
really appeared more a want of connexion between the mind and the
body . . . for he determined rightly what should be done in those
circumstances which he supposed present, and would express his
sentiments in really elegant language'. Moreover, the patient would
become 'sensible of impressions' but would suppose them 'to be in
any other body than his own'.

> Thus, he would tell his nurse or the bystanders that they
> were hungry or thirsty; but upon offering food or drink,
> it appeared plainly by his eagerness that the idea had arisen
> from a sensation of hunger in his own stomach. He would
> show great signs of distress or anxiety, which he would say
> was because his nurse wanted to go to the close stool, but
> was restrained by his presence; and this from his sensations
> also. He had a violent cough, in which he would sympathize
> with some bystander, proceeding in his story after the cough,
> no otherwise disturbed than by sympathizing with the person
> he thought so unfortunate as to have it.

'The objects about him,' adds Hunter, 'were more to him than
his own sensations.'[46] Hunter's achievement, however, has been
to allow his writing to represent this man's peculiarly self-effacing
personality with vitality and sympathetic engagement, rather than
concentrating upon the diagnosis and treatment that constitute the
province and personality of the physician.

Such treatments as were practised by these more endorsive
recorders of case histories were not, in fact, radically different
from those traditional remedies that had been handed down with
the authority of Willis and Sydenham. While Darwin was unusual
in combining progressiveness of attitude towards mental illness with
fierceness in the form of his favourite shock treatments, few other
practitioners took the extreme step of not treating their patients at
all. Even Andrew Harper, a military surgeon, only speculated on
the advantages of such a course.

If it were possible to give full scope to the extravagant humours and excentric vagaries of incipient Insanity, I can conceive it very probable that the mind would pursue the fantastic delusion, through the path of distracted ideas, till the powers of mental action being spent, and the corporal system materially changed, the tumultuary motions would consequently cease, and the calm serenity of established reason resume its natural influence. [47]

However, many avoided, like Battie, the more life-threatening measures of orthodox Bethlem. But Battie himself recommended a significant range of medicines and operations for the patients at St Luke's: 'the lancet and the cupping-glass again and again repeated' in order to reduce the 'delirious pressure of the brain or medullary substance contained in the nerves'; 'neutral salts', such as 'Nitre, Sal Catharticus amarus, Magnesia alba, Tartar', to 'provoke stools and urine'; and the various methods of effecting 'Revulsion' of the 'delirious pressure', which could be 'successfully attempted by the oily and penetrating steams arising from skins and other soft parts of animals newly slain, by tepid fomentations and cataplasms applied to the head legs and feet, by oily and emollient glysters'. He does, however, warn against 'the rougher cathartics, emetics, and volatile diaphoretics', and 'if the subject is either naturally infirm or shattered and exhausted by preceding illness, the lancet must be cautiously used or entirely forbidden'. [48]

The shift in attitudes towards mental illness was achieved through the individual work and publications of all the writers and physicians discussed in this chapter, and by very many others. The walls of madness were broached not so much by the mad attempting to get out as by the sane trying, through observation and dialogue, through medical and linguistic adaptability, to get in. Each case history represents one crack in the silence. Each account opens a small section of the inner world of the mad, picked out under the torch of language. But the overriding reason why William Battie, who published no case histories, gave no specific examples in the *Treatise on Madness*, and had nothing to say about the language of the insane, was so significant a force in giving direction and respectability to the work of these predecessors and contemporaries was that he alone ran a public asylum.

The third major aspect of Battie's significance, then, was in the impetus he gave to the growth of asylums. Yet the irony of Battie's achievement was that in bringing the physician closer to the individuality of the mad he actually closed the doors on madness in a way that Bethlem, with its tradition of admitting spectators, had never done. Battie's patients were behind walls, deliberately separated from family, friends, way of life, the public world. The management of the mad meant confinement, even if it also meant a real attempt to understand the structure and texture of madness. Because of his position, Battie's publication and influence made attitudes towards madness more open, less confined by tradition and prejudice. But his model asylum of St Luke's was also the stimulus for the founding of similar institutions between the 1760s and the end of the century. The Manchester Lunatic Hospital began taking patients in 1766, and by 1769 had expanded to accommodate over 300. A 'Hospital for Lunaticks for the Counties of Northumberland, Newcastle upon Tyne and Durham' opened in 1765, the York Asylum in 1777 and Liverpool Asylum in 1790.[49] In particular, the stress given to management, to regimen, to obliging madness to take responsibility for itself rather than suffering treatment as the object of the physician's authority, became the moral management movement of the late eighteenth and early nineteenth centuries.

Moral management was enlightened, humane and intrusive. On one hand no other therapy was more endorsive of individual madness, for the whole personality of the patient was implicated in a shared responsibility for the progress and pace of his or her own recovery. On the other, no regimen was more restrictive in fixing the range permitted for individual eccentricities or in its definition of cure. As Roy Porter describes, a new relationship developed between physican and patient.

> The precise inflection of the madman's demeanour and disposition, attitudes and ideas, address and responses, had all to be digested and then handled in ways appropriate to the particular case – sometimes by soothing, sometimes by shocking, perhaps by rest, maybe by exertion. By nice calculation of means and ends, the physician had to achieve command, substituting his control for that of the disease controlling the lunatic.[50]

Nevertheless, the physician as observer and guide was able to develop, like Francis Willis, or William Pargeter, who practised in London and Oxford, into the physician as lion-tamer. There were even physicians whose roles included that of actor-manager. Joseph Mason Cox, who owned and ran the large private madhouse at Fishponds in Bristol, devised carefully individualised deceptions and illusions as part of the therapies intended to jolt his patients into their senses – 'imitated thunder or soft music', or 'signs executed in phosphorus upon the wall of the bedchamber'.[51] The authority of the doctor who handed down traditional repressive remedies became another kind of authority, less damaging to the patient's health and to his chances of survival, but more all-embracing in that every aspect of the patient's life and personality was subject to observation and to utilisation in the quest for sanity. Whereas the traditional lunatic was simply required to take the treatment, the morally managed madman was held accountable for everything that had made him ill, and for each step forwards and backwards on the eccentric road to recovery. This included what he said and how he said it as well as what he did or did not do. The physician was now the all-seeing eye, and his disapproval the ultimate deterrent.

The institution that was most closely based on the principles of moral management, and that best illustrates the dilemma at the heart of this movement, was the York Retreat. The Retreat was founded by William Tuke, a Quaker, and opened in 1796 for members of the Society of Friends, and its name was intended to reflect the principles upon which were based its attitude towards and treatment of inmates. These were described by Samuel Tuke, grandson of the founder, in *Description of The Retreat*, which was published in 1813.

It was conceived that peculiar advantage would be derived to the Society of Friends, by having an Institution of this kind under their own care, in which a milder and more appropriate system of treatment, than that usually practised, might be adopted; and where, during lucid intervals or the state of convalescence, the patient might enjoy the society of those who were of similar habits and opinions. It was thought, very justly, that the indiscriminate mixture, which must occur in large public establishments, of persons of opposite religious sentiments and practices; of the profligate and the virtuous; the profane and the serious; was calculated to check the progress of returning reason, and to fix, still deeper, the melancholy and misanthropic train of ideas, which, in some descriptions of insanity, impress the mind. It was believed also, that the general treatment of insane persons was, too frequently, calculated to depress and degrade, rather than to awaken the slumbering reason, or correct its wild hallucinations.[52]

Retreat was confinement, but confinement from those pressures and principles against which the Friends were dedicated. Retreat was protection by the presence and support of those whose friendship and beliefs were of highest value when sane. Patients enjoyed a minimum of medication and physical restraint, ate well, were properly housed and clothed, and were induced to take such remedies as warm baths, reading and exercise. Convalescent patients were allowed out to take tea with local Quaker families, and neighbouring Friends visited the asylum to mix with and sustain the patients at formal gatherings and meals. The grounds were attractive and varied, while the proportion of attendants to patients was higher than in the large public establishments.[53]

Treatment of the Quaker insane relied above all on one principle: 'By what means the power of the patient to control the disorder, is strengthened and assisted.' The source for this strengthening was found in the model of the family. Thus 'fear' was 'considered as of great importance in the management of the patients', but not 'beyond that degree which naturally arises from the necessary regulations of the family'. This meant that each inmate was expected to restrain him or herself from 'offensive conduct, towards their fellow sufferers'. Patients were also 'considered capable of rational and honourable inducement', of which '*desire of esteem*' was regarded as the most powerful. This, too, operated upon the minds of inmates to produce 'a salutary habit of self-restraint'.[54] Unruly patients were denied the company of their fellows, but the word of the patient was accepted as to future behaviour or in regard to likely offence. So, as the Retreat records show, Samuel W. 'at his own request with promises of good behaviour had the waistcoat taken off', while William W. requested that his arms be restrained to prevent his beating the wall with them.[55]

The privileging of the patient's word, however, was itself strictly confined, and this confinement is indicative of the dilemma of moral management. Samuel Tuke, like Haslam and Nicholas Robinson, was adamant that there could be no entering the world of the patient's madness:

The persuasion which is extended to the patients is confined to those points which affect their liberty and comfort. No

74

advantage has been found to arise from reasoning with them, on their particular hallucinations.[56]

The sentence comes like a blow to the head. The line of opinion that has come closer and closer to the endorsement of individual madness is suddenly brought to an abrupt halt in the institution that above all others was made possible by the new orthodoxy of William Battie and the managers of madness. Tuke actually speaks of assisting patients, through '*fear*' and 'the *desire of esteem*', in the task of 'confining their deviations'.[57] Madness at the Retreat was ultimately required to be itself in retreat, hidden from detection through behaviour or language. The work of a Hunter or a Woodward, the principles advocated by Reid or contemplated by Harper, were alien to its attitudes and therapies, and to its expectations and definition of cure. Humane, mild, moderate, it nevertheless had no interest in the individuality of madness, in tracing its rise and progress, or in listening to the language by which it sought to express itself. The mad were given respect, treated as capable of making decisions for themselves, of keeping or breaking their word, of behaving in a manner that made them fit for each other's company and for the society of Friends, but the price of this was the denial of their madness. Sanity was achieved by silencing mad language, by stilling mad behaviour. In order to be mad, patients had to be seen and heard to be mad, otherwise they were obliged to take to themselves the terrible responsibility of being sane.[58]

The treatment of patients at the Retreat was, of course, infinitely better than that suffered for generations by the inmates at Bethlem hospital, or at the hands of private physicians and madhouse owners. But when Patrick Blair took his patients closer and closer to drowning until they said what he wanted, and kept to what they said, he was doing by violent means what the Friends at the Retreat achieved through kindness and philanthropy. If Blair's patients took home with them the message that they should keep their madness to themselves, and not trouble their husbands and friends with matters they had no wish to hear or see, so too did the Quaker insane return from the Retreat to their families and Friends. Madness, if unseen and unheard, was no madness at all, until Sigmund Freud, like Dr Johnson, began to demonstrate that to 'speak with rigorous exactness, no human mind is in its right state'.[59]

★

Jeremy Bentham in 1791 published a work called *Panopticon; or, the Inspection-House: Containing the Idea of a New Principle of Construction Applicable to Any Sort of Establishment, in which Persons of Any Description Are To Be Kept under Inspection.* Doerner describes the basis of the plan and its influence:

> He conceived of a cobweblike design for prisons, houses of correction, poorhouses, workhouses, insane asylums, and industrial installations. From a central room permitting an overview, corridors running along rows of workrooms or cells are to radiate out as from a star to facilitate surveillance by a single person, or two or three at most . . . Every cell was to have a barred window to the outside. Bentham saw his plan as a gesture of liberalization for the insane: chains and other such physical restraints were supplanted by a more efficient architectonic–organization restraint. Until 1851, numerous institutions based on Bentham's star-shaped, H-shaped, or semi-circular model were built throughout England – huge domed structures of unparalleled dimensions.[60]

Madness as a public spectacle to be witnessed in Bethlem upon appropriate payment, madness as a visual entertainment, had been replaced by madness confined, but kept under constant surveillance. Madness was still something to be inspected, but the eye of the beholder had changed. In a more enlightened age, the principle that the insane were only insane when observed to be so was now firmly enshrined in the very architecture, the bricks and bars, of the houses built for fools and mad. The cracks in the walls had closed.

4

BORROWED ROBES

In Letter XXVII of *The Natural History of Selborne*, Gilbert White recalls one of the human curiosities formerly to be seen in his village.

We had in this village more than twenty years ago an idiot-boy, whom I well remember, who, from a child, shewed a strong propensity to bees; they were his food, his amusement, his sole object. And as people of this cast have seldom more than one point in view, so this lad exerted all his few faculties on this one pursuit. In the winter he dosed away his time, within his father's house, by the fireside, in a kind of torpid state, seldom departing from the chimney-corner; but in the summer he was all alert, and in quest of his game in the fields, and on sunny banks. Honey-bees, humble-bees, and wasps, were his prey wherever he found them: he had no apprehensions from their stings, but would seize them *nudis manibus*, and at once disarm them of their weapons, and suck their bodies for the sake of their honey-bags. Sometimes he would fill his bosom between his shirt and his skin with a number of these captives; and sometimes would confine them in bottles. He was a very *merops apiaster*, or bee-bird; and very injurious to men that kept bees; for he would slide into their bee-gardens, and, sitting down before the stools, would rap with his finger on the hives, and so take the bees as they came out. He has been known to overturn hives for the sake of honey, of which he was passionately fond. Where metheglin was making he would linger round the tubs and vessels, begging a draught of what he called *bee-wine*. As he ran about he used to make a humming noise with his lips, resembling the buzzing of bees. This lad was lean and sallow, and of a cadaverous complexion; and, except in his favourite pursuit, in which he was wonderfully adroit, discovered no manner of understanding. Had his capacity been better, and directed to the same object, he had perhaps abated much of our wonder at the feats of a more modern exhibitor of bees: and we may justly say of him now,

> . . . *Thou,*
> *Had thy presiding star propitious shone,*
> *Should'st Wildman be . . .*

When a tall youth he was removed from hence to a distant village, where he died, as I understand, before he arrived at manhood.[1]

Here, described with White's characteristic directness, is a particularly lively example of Bernstein's 'alternative realities, alternative arrangements in the affairs of men', but one that is framed both by White's memory of 'more than twenty years ago' and by the semi-formal style of the letter (addressed to Daines Barrington). The perspectives that are available for writing about the bee-boy are therefore constrained by distance and by language. If that means that the 'alternative reality' finally escapes, it also means that we can read unusually clearly the features of our mental and linguistic processes that tend to inhibit our laying firm hold on other mental and linguistic 'arrangements'. As such, White's letter exemplifies much eighteenth-century endeavour in writing about madness.

White's is language that unashamedly presents its object as a curiosity, thus justifying its inclusion within the letter form, and within the wider form of a work of natural history intended for popular readership. There is stress on the community, not only the village community – 'We had in this village' – but those activities that identify sub-groups, such as bee-keeping, the making of metheglin, and even the appreciation of poetry. There is also the endorsing of assumptions likely to be held concerning idiots – 'as people of this cast have seldom more than one point in view' – against which the boy can be depicted as lacking many of the attributes that make for inclusion within such a community, as in fact scarcely human. He is truly a 'natural' in that he virtually hibernates for the winter (a subject in which White had a great curiosity, especially with regard to swallows), and returns to life in the warmth of summer. The word 'alert', which in a different context would suggest mental preparedness, has here to be read as identifying the boy with animal alertness. He disarms bees with all the skill and invulnerability of some wild creature, and buzzes as he runs about, which is read less as evidence of his desire to mimic his prey than as an indication of his incapacity for normal human speech. To this extent, the writing act that frames him also excludes him.

One dimension of the curiosity of the bee-boy, however, and one that is rendered especially well through the style of the letter, is the uncanny likeness that he bears to normal human life. It is, for example, a shock to find, late in the letter, that he 'was lean and sallow, and of a cadaverous complexion': White, we realise, had described the boy in terms of his activities and of the ways the village viewed them, rather than for his personal appearance. If this initially liberates the reader's imagination, it is equally a jolt to be told that the frenetically single-minded quality of his activity is not matched by his physique, which is suggestive of a more conventional human lot, of illness and death. Other details fill in the human aspect of this curiosity: he has been known as a child, has a father, sits in the chimney-corner, wears a shirt. He grows, like other boys, becomes 'a tall youth', and, like others, proves mortal, despite his deceptive invulnerability. He even, after all, turns out to have some capacity for language, although White chooses not to draw attention to it, slipping it in almost as an aside: he begs for a draught 'of what he called *bee-wine*'. This tantalising glimpse, two words, is the closest we are allowed to approach to the reality of the bee-boy. He *can* speak for himself, but his speaking has been rendered safe within the conventions of reported speech, within the confines of a letter where this kind of casual selectivity is wholly acceptable, even appropriate.

If the language of the bee-boy is confined within an aside, this is completely in keeping with the other kinds of stylistic closure practised in the letter. The balance and pattern of White's writing has nothing in common with its subject, and everything to share with its recipient and reader. The ready-made label, 'idiot-boy', immediately signals a range of expectation (a range that Wordsworth was to take such pains to extend not only through his poem 'The Idiot Boy' but through the various letters and defences of it written afterwards). Our access to this boy is through the safe medium of White's own memory, where the knowledge has lain for many years, and any unruliness the subject may retain in the opening sentence (the slight awkwardness of the 'whom I well remember, who . . .' structure) is put to rest by the firmness of an additional two main clauses. One, 'showed a strong propensity to bees', is fortified against idiotism by both alliteration and the strong Latinate diction of 'propensity'. The other musters a tripartite structure in describing the nature of the boy's passion: 'they were his food, his amusement, his sole object', where the repetition of the personal pronoun enforces the deployment of two subordinate complements. The unusual, even threatening, nature of the subject is comfortably accommodated within the grammatical capacities of the English language. This first sentence is a model for the overall strategy of the letter. That which is at bottom a disturbing parody of human life, an animal in human form, an alternative set of passions, actions, linguistic arrangements, is so far modified by the form of its expression as to become a matter rather of leisured report, of something less than scientific interest, of curiosity. The ultimate distance between the writing and its subject is visible with White's use of Latin, the 'nudis manibus' and the 'merops apiaster', for here we find not only the causal phrase-dropping of a semi-learned correspondence but a hint of the systematic classification that White was adopting from Linnaeus for itemising scientific specimens.

The attitudes towards mental derangement that underlie the structure and tone of White's language are made more explicit in a letter by Edward Young, written on 16 October 1746, concerning the madness of an acquaintance, Grace Cole. Miss Cole had been badly affected by the death of her father, Captain John Cole, in March and her mother was dying as Young wrote. (Her burial is recorded in the Chelsea parish register as 17 October.)[2] Young's letter is to Margaret, Duchess of Portland. (Both the Duchess and her mother, Henrietta, Countess of Oxford, left money to help pay for the care of 'Mrs Grace Cole a lunatick'.)[3] After remarks about the need for trust in the Father of all, that would have 'softend her Affliction, & have prevented the Calamity' of Miss Cole's madness, Young continues:

A Calamity, I mean, to Us; for what it is to her, God only knows. We know no more of her, than of ye state of the Dead. She is actually dead to our Manner of Life, nor know we at all what her present Condition is as to Happiness or Misery. That, doubtless, depends on ye Nature of the Ideas that pass thro her Mind; & that we know no more of, than of ye Dreams of those yt sleep. The Beggar in his Dream

> may be a King; & she, under this melancholy Appearance, may be Happy for ought we know to ye Contrary. For *now* Madam, she exists in a *Separate State*. We exist under ye Reign of *Reason*; She is in the Kingdom of wild Imaginations only.[4]

Here is the acknowledgement that the 'alternative arrangement' that is madness is so complete that all human definitions are likely to be overturned by it. So, conventional notions and expectations of happiness and 'Calamity' no longer have any validity when thinking of the experience of madness. The mad have passed beyond what normal language can say of the emotions and thoughts of those who are left 'under ye Reign of *Reason*'. Young can make no effort to follow Miss Cole, or to begin to understand her state of mind. He cannot even think of her as having a mind capable of exercising anything resembling thought, but rather suggests that she has become a passive receptacle, or channel, through which 'Ideas' are able to 'pass'. Human life can be no further removed from social fellowship than to be regarded as if dead, while to be 'actually dead to our Manner of Life' is, like the bee-boy, to be if anything more distant than the dead themselves. Miss Cole's father, though dead, is remembered as Captain John Cole, with the identity and characteristics by which he was known when alive. His daughter, however, though still alive, has no identity or characteristics by which to be known, but only a frame and a name which provide a label for this example of non-life.

Two particular messages are pointed by Young for those of us who remain in the realm of reason and language. One is quite explicit, and concerns the reading we must make of madness and the conclusion our reading should enforce. He continues,

> Let this consideration, Madam, comfort us; let us hope ye Best of Her; as we do of Friends departed in *Another* way. Let us look on her, as a *Living* Monument of ye *realy* Deceased; & then, like other Monuments, it will naturally put us in mind of ye Vanity of human Life. And it will do yt Kind, & Needfull Office in a Manner as much more Effectual than Other monuments, as it is more Uncommon & Surprizing than They. Thus her *reputed* Calamity will be our *real* Benefit; & such, past Dispute God Allmighty designs it to be. For all his *Dispensations* to particular Persons are *Instructions* to Mankind

in General. His good Providence designs One person to be, as it were a Glass to Another; & to show us our *possible* Misfortunes by ye *actual* Misfortunes of Those about us.[5]

The train of thought that Young has developed concerning the living dead is safely resolved by the recollection of God's grace, by which Grace Cole is to be interpreted in a way that has nothing at all to do with her individual madness but solely in terms of a moral lesson to mankind. Her resemblance to human life enables her to be seen as a 'Glass', while her removal from that life is a powerful persuasion for us to put our trust in God and remember human frailty and mortality. Madness has been allowed to exist in order that it may *mean* for those who are sane, and who have reason and language at their disposal. And how much preferable, says Young, is an actual death – 'A fine *Deathbed Suit* we shd purchase at any rate. It is by far ye most glorious Apparel we can put on'[6] – to this living death with which God has visited Miss Cole.

The close resemblance between the mad and the sane, the 'Glass' for mankind, provides a second message that is implicit in Young's writing. In choosing to compare access to a mad mind to access to a sleeping one, he is bringing the experience of madness much closer to home, and almost saying that each of us, while spending our lives 'under ye Reign of *Reason*', nevertheless approaches a 'Kingdom of wild Imagination' whenever we sleep. The beggar who dreams he is a king while asleep will be pronounced mad if he persists with this view once he is awake. The line between madness and sanity, then, begins to look as fragile as the difference between sleeping and waking, or the ability to distinguish between oneself as a coherent identity and as an image in a mirror. This aspect of Miss Cole's case is picked out again in a slightly later letter to Samuel Richardson.

As to the melancholy part of your letter, our Chelsea friend, poor soul! But God is good. And we know not what we pity. She is dead to us; she is in another state of existence; we are in the world of reason; she is in the kingdom of imagination; nor can we more judge of her happiness or misery, than we can judge of the joy or sorrow of a person that is asleep. The persons that sleep are (for the time) in the kingdom of the imagination too; and she, as they, suffers, or enjoys, according to the nature of the dreams that prevail.[7]

Young is abridging his letter to the Duchess, but in doing so makes more explicit the close relation between dreaming and madness, between sanity and the insanity beneath the routine surface of domestic and everyday life that so fascinated and appalled the eighteenth-century mind, and underwrote so many attempts to write in sane language about mad subjects and mad people.

Hester Lynch Piozzi, corresponding with the Reverend Thomas Whalley in January 1789 about the madness of George III and its consequences, typifies the inability to engage with the subject.

> One thick Political Gloom covers us just now – *Art after Art goes out, – and all is Night*. Della Crusca's fine Poem called Diversity breaks thro' however, and flashes with transient Lustre gleaming across the Mist from Time to Time: And Mrs Siddons unites all Parties in *her* Favour twice o'Week . . . May you enjoy many happy returns of this Season Dear Sir, and do rejoyce with me that 88 is past: those two Figures have already brought Confusion and temporary Distress upon this Island twice before.[8]

Mrs Piozzi has no linguistic means of addressing the madness of a king, though she is clearly attracted by the topic and wishes to be able to write something suitably stylish to her correspondent in Bath. A self-conscious literariness is therefore adopted in substitution for real opinion or concern, though the kinds of allusion chosen are indicative of the feelings supposed appropriate for a matter of such weight. Her first remark, for example, hides both George's illness and its repercussions with a thick metaphorical cover, rendered all the more impenetrable through the internal echoes that bind the two adjectives, the figurative 'thick' and the momentary promise of meaning in 'Political'. Thereafter, however, no attempt is made to generate meaning, but rather the quotation from the final lines of *The Dunciad* is allowed to stand in for a sense of apocalyptic threat, to state, to sanity, while Pope's imagery is retained for the remarks about Robert Merry's poem. Only with the pretty compliment to Sarah Siddons, who was performing the roles of Queen Katherine in *King Henry the Eighth*, Jane Shore, and Lady Randolph in John Home's tragedy *Douglas*,[9] is there some hint of the real political consequences of George's condition. And Mrs Piozzi concludes this section of her letter by indulging in a piece of current superstition that signals the end of any serious attempt to give personal or social comment, while offering some insight into the appeal exerted on the popular mind by the nature of the sovereign's indisposition, and hinting again at the threat to national sanity thereby presented.

Such remarks and their structure are characteristic of many more serious efforts to write about madness. Thomas Gray, in a letter to Richard West written in May 1742, attempts to describe the nature of his own melancholy.

> Mine, you are to know, is a white Melancholy, or rather *Leucocholy* . . . which though it seldom laughs or dances, nor ever amounts to what one calls Joy or Pleasure, yet is a good easy sort of a state, and *ca ne laisse que de s'amuser*. The only fault of it is *insipidity*; which is apt now and then to give a sort of Ennui, which makes one form certain little wishes that signify nothing. But there is another sort, black indeed, which I have now and then felt, that has something in it like Tertullian's rule of faith, *Credo quia impossible est*; for it believes, nay, is sure of everything that is unlikely, so it be but frightful; and on the other hand excludes and shuts its eyes to the most possible hopes, and everything that is pleasurable; from this the Lord deliver us![10]

Here is a description that genuinely tries to communicate a personal experience, and to explore the differences between two kinds of mental unease. But Gray's remarks, far more than Mrs Piozzi's, are framed within a pattern of articulacy and learning that always inhibits his closing with his subject. It is a kind of writing that for the most part confines itself to the shared culture and tastes of its two participants: the playful coining of '*Leucocholy*', the effortless lapsing into French and Latin, the citing or alluding to Tertullian and Shakespeare. The hint of *Macbeth* is particularly neat, drawing a veil over the reality of personal experience at the moment when a touch of the real seemed about to be given – 'which makes one form certain little wishes that signify nothing'. Other passages and phrases look not to learning but to the commonplaces of everyday expression: 'you are to know', 'what one calls', 'a good easy sort of a state', 'which is apt now and then', 'a sort of Ennui', 'certain little wishes', 'I have now and then felt', 'something in it', 'the Lord deliver us!' This mixture of the coy, the self-conscious and the colloquial that accounts for virtually the whole of the rest of the passage means, in effect, that Gray has allowed the norms of informal English prose to write his letter for him. The experience that is alluded to is not within the writing but rather beneath the surface of it, hiding itself behind quotation, allusion, the conventional language of conversation and correspondence that has been deliberately put on as a show between two highly articulate friends. Gray has cultivated the means of evading the truth of his feelings, and his words consequently express themselves and their own patterns rather than the experienced anguish of true melancholy.

What we are seeing with Gray is the polished manipulation of socially acceptable signals that stand in for personal experience, and are understood to do so by both writer and recipient. Language is thereby enabled to exist within the narrowest of frameworks, and to perform a very limited number of functions, albeit in the hands of members of an articulate elite. If this is to accuse a writer like Gray of failing to exercise a writer's responsibility to the potential and resources of his native language, it is also, more importantly, to point to the perils of articulacy in successfully hiding the horror of experience. Language is adept at seducing the writer with substitutes for himself, and the narrower the intended readership the more difficult that seduction is to resist, or even to recognise. The sincerity of Gray's letter is suggested by the last lines of the paragraph, where for a moment he talks unaffectedly of the real nature of melancholy. But he cannot sustain the reality for long enough to expand on what is believed by the sufferer, or the nature of the truly 'frightful', and veers away to the haven of a prayer, or mock prayer. It is enough, however, to guarantee that this is not intended as a playful letter, but rather that linguistic playfulness has intervened to offer a surface distraction from the depths of confrontation with suffering.

The example of Gray's letter shows particularly clearly how madness, or most forms of mental disturbance, contrive to remain, in Foucault's phrase, in perpetual retreat[11] in conventional writing of the eighteenth century, and how formal and informal arrangements of language consist so much of borrowed patterns of syntax and diction that can be recognised as standing for socially acceptable forms of experience. Signals of madness pervade these linguistic representations, while madness itself, as an idea, an attraction, even as an experience, both compels and withdraws from the grammar of its own description.

The drama occupies a bluntly revealing position in this respect, with a measurable audience, actors and actresses of known appeal, and a necessity for easily recognisable signals through text and performance that certain subjects are being offered and developed as spectacle. Nicholas Rowe's popular play, *The Tragedy of Jane Shore*,[12] which was first performed in 1714, offers satisfaction to a taste for depictions of madness, and more particularly of mad women, with its only two female characters gradually pushed towards the brink of insanity through suffering and jealousy. Of the two, Alicia became a standard of the stage representation of female insanity, and provided a vehicle for a succession of actresses to demonstrate extreme passion. This is Alicia at the height of her madness in Act V:

> I'll give thee misery, for here she dwells;
> This is her house, where the sun never dawns,
> The bird of night sits screaming o'er the roof,
> Grim spectres sweep along the horrid gloom,
> And naught is heard but wailings and lamentings.
> Hark! something cracks above! it shakes, it totters!
> And see the nodding ruin falls to crush me!
> 'Tis fallen, 'tis here! I feel it on my brain!. . .
> A waving flood of bluish fire swells o'er me;
> And now 'tis out, and I am drowned in blood.
> Ha! what art thou! thou horrid headless trunk?
> It is my Hastings! See! he wafts me on!
> Away! I go! I fly! I follow thee.[13]

Jane Shore, herself presented with 'her hair hanging loose on her shoulders, and barefooted', points up the spectacle: 'Alas! she raves; her brain, I fear, is turned.'

This is madness treated as display, the dramatic equivalent of the literary or actual sightseeing tour of lunacy. Alicia, who is also shown 'in disorder', is made to speak her own analysis of her madness which, at the same time, is also the visual and aural evidence of derangement. She attributes her condition to the force of 'misery', yet her own mind is the 'house', now inhabited by misery, that is thrown into relief by the traditional images of madness: darkness beyond the light of sanity, noise beyond language, extremes of suffering, visions beyond the range of sane eyesight or sane imagining. The most dramatic turn in the portrayal is achieved by Alicia's dizzy shift in perspective from the house as a mind to a house that is also tottering above her and collapsing about that mind. The image of the house that has contained her madness has suddenly been returned to reality, but only in order to double back upon itself and reinforce the instability of a madness that cannot be held by any single image. And Rowe, indeed, then gives his character a chilling mix of images, as if to suggest the fecundity of the mad mind: a 'waving flood of bluish fire', succeeded by drowning in 'blood', and finally a meeting with a 'horrid headless trunk'.

Rowe's play was quite explicitly 'Written in Imitation of Shakespear's Style', and his portrayal of a mad character has been filtered through a variety of scenes of madness, and of visitations upon disturbed minds, from *Macbeth*, *Hamlet*, *Richard III* and others. But the signals do not require an audience closely familiar with Shakespeare, for diction and style are less important here than the stereotypes with which Rowe is dealing. Alicia sees ghosts and follows them, she raves, her speech is marked by abrupt changes in pace, and by an extravagant insistence that would draw her listeners into the pattern of her derangement with 'I'll give thee misery', 'Hark!', 'And see', 'See!' These are not distinguishing features of an individual madness but characteristics of received ideas of the insane. There is no grasp within the language of why people go mad or how they behave and express themselves when they do, but there is instead a sure sense of the kind of behaviour and speech that people expect when they pay to see a theatrical presentation of human emotions at their most extreme.

One spectator, at least, of Rowe's play has testified to the power of this portrayal of madness. Charles Churchill's *The Rosciad*, published in 1761, contains a tribute to Susannah Cibber's playing of Alicia.

> When poor Alicia's madd'ning brains are rack'd,
> And strongly imaged griefs her mind distract,
> Struck with her grief, I catch the madness too:
> My brain turns round, the headless trunk I view!
> The roof cracks, shakes, and falls! new horrors rise,
> And Reason buried in the ruin lies.[14]

Character is a medium whereby readers or spectators are given space to indulge for a while their fascination for the abomination without losing hold of the structures and security of their own language. Insanity can be encountered with the confidence and sense of consistent personal identity that is based in retaining the form of the iambic pentameter, and in being able to find a rhyme for 'distract'. Pope's 'Codrus' stands at one extreme in this respect, for 'Codrus' is character as icon:

> You think this cruel? take it for a rule,
> No creature smarts so little as a Fool.
> Let Peals of Laughter, *Codrus!* round thee break,
> Thou unconcern'd canst hear the mighty Crack.
> Pit, Box and Gall'ry in convulsions hurl'd,
> Thou stand'st unshook amidst a bursting World.[15]

At the very heart of Pope's lines is the emblem of madness, silent now, self-contained, an alternative order quite apart from the order of the language that holds, and then drops, him. He is a still centre while the world breaks up in laughter, undizzy while rhyme and syntax break and reform in a poetic display around him. He offers no mental or linguistic access, yet is a focus of fascinated attention.

The madman as icon is a figure that is openly exploited by the satirists.[16] In satire, madness is adapted for its capacity to reveal a moral meaning, and its linguistic rendering is therefore motivated not by the inner compulsions of individual or group insanity, but by virtue of occupying a premeditated place in a given order of transgression and redemption. Dryden's Zimri, Pope's Theobald and Cibber, Swift's Partridge, Wharton, Gulliver, Fielding's Wild and Johnson's astronomer are emblems of madness and as such are mad with a meaning. They are wholly absorbed by the purpose of their portrayal, by the message that is to be understood through their transgression, and the language that marks them out as different does so in order to recall the reader to the redemption of a recognisable order of sane English. If Alicia allows a Churchill to relish a momentary turning of the brain, Gulliver and the astronomer ultimately resist such an indulgence to the extent that they require interpretation if their reading is to be successfully completed. Madness, for the satirists, is not madness at all, but a strategy for enforcing understanding of what is being satirised and of what is being endorsed. The madman is reduced to a tool of sane writing, a figure that has been borrowed in order to get the satiric job done.

The appropriation of madness to occupy a significant place within the forms and structures of sane thinking is by no means confined to the work of dramatists and satirists, or even to creative writers.

Inroads into mad territory are most persistently attempted through the language of reason in classifying or codifying for purposes of medical and legal definition. Sir William Blackstone provides one such attempt in his *Commentaries on the Laws of England*, published between 1765 and 1769. Blackstone is concerned to distinguish between idiots and lunatics, and gives both the form and methods for pursuing investigations into the state of mind, and therefore legal state, of each.

I proceed . . . to the eighteenth and last branch of the king's ordinary revenue; which consists in the custody of idiots, from whence we shall be naturally led to consider also the custody of lunatics.

An idiot, or natural fool, is one that hath had no under-standing from his nativity; and therefore is by law presumed never likely to attain any. . . . By the old common law there is a writ *de idiota inquirendo*, to enquire whether a man be an idiot or not: which must be tried by a jury of twelve men; and if they find him *purus idiota*, the profits of his lands, and the custody of his person may be granted by the king to some subject, who has interest enough to obtain them. . . .

A man is not an idiot, if he hath any glimmering of reason, so that he can tell his parents, his age, or the like common matters. But a man who is born deaf, dumb, and blind, is looked upon by the law as in the same state with an idiot; he being supposed incapable of understanding, as wanting those senses which furnish the human mind with ideas.

A lunatic, or *non compos mentis*, is one who hath had understanding, but by disease, grief, or other accident hath lost the use of his reason. A lunatic is indeed properly one that hath lucid intervals; sometimes enjoying his senses, and sometimes not, and that frequently depending upon the change of the moon. But under the general name of *non compos mentis* (which sir Edward Coke says is the most legal name) are comprized not only lunatics, but persons under frenzies; or who lose their intellects by disease; those that *grow* deaf, dumb, and blind, not being *born* so; or such, in short, as are by any means rendered incapable of conducting their own affairs. . . .

The method of proving a person *non compos* is very similar to that of proving him an idiot. The lord chancellor, to whom, by special authority from the king, the custody of idiots and lunatics is intrusted, upon petition or information, grants a commission in nature of the writ *de idiota inquirendo*, to enquire into the party's state of mind; and if he be found *non compos*, he usually commits the care of his person, with a suitable allowance for his maintenance, to some friend, who is then called his committee. However, to prevent sinister practices, the next heir is never permitted to be this committee of the person; because it is his interest that the party should die. [17]

In the logical progression of the law, to which Blackstone draws attention at the outset, idiots and lunatics occupy a minor but significant place in so far as the rights and responsibilities of property ownership may be involved. Legal prose at its best, of course, has its own distinctive patterns and conventions – the frequent Latin terms which provide the incontrovertible definitions to act as markers, or points of stability, within the shifting possibilities of human affairs; the high incidence of grammatical dependency, with a particularly clear relation between the different kinds and ranks of units in the syntactical chain; the provision of alternatives, as if to cover all the likely variants of a hypothetical situation. Such conventions, however, begin to seem remote, matters of merely linguistic interest, when the subject under discussion is one that has itself little relation to the niceties of the ways in which language can be organised. If White's bee-boy has no access to 'nudis manibus', the true idiot or lunatic has no interest in any of the phrases that describe him, the procedures that are intended to ensure that he can be recognised, or the preoccupations with lands and profits that his idiocy or lunacy makes into an issue of interest to the law. Legal endeavour, here, is identical to society's need to protect itself and its traditional forms of inheritance from the potential damage of permanent or spasmodic irresponsibility. That irresponsibility, capable of owning neither parents nor age, must therefore submit to losing its property, and its identity, under the legally provided definitions, 'purus idiota', 'non compos mentis'.

Features of legal prose are indicators of society's attitudes towards kinds of madness, and of the extent to which madness must be pinned down within a sane system of understanding. But other attitudes can also be detected here. To speak of a lunatic as one that is capable at times of 'enjoying his senses' contrasts sharply with Young's private, and more generous, speculation that Grace Cole 'may be Happy for ought we know to ye Contrary'. The refusal to value the experience of being mad, or of enjoying idiocy, is confirmed by the comparison with one 'born deaf, dumb, and blind' and as therefore 'wanting those senses which furnish the human mind with ideas'. Again, Young's attitude is both more generous, and can afford a more honest uncertainty: Miss Cole's happiness or misery 'depends on ye Nature of the Ideas that pass thro her Mind; & that we know no more of, than of ye Dreams of those yt sleep'.

Finally, the 'method of proving', similar for both idiots and lunatics, confirms the extent to which language dominates the investigation of madness. To be considered sane is, first and foremost, to be capable of recognising the structure of a question, and then to have access to those features of identity that society can understand and assimilate: parentage, age, and 'the like common matters'. These are blunt instruments for deciding the fate of a man's property and person, but the law, like any instituted system of knowledge, is inevitably baffled when confronted with that which is insistently absent from the normal grounds of procedure. Questions are suitable for arriving at certain kinds of truth, but depend upon an acknowledged linguistic contract between interrogator and subject. When the grammatical form that is a question may or may not be recognised, when the answer may or may not take a form that can be assimilated or considered relevant, that contract is strained beyond the capacity of any meaningful exchange. One decision or another will be made, because that was the point of the inquiry. But such a decision will necessarily have little to do with the realities of madness and sanity. When the English legal system comes to call, madness will rarely be at home.

An anonymous pamphlet of 1747 describes the proceedings of such a Commission of Lunacy, investigating the case of Henry Roberts, Esq. A Commission had met in 1743, and found Roberts 'a Person of unsound Mind' who 'had not enjoyed a lucid Interval of Reason for 12 Years past'. Doubts about the conduct of the Commission led in 1744 to the granting of a new trial, where Roberts was subjected to questioning a second time, in order to discover any 'glimmering of reason'.

The Day following the trial, Mr Roberts waited upon Dr Mead, Dr Monroe, Dr Nichols and other Gentlemen, who said to him, 'Sir, when you was taken out of the Court . . . and was in private with the Jurymen, what Questions did they ask you? How did they use you?' To this Mr Roberts replyed, 'They came around me and asked their Questions together, without giving me Time to answer. They asked me what a Lamb, and what a Calf was called at one, two and three Years old. They gave me a Sum of Money to tell, which I miscounted; and then I heard them say, he is not capable of managing his Affairs, we will return him incapable.'

Other questions recalled by Roberts were: 'From Doncaster, Sir, to Ferry-Bridge was ten Miles, but now there are fifteen Mile-Posts set up, is it not further now than before?' 'Pray, take three Shillings out of a Guinea, how much change must you have?' And snatches of dialogue are also recollected:

Mr Geo. Newport. Pray, how many Pots of Sugar did your Plantation in Barbadoes yield you last Year? Mr Roberts. I have forgot. I cannot tell. Mr Newport, Pray how many Pots of Sugar go to fill a Hogshead? Mr Roberts. I can't tell. Mr Newport. Is this man capable of managing his Affairs? It's plain he may be imposed upon.[18]

The second Commission confirmed the verdict of the first, and Roberts's trustees retained their control over his estates.

One of the ironies of this case is the ready recall Roberts has of the details of the question and answer exchanges with the jurymen, in spite of the pace and difficulty of their questions, even in front of the impressive collection of physicians involved. (Richard Mead was George III's physician, Frank Nicholls had been physician to George II, and James Monro was the first of his line to specialise in insanity.) He has no trouble with 'what Questions did they ask you', and was apparently expected by the physicians to be able to supply this information. But what is particularly striking is that the professionals have had no part in the inquiry. The questioning and the duty of reaching a verdict belong to amateurs, representatives of common sense, not of expert knowledge. Madness is taken to be recognisable not by the diagnosis of medical science, but through the observation and intelligence of any rational gentleman. If this increases the risk of interested parties manipulating the proceedings for private reasons, it also means that the language to which the lunatic or idiot must give an account of himself is language that has taken its form and focus from the affairs of everyday life. If, as in the case of Henry Roberts, that language emerges as oblique to the personality of a man who was probably simple-minded but sane, it is indicative of the limits of the law's interest. In deciding a man's capacity for assuming his responsibilities, neither the language of the legal commentator nor the language of the juryman has the scope to accommodate the cast and character of the individual. He is to be judged solely against the measure of the position in society to which he has claim. That position dictates the terms of the investigation and means that his identity is inevitably assimilated within a recognisable social role and the language that is considered appropriate to it.

Where the law did begin to acknowledge the intricacies of the madman's madness, and, as Joel Peter Eigen has shown,[19] increasingly so during the course of the eighteenth century, was in recognising in criminal trials the plea of 'Guilty but insane'. This had two important accompaniments for the handling of criminal cases involving insanity: madness was granted a spokesman who was entrusted with proving the insanity of the defendant; and the expert witness became a frequent visitor in courts of law, for, as Eigen puts it,

> The classic raving madman could of course be identified without 'expert' guidance; it was the subtle twists and turns of moral insanity, of inhibitory insanity, and of irresistible will which required the special insight of a physician to 'bring the pathology to light'.[20]

In the eloquence of an Erskine pleading for James Hadfield, the would-be assassin of George III, we see the ultimate separateness of madness from the language that successfully communicates the reality of that madness:

> Lord Coke, in speaking of the expression *non compos mentis*, says, 'Many times, as here, the Latin word expresses the true sense, and calleth him not *amens*, *demens*, *furiosus*, *lunaticus*, *fatuus*, *stultus*, or the like, for *non compos mentis* is the most sure and legal'. . . . Gentlemen, it has pleased God so to visit the unhappy man before you; to shake his reason in its citadel; to cause him to build up as realities, the most

impossible phantoms of the mind, and to be impelled by them as motives *irresistible*; the whole fabric being nothing but the unhappy vision of his disease – existing no where else – having no foundation whatsoever in the very nature of things.[21]

The law can recognise madness, but finds it easier to do so if madness is presented in a language the law can understand. Similarly, delusion is acceptable as evidence of madness, but only after the law has been prepared to acknowledge its own limitations, the limitations of common sense, and to call in the experts. If professional questioning can expose the delusional system to the understanding of a jury, as it did when William Battie appeared for his rival John Monro in an action in 1763 when Monro was sued by a former patient for illegal detention, this at least represents an opening up of an alternative system of logic, of conducting human affairs. To this extent, madness is being afforded a reality of its own, and on its own terms. But this is necessarily a severely curtailed freedom. Inevitably this form of recognition for what madness had to say for itself was accompanied by confinement and treatment: to be found guilty but insane does not mean that mad language has won the right to proclaim itself.

In 1809, James Tilley Matthews, confined in Bethlem since 1797, petitioned for release before the King's Bench. John Haslam, in his deposition against the release, gives one form of access to a system of delusion. Matthews, according to Haslam, believed

that he had been employed by the French and English Governments to negotiate a peace but that he had never received any reward, not even his travelling expences. That he had been Four times backwards and forwards from France to England. That at his suggestion of its propriety, the Committee of Public Safety in France was formed and that it was in order to prevent his letters from reaching France and himself from going over there that the Traitorous Correspondence Bill in this country was received. That when he communicated to the Ministry of this Country some valuable and important secrets they betrayed him. . . . That when he was in Flanders the Duke of York caused his army to make various marches and countermarches to beset him, and wished to deliver him over to the Enemy as a spy. . . . That the King of Prussia . . . had formed a plan of destroying

94

General Washington and to have divided America into two Monarchies.[22]

The very colourlessness of the legal deposition, the relentlessness of the simple order of ever more extravagant items of belief, carries conviction. The logic whereby a wide range of events, real and imagined, is made coherent by the force of a single overpowering obsession is brought out by the simple device of allowing each piece in the chain a moment of attention before it is capped by the next. No commentary is necessary, for each succeeding item is a commentary on its predecessor: a man who believes the latter will certainly have believed the former, and what will he believe next? The focus is on the mind of the lunatic, his delusions constitute the whole document. The tone of the piece, however, or rather the absence of tone, is in fact the stylistic equivalent of the stunned silence. On to the lack of colour the reader or listener can inscribe the incredulity of his own conviction, his astonishment at any man's believing these things. Matthews's beliefs may make up the entire document, but Haslam's presentation of them sets its sights not on the mad mind but on the sane one. The petition was refused, and Matthews stayed in Bethlem.

The presentation of a mad mind for a court of law is obliged to meet certain forms of expression, and, in the case of Matthews, those forms enabled a cast to be given to his state of mind that virtually guaranteed conviction. In a document like Haslam's, the reader's conviction depends upon a growing distance between text and subject, with language as the apparently neutral medium that is actually in conspiracy with sanity, showing up lunacy for what it is, and helping to bring about the judgment. But other expressions of obsessional states work, on the contrary, by unobtrusively drawing the reader into the system of delusion, and indeed by obliging the reader to question the status of delusion itself. A Tale of a Tub and Gulliver's Travels, for example, operate by drawing the reader in and by presenting distance at the same time. But it is in the novel, rather than in the moral schemes of works of satire, that interest in obsessive states of mind becomes genuine. William Godwin's Caleb Williams, dealing like the Matthews case with the excitement and anxiety surrounding the French Revolution, is of particular interest in that two interconnected, and eventually complementary, obsessions are presented and endorsed.

In the 1832 preface, written thirty-eight years after the book's first publication, Godwin discusses his reason for 'making the hero of my tale his own historian':

> It is infinitely the best adapted, at least, to my vein of delineation, where the thing in which my imagination revelled the most freely was the analysis of the private and internal operations of the mind, employing my metaphysical dissecting knife in tracing and laying bare the involutions of motive, and recording the gradually accumulating impulses which led the personages I had to describe primarily to adopt the particular way of proceeding in which they afterwards embarked.[23]

The creation of character in fiction is first and foremost undertaken with a view to convince that the unreal person is in fact real, while the intention of a Haslam in writing about a Matthews is to convince that the personality of a real man is wholly taken up in believing what is unreal. Mind, for Haslam, must be made strange, as if running according to non-human principles. For the novelist, the primary duty is to achieve association with the alien mind, understanding for those involutions and impulses that authenticate the created character's identity. Language is therefore far from neutral, but is required to speak on behalf of the alien, even, as in *Caleb Williams*, to become one with him.

Language, in Williams's voice, is the way into his obsession:

> The spring of action which, perhaps more than any other, characterised the whole train of my life, was curiosity. It was this that gave me my mechanical turn; I was desirous of tracing the variety of effects which might be produced from given causes. It was this that made me a sort of natural philosopher; I could not rest till I had acquainted myself with the solutions that had been invented for the phenomena of the universe. In fine, this produced in me an invincible attachment to books of narrative and romance. I panted for the unravelling of an adventure with an anxiety, perhaps almost equal to that of the man whose future happiness depended on its issue. I read, I devoured compositions of this sort. They took possession of my soul.[24]

Even here, on the second page of the novel, the language of obsession is identifying itself not only with the mind but with the physical impulses and cravings of the protagonist. Language thus embodied not only carries its own authenticity, but can be recognised as prefiguring the action of the narrative that is expected to compel the reader as much as 'the man whose future happiness or misery depended on its issue'. If this is the voice of an obsession proclaiming, or confessing, itself, it finds its counterpart, at the moment of its supreme satisfaction, in Falkland's confirmation of the guilty secret that has constituted the greatest challenge to Williams's curiosity – not only the secret, but the 'involutions of motive' from which the secret arose:

> This it is to be a gentleman! a man of honour! I was the fool of fame. My virtue, my honesty, my everlasting peace of mind, were cheap sacrifices to be made at the shrine of this divinity. But, what is worse, there is nothing that has happened that has in any degree contributed to my cure. I am as much the fool of fame as ever. I cling to it to my last breath. Though I be the blackest of villains, I will leave behind me a spotless and illustrious name. There is no crime so malignant, no scene of blood so horrible, in which that object cannot engage me. It is no matter that I regard these things at a distance with aversion – I am sure of it; bring me to the test, and I shall yield. I despise myself, but thus I am; things are gone too far to be recalled.[25]

Neither Williams nor Falkland are deluded, of course, in points of fact: Williams *has* discovered a dreadful secret, Falkland *is* a murderer, a victim of his own sense of honour, and, subsequently, Williams *is* hounded across the breadth of the kingdom by Falkland's enmity. Where they are deluded is in investing their obsessions with such overwhelming importance. The madness in Falkland's remarks is the degree to which he is acknowledging himself as a man intent on pursuing two incompatible ways of life, prepared to commit any crime in order to appear spotless. The moment of triumph for Williams is also a moment of relief for Falkland: 'My tongue has now for the first time for several years spoken the language of my heart.'[26] But the moment is pivotal. From now on Williams is enforced to live out Falkland's madness, or rather the antithesis of his madness, for the consequence of Williams's obsession is to flee the country under the name of 'the blackest of villains' while actually innocent.

What affords Godwin his success is the peculiar aptness of the novel form to the forms and structure of persecution. An elaborate and tightly controlled plot will always strain the reader's readiness to believe, unless the main character is being persecuted. If Tom Jones had any sense, he might suspect that someone was pulling his strings. Having only a good heart, he retains his sanity and wins out in the end. Caleb Williams, telling his own story, tracing 'the variety of effects from given causes', has the freedom of the English language but is trapped within a single focus on events which move dramatically out of his control. His flight from Falkland is his attempt to escape from the plot to which his own obsession has given potency. The particular agony of his persecution is not that it is unreal, or even that he believes it undeserved, but that he comes to value his persecutor more highly than himself. In other words, the story he has to tell should by rights be not his own but Falkland's.

> I began these memoirs with the idea of vindicating my character. I have now no character that I wish to vindicate: but I will finish them that thy story may be fully understood; and that, if those errors of thy life be known which thou so ardently desiredst to conceal, the world may at least not hear and repeat a half-told and mangled tale.[27]

Here is Williams's 'possession': the tale which he feels obliged to tell to the end is no longer his own, the memoirs are such that he would prefer not to remember them, the language he writes gives access to nothing that is of any value. His 'invincible attachment to books of narrative' has culminated in his inability to finish his own story.

Caleb Williams is unusual in that through the narrative of one obsessed character it contrives to involve the reader in the construction and endorsement of two forms of delusion, one of which brings about the collapse of the narrative itself and therefore of the language that secured the endorsement in the first place. Few novels of the period are so radical as Godwin's, even though an interest in madness can involve protagonists and readers in unsettling experiences. Smollett, for example, writes a deft display of mad language into *Sir Launcelot Greaves* when he has his 'adventurer' forcibly removed to a private madhouse. As he 'resigns himself to slumber' on his first night, Sir Launcelot is disturbed by voices from different rooms in the house:

> His ears were all at once saluted with a noise from the next room, conveyed in distant bounces against the wainscot;

then an hoarse voice exclaimed: 'Bring up the artillery –
let Brutandorf's brigade advance – detach my black hussars
to ravage the country . . . I'll lay all the shoes in my shop,
the breach will be practicable in four and twenty hours. . . .'
'Assuredly, (cried another voice from a different quarter)
he that thinks to be saved by works is in a state of utter
reprobation – I myself was a profane weaver, and trusted to
the rottenness of works . . . but now I have got a glimpse of
the new-light – I feel the operations of grace – I am of the new
birth. . . .'

This dialogue operated like a train upon many other inhabitants of the place: one swore he was within three vibrations
of finding the longitude, when this noise confounded his
calculation: a second, in broken English, complained he
was distorped in the moment of de proshection – a third,
in the character of his holiness, denounced interdiction,
excommunication, and anathemas. . . . A fourth began to
hollow in all the vociferation of a fox-hunter in the chace; and
in an instant the whole house was in an uproar – The clamour,
however, was of a short duration. The different chambers
being opened successively, every individual was effectually
silenced by the sound of one cabalistic word, which was no
other than *waistcoat*: a charm which at once cowed the king of
P——, dispossessed the fanatic, dumbfounded the magician,
dismayed the alchemist, deposed the pope, and deprived the
'squire of all utterance.[28]

Smollett, as a surgeon, had, of course, a closer awareness of
illness and medicine than most novelists, and his recording of
the voices of the mad may well be authentic. But his madmen
nevertheless fall into readily recognisable types, and the language
spoken owes its construction as much to the necessity to entertain
the reader as the desire to allow different forms of madness
to proclaim themselves. So, the king of Prussia must have his
English misspelt, to point the joke that this mad Englishman feels it
necessary to authenticate his delusion by speaking 'broken English',
while the fanatic gives Smollett the opportunity to engage in satiric
portrayal of Methodism. The description of order being reimposed
allows the humorous intention to surface and take over the language
of the narrative itself: the mock mystery of the word and its power
to 'charm' into silence; the recapitulatory listing of the range and

kinds of inmate; the self-consciously alliterative verbs that impose identical structures on the variety of supposedly mad experience. This is one kind of display, not far removed from the Lady Alicia, and no degree of proximity is encouraged either in Sir Launcelot or in the reader.

Yet Smollett is a more sophisticated novelist than this would suggest, and the following chapter adopts a quite different linguistic strategy when the protagonist attempts to 'explain himself' to the physician 'in such a manner, as should make an impression upon him'.

> When the doctor made his next appearance in Sir Launcelot's apartment, the knight addressed him in these words: 'Sir, the practice of medicine is one of the most honourable professions exercised among the sons of men; a profession which hath been revered at all periods and in all nations. . . . The character of a physician, therefore, not only supposes natural sagacity, and acquired erudition, but it also implies every delicacy of sentiment, every tenderness of nature, and every virtue of humanity. That these qualities are centered in you, doctor, I would willingly believe. . . . If you understand the art of medicine, you must be sensible by this time, that with respect to me your prescriptions are altogether unnecessary – come, Sir, you cannot – you don't believe that my intellects are disordered. . . . That you may not plead ignorance of my name and family, you shall understand that I am Sir Launcelot Greaves, of the county of York, baronet; and that my nearest relation is Sir Reginald Meadows, of Cheshire, the eldest son of my mother's sister.'[29]

Having heard the voices of the real mad, their claims, pretensions, reasoning, the reader is now obliged to consider how sanity can prove itself in a context of expectation of madness. Sir Launcelot is sane, but how can sane language be recognised? He relies on his power of eloquence, on his name and family, on the attempt to share an outlook based on common sense with the doctor. Who could do more? How could it be enough? The doctor is unconvinced: he 'assured our adventurer he would do him all the service in his power; but, in the mean time, advised him to take the potion he had prescribed'. Upon which Sir Launcelot immediately lapses into a stereotype of the raving madman.

'I am now convinced, (cried he) that you are an accomplice
in the villainy which has been practised upon me . . . yes,
sirrah, you are the most perfidious of all assassins . . . but I
will be calm . . . I demand the protection of the legislature
– if I am refused . . . in the mean time, begone, lest my
just resentments impel me to dash out your brains upon that
marble – away. –'[30]

By placing language that has for many chapters been taken as un-
questionably sane in a situation where it is heard as insane, Smollett
has for a moment turned reading *Sir Launcelot Greaves* into a different
kind of experience. The safety afforded by a secure character, a
stable discourse, is shaken when language itself is interrogated,
and found unconvincing. And the dilemma allows of no solution,
each step only confirming the suspicions aroused by the step before.
Because Smollett is not writing *Caleb Williams*, or anything like it,
his 'adventurer' is obliged to be rescued by his 'trusty friends', thus
endorsing sanity and restoring the reader's security in this particular
narrative. The novel is enabled to proceed rapidly to a conclusion of
marriage and family that validates Sir Launcelot's declaration, 'I am
Sir Launcelot Greaves, of the county of York'.

A kind of authentication of mad experience, mad language,
can therefore be achieved through fiction, when novelists are
prepared to subvert expectations of narrative, of voice, of plot.
The dimensions of Smollett's madhouse are revealed through
the voices of the mad, speaking of their own delusions, and
emanating from an apparently endless series of apartments. Each
room is another example of the ways by which the human mind
has found it possible to become deranged. But just when the house
seems fully proportioned, and stands as a finished structure capable
of containing representatives of all species of madness, the turning
of sane language against itself deftly enforces the conclusion that
the house will never be finished. The language of common sense,
of the forms and tones of narrative, the language in which as
readers we participate and unthinkingly endorse, can also be heard
as irredeemably mad. The house built for fools and mad is always
capable of expansion simply by a shift in definition of what is sane,
by a change in the rules that govern the forms of language that are
available to be spoken, and likely to be heard. Madness, in other
words, can never be measured by the dimensions of the house.

★

If these novelists concentrate on the construction of a house of madness in which the reader is brought to participate in supplying the bricks and mortar, poetic form is differently constituted. In 'Sir Eustace Grey', first published in his *Poems* of 1807, Crabbe, like Smollett, places his scene in a madhouse,[31] with an unnamed 'Visitor' discovered near the end of his tour ('I'll know no more; – the heart is torn')[32] under the guidance of the 'Physician'. Unlike the novelist's, however, Crabbe's story is told not by adding several links in a chain of apartments, each signifying a stock species of madness, but through the voice of one 'Patient', Sir Eustace Grey. What that voice is made to encompass is a whole past, in which Sir Eustace, over 'Some twenty years' (l.44), declines from his happy position as 'the young lord of Greyling Hall' (l.51) with 'children, friend, and wife' (l.108), through betrayal, vengeance and loss, the madness of guilt and of religious conversion, to his present confinement. The chronology of his narrative invests Sir Eustace with memory and a sense of sequentiality that authenticate his account of his insanity. Here is one significant difference from Smollett's madmen, each of whom is caught at one typically revealing moment, and allowed no further life or being. Yet the hallmark of Sir Eustace's individual identity is not his story, which is itself fairly commonplace, but the fact that its chronology is cut across by the speaker's recalling not only the sequence of his downfall but also, within that sequence, an overwhelming experience of oblivion that both defies chronology and, through the strength of the images in which oblivion resides, resists incorporation into the time sequence of the poem.

The centrepiece of Sir Eustace's madness is his being placed at the disposal of 'Two fiends of darkness' who make him 'their sport, their play, Through many a stormy troubled year' (ll.173, 176–7). He is placed 'on a boundless plain; Where nothing fed, nor breathed, nor grew, But silence ruled the still domain' (ll.193–5).

> Vast ruins in the midst were spread,
>   Pillars and pediments sublime,
> Where the grey moss had form'd a bed,
>   And clothed the crumbling spoils of time.
>
> There was I fix'd, I know not how,
>   Condemn'd for untold years to stay:
> Yet years were not; – one dreadful *Now*
>   Endured no change of night or day. (ll.200–7)

If Crabbe is finding for Sir Eustace, as Rowe does for Lady Alicia,
a suitable image for the decaying mind in a prospect of ruined
buildings, he is going beyond the confines of a single image
in suggesting that other items in this landscape also participate
in his derangement. Sir Eustace, unable to experience passing
time, knowing only that the 'years were not', is himself one of
the 'crumbling spoils of time' that is 'clothed' in the form of
Grey, while the timeless nature of his suffering obliges him to
partake, too, of the 'boundless plain' on which he is now 'fix'd'.
This fixity, in which mad identity is located in the remorseless
reality of a landscape without limit, is responsible for holding
back the sequence of narration that the form of the story, and
the expectation of its listener, would otherwise demand. But
the reality of that landscape is itself under suspicion in so far
as it is only perceived and conceived through the experience of
madness. The story moves on, but only to reveal newly conceived
landscapes that give endless representation to the timelessness of
mental suffering.

> They hung me on a bough so small,
>   The rook could build her nest no higher;
> They fix'd me on the trembling ball
>   That crowns the steeple's quiv'ring spire;
> They set me where the seas retire,
>   But drown with their returning tide;
> And made me flee the mountain's fire,
>   When rolling from its burning side. . . .
>
> I've furl'd in storms the flapping sail,
>   By hanging from the topmast-head;
> I've served the vilest slaves in jail,
>   And pick'd the dunghill's spoil for bread;
> I've made the badger's hole my bed,
>   I've wander'd with a gipsy crew;
> I've dreaded all the guilty dread,
>   And done what they would fear to do. (ll. 276–83, 292–9)

The perspective shifts between third person and first, the speaker
is now complement, now subject. The movement in grammatical
patterns constantly reinforces the endlessness of the mental syntax.
The arrangement of language may change; the reality of suffering,
the experience of madness, stays still.

Crabbe has given imaginative form to Young's suggestion that the reality of madness resembles the experience of the dreaming mind. The connectedness of this central section of Sir Eustace's narration is the connectedness of dream images, and exercises a similar compulsion. Madness, like the dream world, exists in a different dimension of time, of experience, from the perspectives of sanity. The extent to which those perspectives are embodied in the forms of literary language is also the extent to which sane writers inevitably failed in their attempts to make madness mean within the context of sane writing. Crabbe, like Young, and like his own guiding 'Physician', endeavours to close the experience of madness by drawing an exemplary moral lesson.

> Would we not suffer pain and grief,
>   To have our reason sound and sure?
> Then let us keep our bosoms pure,
>   Our fancy's favourite flights suppress;
> Prepare the body to endure,
>   And bend the mind to meet distress;
> And then HIS guardian care implore,
>   Whom demons dread and men adore. (ll. 430–7)

One of the strengths of this disturbing poem, though, is its resistance to moral closure. The more successfully the energies of madness are activated, the less they will tolerate being written into the design of a sane text, as White and as Gray had written them in. Crabbe represents a serious attempt to authenticate the experience of a mad mind, and he exploits the forms and diction of English poetry to give reality to a mental world beyond the normal. Madness, however, has a life of its own and, once arrayed, slips from its borrowed robes and watches while the poem moves to its conventional conclusion without it.

5

THE STRUGGLE FOR LANGUAGE

Erasmus Darwin, writing in the 1790s, gives a tripartite division of the causes of madness from pain of various kinds.

> Madness is sometimes produced by bodily pain, particularly I believe of a diseased liver, like convulsion and epilepsy; at other times it is caused by very painful ideas occasioned by external circumstances, as of grief or disappointment; but the most frequent cause of insanity arises from the pain of some imaginary or mistaken idea; which may be termed *hallucinatio maniacalis*.[1]

The struggle that is the subject of this chapter is one that proceeds between identity and pain, between the necessity to make sense and the resistance to explanation of extreme forms of mental and physical invasion. It involves the attempt by mad patients, or former patients, to articulate an adequate response to the individual experience of suffering, in some cases suffering that is continuing without any prospect of cessation, and in others suffering that is being recalled in the context of an interpretation that has since given meaning to the experience.

A number of significant eighteenth-century medical voices have already been heard testifying to the power of pain in creating mental disturbance. William Battie's 'Consequential' madness arose as a result of 'other disorders or external causes', and could be relieved by the speedy 'removal or correction of such disorders or causes', whereas 'the force and continued action' would effectively render the derangement habitual. Sir Richard Blackmore wrote of his certainty that sufferers from hypochondria and hysteria were 'often afflicted with various Pains and great Disorders', and John Woodward, in 1716, enabled his patient Mrs Holmes to put into words the pain that was, by the time of her consultation with him, already obsessional. Physical pain, of all human afflictions, has the capacity to assume such dimensions that the sufferer is compelled to contrive the means whereby he or she may begin not merely to experience the pain but to negotiate it. This may, ultimately, take the form of contriving to understand some meaning behind such suffering, but in order to arrive here the individual must already have found a way of retaining a private sense of identity, of individual integrity in the face of invasion. An apparent onslaught by an alien mode of existence quickly makes the threat of completely overrunning all personality, all self. Dealing with pain, therefore, involves the discovery of an appropriate language for negotiation.

The speech acts of the mad as recorded by medical practitioners, or by other interested professionals, vary across an enormous range, from the purest nonsense to the soundest sense. Some betray what seems to represent an insupportable degree of pain. At one extreme, a patient, Francis Culham, 'a Chirurgion', observed in 1671 by William Turner, the vicar of Walberton in Sussex, is described as having become 'stupified in his Brain' and subsequently in his whole body, 'so that he was forced to take to his Bed, and immediately grew not only speechless, but lost the use of his Reason'. This man, who alternated between fasting and consuming 'a whole Joynt of Meat at a Meal', was quite incapable of speech at all, 'for he made a dreadful and horrid Noise, but inarticulate, and lay roaring and howling most part of the Day after, (as sometimes he did before he did eat) seeming to covet more Meat, even then when he had fed most plentifully'. The sense of the animal in this description becomes even more explicit. The patient knows nobody, he 'used several sorts of Tones and Cries, all lamentable enough', and 'he would sometimes attempt to bite those that came near him'.[2] This is one response to a pain that would seem to have defied language.

At the other extreme, there are patients whose language reads as perfectly normal English, with the exception that it bears little relation to its conversational context, and apparently little sense of a self in control of the language that is being generated. William Salmon, one of the earliest of practical medical men to have left detailed case notes, wrote at the end of the seventeenth century about 'Sir John Roberts of Bromley by Bow'. Sir John's conversation was normal in terms of the forms of words used, but, argues Salmon, these forms in fact meant nothing to him.

His Discourse was nothing but only questions, and they were generally but two. 1. What was usual with him in the time of his Health and Strength of Reason and Understanding, which was always, *What news, or what news at London?* 2. A question about somthing which was present with him, and which by reason of the trouble thereof, could scarcely go out of his mind, which was, *what he should do about the weakness in his knees?* For he was so weak that he could scarcely go; not well sit down on his Chair without some assistance, nor rise off it again without help.

These Questions, at any time when I have set by him he would frequently ask me, to whom I made what answer I then saw convenient; in a few minutes after, he would ask the same Question again, to which I would reply, Sir John, you asked me that but just now, and I gave you an Answer: he would reply again, did you? I don't remember, I have forgot, What did you say? or words to the like effect; and then presently ask the same question over again.

Salmon has a great deal to say about the first of Sir John's questions.

But tho the Question, *What News at London?* may seem to be rational enough from any man that is *compos mentis;* yet not so in him which is not. . . . The Idea is fixed in his mind, so as he cannot eradicate it, and therefore he still proposes it being mad, as he used to do when rational; save, that he now does it Curtly, and alwaies forgets the answer.

This is language as a mechanical repetition of habitual acts lingering on from the world of sanity, like John Haslam's mad publican, referred to earlier, obsessed with the company's not having paid him. Sir John's senility thoughtlessly repeats phrases which happen to mean something, but might as well be inarticulate sounds, for they actually represent a less significant response to present reality than Francis Culham's roaring. But Salmon also seems seriously to underestimate his patient's second question, simply because it too is endlessly repeated, and because it is accompanied by behaviour for which he is unable to account, or at least which is accountable through the known patterns of one 'decayed in his Intellectuals'. Sir John would foolishly and impertinently ask his second question, with manifold Repetitions, sometimes laughing, and then immediately crying again without any known cause or reason, which was then usual with him. I have asked him what he cryed or wept for? He would sometimes make me no answer, and sometimes he would say he could not tell.[3]

This in fact is a question perfectly well attuned to the circumstances of its asking: a man in distress with physical weakness repeatedly asks his physician for advice. A man's sinking into senility is here taken as a reason for hearing all that he has to say as evidence for his condition. If Salmon was correct to see the repetition and the emotional reactions as part of a recognisable set of symptoms, his predisposition to do so was probably fortified by there being nothing he could do for 'the weakness in his knees'. We should also be aware, however, that sane questions can be asked in the context of mad, or 'decayed', behaviour, and that a response to pain can find its form in a legitimate, even a conversational, use of normal English structures.

Other patients, neither wholly inarticulate nor residing within a fabric of recollected snatches of language, react to pain through the dislocation of their relation to spoken English. William Perfect reports in his *Select Cases* a patient, a 'Gentleman, aged fifty-eight', who was disordered through 'a sudden transition in his circumstances':

his complaints were great pain in the head, almost a continual noise in his ears, and, at intervals, a melancholy depression, or a frantic exaltation of spirits; he was inclined to be costive, his water was very high-coloured, he passed whole nights without sleep, sometimes raved and was convulsed, and his attention was invariably fixed to one object namely, that he was *ruined*, *lost*, and *undone*! which was his incessant exclamation both by night and day.[4]

This speech pattern would seem to display exactly the pattern of mad writing that John Ferriar describes in 1795 in his *Medical Histories and Reflections*.

When lunatics attempt to write, there is a perpetual recurrence of one or two favourite ideas, intermixed with phrases which convey scarcely any meaning, either separately, or in connection with the other parts. It would be a hard task for a man of common understanding, to put such rhapsodies into any intelligible form, yet patients will run their ideas in the same track for many weeks together.[5]

The compound of mental and physical pain suffered by Perfect's patient seems to result in just such a mix of 'recurrence' and meaninglessness, yet Ferriar's 'intelligible form' is a limited response to the perceiving of meaning. Repetition is not an unexpected form of expression for any kind of intense preoccupation, whether real, as in this case, or imaginary, as in many others on record. Nor, as with Culham, is the formlessness of 'raving' necessarily unexpressive as a response to pain, confusion or absolute helplessness. This man's speech is not part of an exchange, and cannot be located, therefore, within the conventional rule systems of meaningful social dialogue, any more than Sir John Roberts's can. That does not prevent it from being expressive of his state of mind. An 'alternative arrangement' necessarily implies a dislocation in relation to more normal arrangements. Perfect's patient is in fact no more conventional as a listener to other speech than he is as a speaker himself. Perfect reports:

> When I undertook the care of this person, he appeared very impatient of contradiction; and, even discoursing with him in the most easy and gentle manner, would often ruffle him into a mis-construction of all that was said.[6]

Dislocation works both ways, and 'mis-construction' of whatever is heard of ordinary speech must be a necessary corollary to discourse that cannot be understood through application of the customary rules of English.

Perfect is rather unusual amongst medical men, of course, in attempting to 'discourse' with his patients at all, and so is privileged in understanding the extent to which normal language is received by the mad according to the nature and distinctiveness of their individual madness. Other patients afford him other insights: the melancholiac who has locked himself into a system of silence, an absolute negation of language, which means that Perfect's asking him 'several questions' receive 'no reply at all'; or the 'middle-aged man' who insists 'upon his being the Lord Chancellor, King of Spain, Duke of Bavaria, or some other great personage' and demands 'reverence and respect accordingly':

he was uniformly vain, formal, stately, gloomy, insolent, and self-important; and at any time, however ridiculous his words and actions appeared to others, they were supported in himself with all the dignity of excessive pride and ostentation, and an entire display of every vanity characteristic of that species of insanity under which he laboured.[7]

These patients are being understood within a linguistic context, and their madness as marking one kind of discourse out of a virtually endless range of possible discourses, some approximating quite closely to meaningful English speech patterns, others private and remote in the realms of inarticulacy, or silence. If this means that mad discourse is measured and judged by the standard of normal arrangements ('however ridiculous his words and actions appeared to others'), it is also the case that individuals are presented in terms of their own linguistic independence, as existing within a language that is more or less adequate to the continuation of their madness, although not to their meaningful relations with society, even with the society of the madhouse.

This represents a revealing contrast with the observations of John Haslam, whose reported cases are full of snatches of speech, but whose judgements are firmly rooted within a monocratic system of language. For Haslam, the efforts he reports his patients making to express pain, or states of mind, are themselves evidence of madness and are simply catalogued as part of the symptoms displayed. One case, 'BH', an aged man, designated 'Incurable', suffered from 'a cough, attended with copious expectoration'. When 'asked respecting his complaints, he said he had a violent pain across the stomach, which arose from his navel string at his birth having been tied too short'. This man 'never spoke afterwards'.[8] A woman of 27, 'AM', confined because of religious enthusiasm, 'alternately sang, and cried the greatest part of the night. She conceived her inside full of the most loathsome vermin, and often felt the sensation as if they were crawling into her throat.'[9] In both of these cases there has been an attempt to find a linguistic equivalent for physical sensation, and each is strikingly successful to the extent that a strong idea of a kind and quality of suffering is distinctively conveyed. Both, too, feel themselves to be under the influence of something over which they have no control, in one case an event involving an action that was done to him, in the other of creatures alien to her yet occupying her. Unlike John Woodward's patient, though, neither seems to attribute this control to Satan, preferring, apparently, to preserve their own linguistic responsibility rather than submit to a form and structure of language that would offer a ready explanation. ('AM' does, however, believe that 'God had inflicted this punishment on her'.) The result is the generating of an image that genuinely encapsulates the nature of their experience.

Other patients can be observed in the act of constructing not an image but a scenario by way of explanation for what is happening to them. 'MW', a middle-aged woman referred to earlier, constantly affirmed 'that she should live but a short time' and believed that she was being poisoned by 'some malevolent person', as evidence of which she would always be 'shewing her teeth, which had decayed naturally, as if this effect had been produced by that medicine'.[10] Here the scenario has to incorporate the known facts of the case, the decayed teeth, as well, no doubt, as the medicines administered at Bethlem, which are then used as evidence for the validity of the construction. Another, 'WC', a man of 53 in grief for the death of his son, suffers from perpetual hurry and restlessness, which he explains to himself through the invention of constantly pressing reasons for his activity.

> He passed about with an hurried step; was often suddenly struck with the idea of having important business to adjust in some distant place, and which would not admit of a moment's delay. Presently after, he would conceive his house to be on fire, and would hastily endeavour to rescue his property from the flames. Then he would fancy that his son was drowning, that he had twice sunk: he was prepared to plunge into the river to save him, as he floated for the last time: every moment appeared an hour until he rose.

Eventually, 'with great perturbation, he suddenly ran into his room, threw himself on the bed, and in a few minutes expired'.[11] Language here is conceived, as reported by Haslam, as a kind of stand-in, a medium on which the patient is able to read a plausible set of reasons that explain his feeling of physical restlessness, rather than an opportunity to attempt to describe the feeling itself.

Yet another case involving grief displays a similarly inventive construction of beliefs. 'ML', a woman of 38, had been a widow for six weeks.

She conceived that the overseers of the parish, to which she belonged, meditated her destruction: afterwards she supposed them deeply enamoured of her, and that they were to decide their claims by a battle. . . . She fancied that a young man, for whom she had formerly entertained a partiality, but who had been dead some years, appeared frequently at her bed-side in a state of putrefaction, which left an abominable stench in her room. Soon after she grew suspicious, and became apprehensive of evil intentions in the people about her. She would frequently watch at her door, and, when asked the reason, replied, that she was fully aware of a design, which had been formed, to put her secretly to death.[12]

Again, language seems to be deployed in order to present as coherently as possible the system of ideas that has been constructed by way of justification for emotions that are not accessible in their own right. The facts of this case, as they appear to the patient, apparently include the behaviour of the hospital staff at Bethlem, and also its sanitary arrangements, and these therefore demand inclusion within the scenario at the same time as they prove that scenario to be the correct interpretation.

Some of these examples quite clearly represent the attempt to come to terms with physical suffering, while in others the suffering involves as well a high degree of mental or emotional pain, such as that arising from loss or bereavement. The stylistic features of mad discourse that accompany these kinds of insanity include, as we have seen, the striking of images of pain, repetition of obsessive ideas, and the inscribing of explanations broad enough to embrace the salient features of a state of mind as perceived by the sufferer. Inevitably, such explanations frequently have recourse either to divine interference or to conspiracy. One particularly monumental and impressive theory is that developed by James Tilley Matthews.

Matthews's theory was presented to the world by Haslam in his publication *Illustrations of Madness* in 1810 in order to ensure that the patient's plea for release from Bethlem Hospital was unsuccessful. It is thus a tendentious document, but one in which Haslam claims to use Matthews's own words to condemn him. Briefly, Matthews 'insists that in some apartment near London Wall, there is a gang of villains profoundly skilled in Pneumatic Chemistry, who assail him by means of an Air Loom'.[13] The processes this machine is capable of effecting are truly horrendous, but the expression of them demonstrates a genuine, if far-fetched, attempt by Matthews to provide a coherent explanation for a large range of bodily sensations and thought patterns. These 'effects' are described:

Fluid Locking. – A locking or constriction of the fibres of the root of the tongue, laterally, by which the readiness of speech is impeded.

Thigh-talking. – To effect this, they contrive so to direct their *voice-sayings* on the external part of the thigh, that the person assailed is conscious that his organ of hearing, with all its sensibility, is lodged in that situation. The sensation is distinctly felt in the thigh, and the subject understood in the brain.

Sudden death-squeezing; by them termed *Lobster-cracking.* – This is an external pressure of the magnetic atmosphere surrounding the person assailed, so as to stagnate his circulation, impede his vital motions, and produce instant death.

Bomb-bursting is one of the most dreadful inflictions performed by the infernal agency of the air-loom. The fluid which resides in the brain and nerves, the vapor floating in the blood-vessels, and the gaz which occupies the stomach and intestines, become highly rarified and rendered inflammable, occasioning a very painful distension over the whole body. Whilst the assailed person is thus labouring, a powerful charge of the electrical battery . . . is let off, which produces a terrible explosion, and lacerates the whole system. A horrid crash is heard in the head.[14]

Matthews adds, 'I do not know any better way for a person to comprehend the general nature of such lobster-cracking operation, than by supposing himself in a sufficiently large pair of nut-crackers or lobster-crackers, with teeth, which should pierce as well as press him through every particle within and without'.

At the level of physical pain, Matthews gives a most vivid rendering of the sensations of suffering based on a dynamic, mechanistic view of the human body and a strong conviction of its susceptibility to the influence of modern scientific apparatus. Here is a potent model both of the vulnerability of the body and of the alienation from one's own physical identity that suffering can produce. The air loom is the navel cord, the vermin, the conspiracy of hospital staff and the voice of Satan all rolled into one overarching explanation for pain. No bodily event can occur that is not capable of being attributed to the air loom. At the same time the body is turned, as it was in the language of Thomas Willis, into a battleground, inhabited by Matthews, but over which alien forces are constantly driving in the attempt to subdue him. As in earlier cases, Matthews's relation to his own body is disjointed by frequent exposure to externally engendered pain, to the extent that he can catalogue his pains with apparent detachment, attributing each one to a separate process with a distinct description of its scientific cause and the nature of its effect. This includes even the extraordinary experience of some of his limbs and organs performing each others' functions.

This sense of detachment from himself, or of division into a self for which he is responsible and one that has been occupied, is consolidated with the gang's attempts at Matthews's own mind.

Kiteing. – This is a very singular and distressing mode of assailment, and much practised by the gang. As boys raise a kite in the air, so these wretches, by means of the air-loom and magnetic impregnations, contrive to lift into the brain some particular idea, which floats and undulates in the intellect for hours together; and how much soever the person assailed may wish to direct his mind to other objects, and banish the idea forced upon him, he finds himself unable; as the idea which they have kited keeps wavering in his mind, and fixes his attention to the exclusion of other thoughts. He is, during the whole time, conscious that the kited idea is extraneous, and does not belong to the train of his own cogitations.

Lengthening the brain. – As the cylindrical mirror lengthens the countenance of the person who views himself in such glass, so the assailants have a method by which they contrive to elongate the brain. The effect produced by this process is a distortion of any idea in the mind, whereby that which had been considered as most serious becomes an object of ridicule. All thoughts are made to assume a grotesque interpretation; and the person assailed is surprised that his fixed and solemn opinions should take a form which compels him to distrust their identity, and forces him to laugh at the most important subjects. . . .

114

Thought-making. – While one of these villains is sucking at the brain of the person assailed, to extract his existing sentiments, another of the gang, in order to lead astray the sucker . . . will force into his mind a train of ideas very different from the real subject of his thoughts. . . .

Tying-down; fettering the energy of the assailed's judgment on his thoughts.[15]

Matthews's theory shows an acute perception of the internal workings of his own systems of thought and their relations to feeling and to identification with self, right down to explaining conflicting trains of ideas as the consequence of members of the gang working to subvert the efforts of each other. He is obviously aware of suffering a removal of his own agency for the generation of thought processes, not least because there remains a sense of identity which is 'conscious that the kited idea is extraneous', that he should 'distrust' his own thoughts, and that there nevertheless exists a 'real subject of his thoughts'. The clarity and force of his imaginative rendering of his beliefs in fact give an irresisitible impression of a strong sense of self capable of retaining its own integrity in the face of torture, persecution and villainy. This is due both to the absolute certainty of his descriptions, rooted as they are in personal experience, and to the outrageous daring of the theory itself. Only a very robust identity could have come up with such a self-reliant explanation.

Matthews also displays a considerable degree of self-awareness, of the ability to see himself from the outside, in accommodating within this most lavish of conspiracy theories such evidence as is available to be perceived by an objective observer. '*Apoplexy-working with the nutmeg-grater*', for example, is 'violently forcing the fluids into the head' and thereby 'producing small pimples on the temples, which are raised, and rough like the holes in a nutmeg-grater: in a day or two they gradually die away'.[16] Similarly, '*Laugh-making*' is the 'forcing' of 'the magnetic fluid, rarified and subtilized, on the vitals, [*vital touching*] so that the muscles of the face become screwed into a laugh or grin'.[17] Matthews quite explicitly offers detailed description of the visible effects of 'lobster-cracking' as an explanation of certain distinctive features of his observable and otherwise peculiar behaviour. This is in the course of explaining the management of the 'levers' on the air loom:

115

The levers are placed at those points of elevation, *viz.* the one nearly down, at which I begin to let go my breath, taking care to make it a regular, not in any way a hurried breathing. The other, the highest, is where it begins to strain the warp, and by which time it becomes necessary to have taken full breath, to hold till the lever was so far down again. . . . But in that dreadful operation by them termed lobster-cracking, I always found it necessary to open my mouth somewhat sooner than I began to take in breath: I found great relief by so doing. . . . I always thought that by so opening my mouth, which many strangers, and those familiar or about me, called sometimes singularity, at others affectation and pretext, and at others asthmatic . . . enabled me sooner, easier, and with more certainty, to fill my lungs without straining them.[18]

At other times, Matthews, when he has 'perceived them about to make the wrench by suction', has 'recoiled as one expecting to receive a blow shrinks back in order to avoid it'.[19]

This provides an insight into the discourse of the mad that includes some mapping of bodily movements and habitual mannerisms such as Foucault required. Matthews's opening of his mouth, his 'grin', his recoiling, are all features of stock mad antics, here described from the other side of the fence. They are not to be understood in the context of everyday life, the context in which the reader reads and Haslam writes. Matthews's world is a reality in which remorseless human malice and the enjoyment of inflicting pain are made manifest in the powerful figure of the air loom and its conspiratorial gang of operators. In this context, everything makes such sense that it would be insane to behave in any other way. Behaviour such as Matthews's may look mad, but in fact is the consequence of 'strength of . . . intellect and unremitting vigilance', and should be regarded as a personal 'triumph' in the face of 'formidable assailments'.[20] Indeed, it is a considerable vindication of the suffering personality that *he* has been selected as the recipient of such extraordinary malice, and that *he* therefore bears a responsibility for resistance on behalf of the human race. (This is a feature of Matthews's beliefs that I shall pick up again in the next chapter.)

Matthews's theory is impressive both in its inventiveness, which goes some way towards satisfying Thomas Reid's call for 'new words and phrases' in describing 'the mind and its operations', and in its immediacy. His beliefs demand acceptance, there is nowhere any allowance for scepticism. These events are happening here and now, and what Matthews suffers could be turned against anyone – have been turned, and the victims, he claims, include several of the most notable public figures of his time.

This immediacy is a feature of many of the accounts so far looked at – not unexpectedly, in that pain, either physical or mental, is itself an experience that allows of no distraction. Sufferers cannot conceive of a time to come when the navel cord will not be too tightly tied, when the vermin will have disappeared, Satan will have retreated or the gang have packed up their apparatus and vanished into thin air. The here and now is therefore a vital ingredient of this kind of mad language. Madness is in a perpetual present, and makes of the past only what can contribute to the chosen explanation for the reality of pain. This may take the form of blocking out key events, particularly those that have most obviously brought about the present suffering – the death of the son, of the husband. But equally, because those features of the here and now that require explanation (the decayed teeth, the smell, the variety of pains, the confusion of thoughts, the very fact of confinement itself) are then used as supporting evidence for the validity of the theory, what has been fabricated also displays a constant confusing of cause and effect.

The effects of this are immediately visible in a work like Alexander Cruden's account, published in 1739 and therefore much earlier than most of the examples so far discussed, of his confinement in a private madhouse. Cruden's pamphlet, the first of several written over several years, is, as its full title proclaims, a work of protest: *The London-Citizen Exceedingly Injured; Or, A British Inquisition Display'd, in an Account of the Unparallel'd Case of a Citizen of London, Bookseller to the Late Queen, Who Was in a Most Unjust and Arbitrary Manner Sent on the 23rd of March Last, 1738, by One Robert Wightman, a Mere Stranger, to a Private Madhouse.* Cruden, in other words, is resting his case on his obvious sanity, and in so doing is in serious danger of overplaying his hand. What is apparent, even in the title, is the force of outrage that is motivating this work, and the desire to set every single aspect of his maltreatment before the objective reader, and at one go in order to prevent any possible shade of misunderstanding. The facts speak for themselves, but for them to do so requires every fact to be seen in the proper context of every other fact.

The stylistic consequences emerge in the very first paragraph of Cruden's account:

> A short narrative is here given of the horrid sufferings of a *London-Citizen* in *Wright's* private Madhouse at *Bethnal-Green*, during nine weeks and six days, (till he made his wonderful Escape) by the Combination of *Robert Wightman* Merchant at *Edinburgh*, a stranger in *London*, and others, who had no right, warrant or authority in Law, Equity or Consanguinity, or any other manner whatsoever, to concern themselves with him or his affairs; and yet most unjustly imprisoned him in that dismal place. How unjustly and unaccountably they acted in first sending Mr C. to *Bethnal-Green*, and how cruel and barbarous they were in their bold and desperate Design to fix him in *Bethlehem*, (after Mr C. refused to sign their Pardon) that they might screen themselves from punishment, by covering one heinous crime with another more heinous, will appear by the following Journal of Mr C.'s Sufferings.[21]

The most striking feature of Cruden's writing is the compression of a large amount of information within the parameters of only two sentences. To enable him to do this, those parameters are stretched far beyond the bounds of what is comfortable by the addition of subordinate phrases and clauses. Cruden's eye is initially fixed on the here and now of his telling, 'A short narrative is here given'. Very quickly, though, he is led away from a manageable time scheme. The phrase 'during nine weeks and six days', with its strict attention to accuracy, causes a distraction from the main current of the sentence in obliging him to insert parenthetically a note on the means and quality of the termination of his 'sufferings' before proceeding with the direct cause of his confinement, '*Robert Wightman*'. Even here, the mention of Wightman necessitates the giving of facts that place him in terms of occupation and origins, as if the reader cannot fully appreciate the extent of the man's barbarity without knowing that he was a merchant, and from Edinburgh.

The thrust of the sentence has by now moved some way from the 'is' of the opening, and the tense has shifted from present to past as Cruden deals more specifically with the background to his wrongs. What is more, the main verb, 'is . . . given', has become so distant that it requires additional verbal support if the structure is to do justice to Cruden's indignation. Two dependent verbs are therefore deployed. The first of these, in the subordinate clause 'who had no right', is used to sustain a trail of dependent items, 'warrant or authority in Law, Equity or Consanguinity, or any other manner whatsoever', apparently intended to bolster the legal arguments behind Cruden's case. The second, 'imprisoned', like 'had', refers to '*Wightman* . . . and others, who . . .', and brings the sentence back at last to the central event of the pamphlet, and to the main emotional preoccupation of Cruden's writing.

The attempt to take a single perspective on a range of times and motivations is even more apparent in the second sentence. Here the governing tense is future, 'will appear', but the narrative impulsion is from the past, and Cruden cannot prevent the matter for the story from intruding into his promise of what the story will contain. So, events and intentions come thick and fast: 'they' acted 'unjustly and unaccountably', they sent 'Mr C. to *Bethnal-Green*', they were not only 'cruel and barbarous' but 'bold and desperate', their 'Design' was to 'fix him in *Bethlehem*', but this was preceded by 'Mr C.' having 'refused to sign their Pardon', and they had therefore 'to screen themselves', and decided to cover 'one heinous crime with another more heinous'. The 'How . . . how . . . will appear' structure of this sentence is a sign of its intended function as a kind of proclamation and advertisement. The intricacies of its temporal patterns, and the cross-currents of its dealings with what happened and why, turn it into a pocket narrative in its own right.

Cruden's account, like Matthews's, allows of no second interpretation. It is a declaration in which every single aspect is turned towards one reading of events. To this extent nearly all of past time, for Cruden, is the cause of his confinement, and should therefore have its place within the narrative, and if possible within each sentence of it, even within the sentences of the 'Journal' that forms the bulk of the document ('A Tool of *Wightman's* formerly an Apprentice to a Taylor, but lately a Coffin-breaker and Grave-digger in St *Andrew's* Burying-ground, and a few months before a pretended Physician of no figure, came in . . .').[22] The forms and structures of English are distorted in order to accommodate a single-minded perspective on past time in which everything is cause, and cause is all that is of interest in the attempt to deal with the fact of his confinement. That such a perspective is itself insane is not a possible reading for Cruden, for that would mean that he had been rendered mad by the very events he now sees so clearly, and that the clarity of his seeing was a consequence not of sanity but of obsession.

★

The finding of perspective is a particularly telling issue in the struggle for a language, for perspective not only embraces cause and effect and therefore the narrative handling of time, but is also at the core of the relation between madness and language. Cruden's single perspective, in which he tries to do justice to everything at once, is that of a man who refuses to acknowledge any truth in the suspicion that he might in fact have been mad, or might now be mad. His writing, therefore, represents an inverse position to those narratives that tell of past madness from a perspective of recovered sanity. Where he protests, and thereby inadvertently offers evidence that he might in fact be mad, writers like Hannah Allen, George Trosse and William Cowper present their madness within a sane structure, and risk losing the truth of their experience in the sanity of their interpretation and expression of it.

Hannah Allen's pamphlet telling of her experience of madness was published in 1683, under the title *A Narrative of God's Gracious Dealings With That Choice Christian Mrs Hannah Allen, (Afterwards Married to Mr Hatt,) Reciting The great Advantages the Devil made of her deep Melancholy, and the Triumphant Victories, Rich and Sovereign Graces, God gave her over all his Stratagems and Devices. The Life of the Reverend Mr George Trosse* was written by 1693, and posthumously published in 1714, while Cowper's *Memoir of the Early Life of William Cowper Esq.* was written around 1767 and published in two versions in 1816, sixteen years after the poet's death. All three find their natural home within a strong tradition of spiritual autobiography[23] and offer, therefore, accounts of madness that are firmly enclosed by the perspective of their redemption through God. Suffering is dealt with, both physical and mental, but its presence is unproblematic in so far as its telling is able to make it mean in a context of temptation, transgression and salvation. So Hannah Allen concludes her account with a statement of her own recovered mind and of the exemplary nature of her experience.

> As my Melancholy came by degrees, so it wore off by degrees, and as my dark Melancholy bodily distempers abated, so did my spiritual Maladies also, and God convinced me by degrees; that all this was from Satan, his delusions and temptations, working in those dark and black humors, and not from my self, and this God cleared up to me more and more; and

accordingly my love to, and delight in Religion, increased; and it is my desire that, lest this great Affliction should be a stumbling-block to any, it may be known, (seeing my case is publish'd) that I evidently perceive that God did it in much mercy and faithfulness to my Soul; and though for the present it was a bitter Cup, yet that it was but what the only wise God saw I had need of according to that place, I *Pet*. i. 6. *Tho' now for a season, if need be, ye are in heaviness through manifold Temptations.*[24]

The frame adopted to make meaning from the experience dictates the linguistic range and register that now narrates what then took place, and the stock phrases and constructions of redemption stand in for the reality of individual suffering. Just as Satan's work is designated by the traditional labels, 'delusions and temptations' ('Stratagems and Devices' on the title-page), and God's is 'much mercy and faithfulness to my Soul' ('Triumphant Victories, Rich and Sovereign Graces' on the title-page), so Hannah Allen's madness is now her 'dark and black humors' and 'a bitter Cup' that is given endorsement by the language of the biblical quotation.

Trosse, by now a Nonconformist minister in Exeter, brings his much more elaborate account to an end with a similarly uncontrovertible closure:

> By my *Sins* and *Sensualities*, I had brought my self into horrible *Distractions* and perfect *Madness*, I was for a Time depriv'd of the regular Use of Reason, and by the Disturbance of my *Imagination* I became *wild* and *outragious*.
>
> But now, my *Brain* is compos'd, my *Mind* calm, my *Thoughts* orderly, I have a *Fancy* to *invent*, and a *Memory* to *retain* what I clearly understand: I can well remember *others Sermons* and my *own*: I acknowledge *Divine Goodness* and *Mercy* in all. . . .
>
> By my *brutish* and *carnal* Way of Life, I had cast my self into the Depths of *Despair* and *Horrour; absolutely concluding upon an Impossibility* of being receiv'd into God's Favour, or of being sav'd.
>
> But now, I hope I have a well-grounded Peace in my Conscience, and, thro' Grace, a comfortable Prospect of Eternal Life.[25]

The greater sophistication of the writing is evident in the self-conscious patterning of Trosse's paragraphs (these extracts are part of a series of ten pairs of 'then and now' summaries that conclude his book) and in the emphatic typographical arrangement, all of which stress the significance the experience now assumes in the divine arrangement of Trosse's life. Cowper's closure is less elaborate, more conditional, but equally resistant to any alternative interpretation of the meaning of the experience he had acknowledged as madness:

> I have found a place of rest prepared for me by God's own hand. . . . If the Lord gives me life, I shall not in this place make an end of my testimony to His goodness; at some future time I shall resume the story, and I have lately received a blessing from His hand which shines as bright as most of the foregoing favours, having the evident stamp of His love upon it, and well deserving to be remembered by me with all gratitude and thanksgiving.
>
> Peace be with thee, reader, through faith in the Lord Jesus Christ. Amen.[26]

These conclusions, like Cruden's opening, testify to the here and now, and to a large extent this perspective governs their understanding of the causes of their madness and the reasons for their recovery. The struggle for language was fought and won prior to the writing of the account, and won by relinquishing an individual right to language in glad surrender to the forms of religious conversion and prayer. Indeed, this struggle was in each case a significant feature of the mad experience, for resistance to God's word is, in the telling, picked out for special treatment. Hannah Allen, conceiving herself to be 'a Devil incarnate', and 'a thousand times worse than the Devil', sets herself against the word of God, recalling that 'When I was forc'd to be present at Duty, I would often stop my Ears.'[27] She believed that her sins were such that the Bible had no language to encompass them, and even chose her own description of her spiritual state as against the silence of religion:

> I would often say, . . . I had committed worse Sins than the Sin against the Holy-Ghost: some would answer, The Scripture speaks not of worse sins, and can you be guilty of greater Sins than the Scripture mentions? Yes, said I, . . . There is no word comes so near the comprehension of the dreadfulness of my Condition; as

that, I am the Monster of the Creation: in this word *I* much delighted.[28]

Allen had to go beyond the bounds of sanctified language in order to find a satisfactory term for her sinful identity, and 'delighted' in the creativity of doing so. But from the perspective of the writing, that delight must, of course, be put down as a measure of her spiritual depravity and of her distance from the language of salvation.

This resistance to the word of God finds a vivid parallel in Trosse. Bound and carried to a madhouse, he

> came to have *direful Apprehensions* of the *Wrath* of God: I was hereupon prompted to *bite off my Tongue*, and (which I desire to mention with *Trembling*) *spit it in the Face of God*. Which Thing I also attempted, thrusting my *Tongue* between my *Teeth* I bit it very hard, with Resolutions to bite it quite through, and that with a *Diabolical Intention*.

If all language is divinely given, then Trosse has chosen a most telling gesture in wishing to spit his tongue in the face of God. However, as reinterpreted from the perspective of sanity, God had other intentions.

> But the Lord graciously prevented so *dreadful* an *Evil*, and would not suffer me to force up my Under-Jaw with so much Strength as to bite it quite off. God would preserve that *Tongue*, tho' it had been so *sinfully abus'd*, and *set on fire of Hell*, that it might be exercis'd in the most *glorious Employment*, even to Preach His *Word* and Celebrate His *Praises*.[29]

The triumph of language over the defiant seeking of silence has led directly to Trosse's career as a preacher and to the writing of the account of his life. In Hannah Allen's case, religious language was eventually instrumental in helping to effect her recovery. She describes the gradual infiltration of her sickened mind by the word of God through the agency of 'Mr *Shorthose*'.

> Mr *Shorthose* having so good encouragement, came the next day again, being Sabbath day after Dinner, and prevailed with me to walk with him into an Arbour in the Orchard, where he had much discourse with me, and amongst the rest he entreated me to go home with him; which after long persuasions, both from him and my Aunt, I consented to, upon this condition, that he promised me, *he would not*

compell me to any thing of the Worship of God, but what he could do by persuasion; and that week I went with them, where I spent that Summer; in which time it pleased God by Mr *Shorthose's* means to do me much good both in Soul and Body.[30]

Lower in key than Trosse, and with a less elevated intention attributed to God, Allen nevertheless offers an interpretation of experience that involves the language acquired to deal with the experience being utilised in an unambiguous narration of it.

That Cowper, over seventy years later, describes the struggle for language if anything more fully than either Allen or Trosse testifies to the abiding nature of the issue in the writing of spiritual autobiographies. An early event, seen as significant in the writing but ignored, apparently, at the time, involved Cowper's recovery from depression during a stay in Southampton. Struck for the first time with God's grace, he offered up prayers of gratitude. However,

> Satan and my own wicked heart quickly persuaded me that I was indebted for my deliverance to nothing but a change of season and the amusing varieties of this place. . . . Upon this hellish principle, as soon as I returned to London, I burnt my prayers and away went all thoughts of devotion and dependence upon God my Saviour.[31]

This act of deliberate linguistic estrangement becomes virtually a primal sin within the pattern of Cowper's relation of madness, for without the language of personal prayer he is cast out on a sea of silence, waiting for signs and words from distant sources. After his failed attempts at suicide, and convinced of his state of sinfulness, his hold on relevant language is sufficient only for him to walk 'to and fro in my chamber' repeating, 'There never was so abandoned a wretch, so great a sinner.' Scriptural images enter his mind, only to be applied immediately and damningly to himself.

> The sword of the Spirit seemed to guard the tree of life from my touch and to flame against me in every avenue by which I attempted to approach it. I particularly remember the barren fig tree was to me a theme of inconceivable misery, and I applied it to myself with a strong persuasion upon my

mind that when Our Saviour pronounced a curse upon it He had me in His eye and pointed that curse directly at me.[32]

He looks in vain for comfort from other men's language – 'all Archbishop Tillotson's sermons', 'a volume of Beaumont and Fletcher' – and finds, rather, 'something that struck me to the heart':

> I cannot but observe that as I found something in every author to condemn me, so it was generally the first sentence I pitched upon. Everything preached to me, and everything preached the curse of the Law.[33]

He dreams of the promise of divinely sanctioned prayer, only to be excluded at the moment when the vision enters the security of language.

> One morning as I lay between sleeping and awake, I seemed to myself to be walking in Westminster Abbey, walking till prayers should begin; presently I thought I heard the minister's voice and hastened towards the Choir; just as I was upon the point of entering, the iron gate under the organ was flung in my face with a jar that made the Abbey ring.[34]

He attempts to repeat the Creed, but finds that 'all traces of the form were struck out of my memory'. His efforts to recover it produce 'a sensation in my brain like a tremulous vibration of all the fibres of it', which Cowper attributes to 'a supernatural interposition to inform me that, having sinned against the Holy Ghost, I had no longer any interest in Christ or in the gifts of the Spirit'.[35] As the language of God is further and further removed from him, the voice of Satan, conversely, grows strong.

> I slept my usual three hours well and then awakened with ten times a stronger sense of my alienation from God than ever. Satan plied me close with horrible visions and more horrible voices. My ears rang with the sound of the torments that seemed to await me and inevitable damnation was denounced upon me in such strains of malice impatient to be gratified that the united world could not have assured me of being reprieved from Hell one hour longer.[36]

In his despair, he feels both physical pain as his 'hands and feet became cold and stiff' and 'a cold sweat stood upon my forehead', and the spiritual agony of imagining 'my soul' seeming 'to cling to my lips as if upon the very point of departure'.[37]

This key image, the soul departing from the lips, epitomises Cowper's linguistic plight: language has been the means and measure of his fall, and in his case the traditional image has a cruel aptness, for the soul that has been divorced from God passes through the tainted organ of speech as it is transported to the inarticulate sufferings of damnation. Having betrayed language, he is now betrayed by language, and his 'thoughts and expressions' become 'more wild and incoherent',[38] until he is carried by his brother John to Dr Nathaniel Cotton's madhouse in St Albans.

Cowper's recovery to the condition in which he is capable of writing his own account as an act of thanksgiving in compensation for the burnt prayers is a painful process of restoration to some degree of confidence in language. In his confinement he experiences visions of beauty and reassurance, one of which enables him to proceed, like Coleridge's Ancient Mariner, to a spontaneous utterance of thanksgiving, albeit with unpromising consequences.

> One evening as I was walking to and fro in my chamber, the day being now shut in, I saw myself suddenly enclosed in a temple as large as a cathedral. It had two cupolas, one at each end, and the roof was supported by tall and straight columns in rows parallel to each other. . . . The whole edifice was built with beams of the purest light, mild and soft indeed, but bright as those of an unclouded sun. I cannot conceive a more regular piece of architecture or imagine to myself a more delightful object. It lasted so long that I had time to consider it attentively. At length I cried aloud, 'Bless me; I see a glory all around me.' At the first word I spoke, the whole disappeared.[39]

Gradually, however, the language of God, of the Bible, of the promise of salvation, is extended to him:

> Something seemed to whisper to me every moment, 'Still there is mercy.'

Having found the Bible upon a bench in the garden, I opened it upon the eleventh of St John's Gospel, where Lazarus is raised from the dead. I saw so much benevolence and mercy, so much goodness and sympathy with miserable mankind in our Saviour's conduct as melted my heart, and I almost shed tears over the relation.[40]

I flung myself into a chair near the window seat and, seeing a Bible there, ventured once more to apply to it for comfort and instruction. The first verse I saw was the twenty-fifth of the third chapter to the Romans where Jesus is set forth as the propitiation for our sins.[41]

As he describes this process he finds his own language inadequate to the emotions dealt with, and consequently the narrative itself comes to rely more and more on biblical allusion and quotation:

I could only look up to Heaven in silence, overwhelmed with love and wonder! But the work of the Holy Ghost is best described in His own words. It was 'joy unspeakable and full of glory'.

My physician, ever watchful and attentive to my welfare, was now alarmed with contrary apprehensions, and began to fear lest the sudden transition from despair to joy should terminate in a fatal frenzy. But 'the Lord was my strength and my song and was become my salvation; the voice of rejoicing and salvation was in my dwelling, for the right hand of the Lord was exalted. I said, I shall not die but live and declare the works of the Lord. . . .'[42]

Even Cowper's acknowledgement of his inarticulacy as a narrator of his own spiritual experience now finds adequate expression through the words of both Old and New Testaments:

How shall I express what the Lord did for me except by saying that He made all His goodness pass before me. I seemed to speak to Him, 'face to face, as a man converseth with his friend', except that my speech was only in tears of joy and 'groanings that cannot be uttered'.[43]

Cowper's recovery of language, like Allen's and Trosse's, is not a restoration to linguistic independence, but a capitulation to a single, all-powerful register that carries with it the capacity to make meaningful every aspect of the experience of derangement. The present that is the time of writing has annexed the immediacy of the suffering that preceded it, and the religious conversion that was the outcome of Cowper's madness is allowed to redraw the parameters of his insanity in order to reduce it to a means to the end that is now celebrated. While Haslam's and Perfect's patients were enclosed within the reality of suffering, and Cruden and Matthews within their respective explanations for the nature of their experiences, Hannah Allen, George Trosse and Cowper's enclosure is more remote from their madness but equally secure in that the here and now is the only perspective that can be taken. Trosse, and apparently Allen, were fortunate to find social and religious contexts to sustain their new-found sanity, and the linguistic frameworks through which they made sense of their sufferings were never themselves subverted by the persistence of yet other 'alternative arrangements'. There is a poignant irony in Cowper's case, in that his assurance of salvation was so short-lived, and from his later and enduring perspective of assured damnation it must have seemed a period of insane hope reflecting cruelly on the remorseless sanity of his life of despair.

6

THE INNER VOICE

The struggle for language, as discussed in the last chapter, was a struggle against physical and mental pain, a fight against succumbing to a silence that would signify the end of belief in the utility of any expression, any self-assertion, in the face of an overwhelmingly alien force. In such circumstances, a hold on language is evidence of a last purchase on a system of human exchange that at least implies a belief in common understanding and fellow feeling. The endeavour of all but the most inarticulate of Haslam's, Salmon's and Perfect's patients is towards expression of an extreme of suffering that appeals for sympathy when perceived and entered into from a perspective of the normal spectrum of human experience. The writing of a Cruden or a Matthews is more remote from this spectrum, and the creating of syntactical space by the former, the inventiveness in diction of the latter, are virtual acknowledgements that here are cases that call for departure from some of the linguistic norms of English prose. Even here, though, we have appeals, explicitly or implicitly made, to an assumed standard of common sense and sympathy, in Cruden's case, quite explicitly, to a standard of outrage at the 'exceeding' nature of his 'injuries', in Matthews's, less obviously, to the conviction carried by such complete and detailed evidence as is offered in his interpretation. Trosse, Allen and Cowper afford different appeals in that they write from the perspective of recovery from suffering, and through the focus of an accepted explanation for the pain they have experienced. It is not understanding of the pain itself that is required, but endorsement of the explanation and its implications for the spiritual welfare of their readers. In many struggles for language, a common tongue is assumed, and some kind of communication is still, therefore, taken as a possibility.

The inner voice is different. In this chapter, the majority of the texts to be looked at are by writers who are locked within a system of madness that is not only self-sufficient but self-justifying. That is, the language used to frame the account also has the tendency to validate the identity of what is mad. Its impulse is inner conviction, and its assumption is not that of sympathetic accessibility from a norm that is just out of reach, but of uniqueness.

If we look again at those writings that are informed by the tradition of spiritual autobiography, we can see that in fact two quite different perspectives are in operation within these texts. One, already discussed, is the given focus of spiritual salvation, a focus that inevitably pulls away from the reality of the experience of madness in providing its interpretation. A second, however, is detectable in those very passages where the most disturbing episodes of madness are described. It seems that the force of recollection is sufficient to enable the writer not only to remember his or her own experience but in a large measure to recover it and to reread it through the structures and diction of the language that it generates. In Trosse's account, for example, the presence of the Devil is never far from his thoughts, and the potency of this force constantly animates the writing, not least because the Devil is capable of taking on any form in order to seduce a potential victim, and particularly the forms of language.

> I then waking, and being alone in the Chamber, fancy'd I heard some *rushing kind of Noise*, and discern'd something at the *Bed's-Foot* like a *Shadow*; which I apprehended to have been a *Spirit*. Hereupon, I was seiz'd with *great Fear* and *Trembling*, rose in Haste, went forth into the *Outer-Chamber* in *great Consternation*, and walk'd up and down in it as one *amaz'd*.[1]

The presence of 'the devil' at this stage in the account is given form only by the sound Trosse 'fancy'd' he heard, and by the shadow 'discern'd' at the end of the bed: the tentativeness of his *experience* of this presence finds *its* form in the precarious verbs, and in the vagueness ('some *rushing kind of Noise*', 'something . . . like a *Shadow*') of the recording of his perceptions. The apprehension of a spiritual presence shakes the firmness of language. Trosse can no longer record with certainly what he saw and what was to be understood by it, and writes instead only his own helplessness before a force with the power to sap his linguistic identity. Immediate recourse is to panic, and therefore to action which itself takes over the text. 'Hereupon' has the gathering energy of terror as Trosse is 'seiz'd' by emotions from within, and the structure of the second sentence sets in desperation a purely physical drive ('rose in Haste, went forth . . . walk'd up and down') against the amorphousness of the demonic.

If 'the devil' has succeeded in unsettling Trosse's hold on his own language, it is, apparently, in order to replace it with a discourse borrowed from legitimate forms of Christian worship.

While I was thus walking up and down . . . I perceiv'd a *Voice*, (*I heard it plainly*) saying unto me, *Who art thou*? Which, knowing it could be the Voice of *no Mortal*, I concluded was the *Voice of God*, and with Tears, as I remember, reply'd, *I am a very great Sinner, Lord*! Hereupon, I withdrew again into the *Inner-Room*, securing and barring the Door upon me, & betook my self to a *very proper* and *seasonable Duty*, namely, *Secret Prayer*. . . .

. . . while I was praying upon my Knees, I heard a Voice, as I fancy'd, as it were just behind me, saying, *Yet more humble; Yet more humble*; with some Continuance. And not knowing the Meaning of the *Voice*, but undoubtedly concluding it came from God, I endeavour'd to comply with it. Considering that I kneel'd upon something, I remov'd it. . . . But the *Voice* still continu'd, *Yet more humble; Yet more humble*. In Compliance with it I proceeded to pluck down my *Stockings*, and to kneel upon my *bare Knees*: But the same *awful Voice* still sounding in mine Ears, I proceeded to pull off my *Stockings*, and then my *Hose*, and my *Doublet*. . . . But *all* I could do was not *low enough*, or *humble enough*. At last, observing that there was an Hole in the Planking of the Room, I lay my self down flat upon the Ground, and thrust in my Head there as far as I could; but because I could not fully do it, I put my Hand into the Hole, and took out *Earth* and *Dust*, and sprinkled it on my *Head*; some *Scripture Expressions* at that Time offering themselves to my Mind, I thought *this* was the *Lying down in Dust and Ashes* thereby prescrib'd.[2]

Once Trosse has accepted the 'Voice' as the voice of God, the form of its language is accepted as legitimate, and the '*awful*' repetition is unquestioningly obeyed so that description of increasingly desperate action alternates with the unyielding injunction of the word to make up the structure of the entire passage. Where the shadowy spiritual presence had disabled the language of the narrative, now that disablement is utilised by 'the devil' in order to ensure compliance with a language that can take over the pattern and development of the text. Trosse has given himself over to a voice whose only form is the language of the Bible, and his act of recall of this self-surrender is so written that the voice of 'God' is visibly directing the reconstruction of his *Life*, so much so, at this point, that '*Written by Himself*', as inscribed on the title-page, becomes part of the evidence of the madness that is described.

Eventually, the true identity of Trosse's instructor dawns upon him.

> At length, standing up before the *Window*, I either *heard a voice*, which bid me, or *had a strong Impulse*, which excited me, to *cut off my Hair*; to which I reply'd, *I have no Scissars*. It was then hinted, that a *Knife would do it*; but I answer'd, *I have none*. Had I one, I verily believe, this *Voice* would have gone from my *Hair* to my *Throat*, and have commanded me to *cut it*: For I have all Reason to conclude, that the *Voice* was the Voice of *Satan*, and that his Design was, to *humble* me as *low as Hell*: But the Absence of a *proper Instrument* prevented it.

From this Trosse draws the inescapably awful conclusion: 'Thus, pretending the *Worship of God*, I fell, in effect, to the *Worshipping* of the *Devil*; and my Falling on my knees before *God* issu'd in a Prostration at the *proud Usurper's* Feet.'[3]

The dawning also involves a restoration to linguistic independence, and Trosse for a while resumes the responsibility for his own text. The voice is heard issuing a wider variety of instructions, but Trosse not only declines the instructions with answers of his own, he also keeps back from the reader his growing suspicion of this voice until the latter part of the paragraph. The telling of his expectation of the command to slit his own throat, and of his conclusion that he was listening to '*Satan*', represents both his own mastery over 'the devil' and his authority over the form and flow of information within his writing. This is in sharp contrast to the narration of his mechanical obedience to the demands for humility, a recollection that tends to recreate the original state of mind, of loss of self within the grip of a powerful and disabling 'usurper'.

Trosse is a writer with a mission. A skilled preacher, his *Life* was framed as a piece of rhetoric from which we have to extract the evidence that can stand as the language of madness from the perspective not of trial and salvation but of a self-contained state of insanity. He acknowledges quite freely that he has been mad, but this in itself is not the same as writing as a madman. Hannah Allen and, much later, Joanna Southcott, are less sophisticated writers, and the madness in their works is consequently far more readily identifiable as subsisting within the language used at the time of their insanity. For example, Allen quite explicitly quotes the language of her madness.

> I would say that *Pashurs* doom belonged to me, that I was *Magor-Missabib*, a Terrour to my self and all my Friends; that I was a Hell upon Earth, and a Devil incarnate. . . . Sometimes when they had told me I had been Prayed for, I would say, *they did not pray for me, for I was not to be prayed for*; for the Scripture said, *That they who had sin'd the sin unto death, were not to be Prayed for*: And when a good friend of mine Mr *Blake* came daily and unweariedly to see me; I would Ask him, *Why he yet came, seeing I rejected his Counsel*; And, *Christ bid his Messengers shake the dust of their Feet off against such*.[4]

The language of the Bible is uniquely adaptable for the expression of passionate states of being, and Allen is obviously attracted to features such as repetition ('*they did not pray for me, for I was not to be prayed for*', '*sin'd the sin unto death*') and strange names and identities. Just as her phrase '*the Monster of the Creation*', in which she 'much delighted', seemed to encapsulate her state of mind, so the words of Jeremiah in cursing and renaming 'Pashur the son of Immer the priest' – 'The Lord hath not called thy name Pashur, but Magor-missabib. For thus saith the Lord, Behold, I will make thee a terror to thyself, and to all thy friends'[5] – seems, if anything, to fuel with the thrill of exotic combinations of syllables the dallying with damnation that is characteristic of her definition of madness.

Allen also describes some of the obsessive states of her period of insanity, as, for example, her unwillingness to eat.

Towards Winter I grew to Eat very little, (much less than I did before) so that I was exceeding Lean; and at last nothing but Skin and Bones; (a Neighbouring Gentlewoman, a very discreet Person that had a great desire to see me, came in at the back-door of the House unawares, who after she had seen me, said to Mrs *Wilson, She cannot live, she hath death in her face*) I would say still that every bit I did Eat hastned my Ruin; and that I had it with a dreadful Curse; and what I Eat encreased the Fire within me, which would at last burn me up; and I would now willingly live out of Hell as long as I could.[6]

Here, too, it is the language of the moment that captures Hannah Allen's state of mind, the language of conviction of damnation, the spilling of spiritual belief into the physicality of everyday life. Allen, believing herself uniquely terrible, has also decided that the act of eating, which sustains life in the rest of mankind, contributes in her to the speed with which she will be consumed into Hell. She therefore, within the logic of her madness, sees that she must starve in order to stay alive.

In a less religiously oriented age, one of John Haslam's Bethlem patients restricted his diet for equally logical but more altruistic reasons:

I remember a patient who conceived, that, although dead men tell no tales, yet their feeling was very acute. This assured principle he extended to inferior animals, and refused to eat meat, because he could not endure to be nourished at the expence of the cruel sufferings, which beef steaks necessarily underwent in their cookery.[7]

Haslam's telling, in sharp contrast to Allen's, apparently preserves none of the language of his patient, paraphrasing the madness of the conception under a self-consciously civilised, and even amused, pattern of phrasing – 'dead men tell no tales', 'very acute', 'assured principle', 'extended to inferior animals', 'endure to be nourished', 'cruel sufferings', 'necessarily underwent'. The original belief is there, recoverable, but any degree of access to the patient's language is denied by the intervention of the language of sanity. Hannah Allen, in the reporting of what she would actually 'say', gives a large measure of the characteristics of mad thinking and speaking. There is the swiftness, even the desperation, with which each phrase succeeds the former, emphasised by the recurring conjunction 'and'. As Haslam observes, some patients

> speak of their disorder as accompanied with great hurry and confusion of mind, where the succession of ideas is so rapid and evanescent, that when they have endeavoured to arrest or contemplate any particular thoughts, they have been carried away by the tide, which was rolling after them.[8]

There is the scale and kind of structural repetition. Above all, there is the mix of one fixed idea variously worked (the obsession with eating) with a logical development from 'Ruin' and 'Curse' through 'the Fire within' to actual damnation, which is the overriding obsession of her insanity. At the same time, a second perspective is present in Allen's writing, parenthetically, with the supplying of information necessary for the reader to appreciate how little she was eating ('(much less than I did before)'), and with the interpolated opinion expressed of Hannah Allen by the neighbour 'to Mrs *Wilson, She cannot live, she hath death in her face*', and expressed of the neighbour by Hannah Allen to the reader that she was 'a very discreet Person'. This neighbour's coming in 'at the back-door of the House unawares' is particularly appropriate in that she enters the text similarly out of the attention of the mad Hannah, and only through the linguistic perspective of the sane telling of the story.

Joanna Southcott, while widely assumed to be mad by many of her contemporaries[9] (she was also, early in her ministry, regarded by some in Exeter as a witch, largely because of her prophecies of bad harvests),[10] rarely makes appearances in recent writing about madness. Her immense popularity and following at the end of the eighteenth century and during the early years of the nineteenth made her into a national figure, with over 7,000 listed believers across the country (there were eight more in Ireland, one in Belgium and one in Swedish Pomerania).[11] On 11 October 1813, at the age of 63, she found herself divinely pregnant with 'Shiloh', whose destiny would be to prepare the way for the Second Coming. This was announced to her followers in 1814, but on 28 December she died without giving birth. There was no child. By the time of her death she had written over sixty publications, the first, *The Strange Effects of Faith*, appearing in 1801.

Even more than George Trosse, Southcott stands as the very type of the divinely inspired prophet, moved by spiritual guidance on behalf of an erring humanity.

> The Lord is coming (as he hath spoken by his Prophets) to be the Mighty Counsellor, the Everlasting Father, the Prince of Peace, and the Desire of every Nation: And this is his Counsel – To deal with Men after the Manner of Men; to have these Writings tried by Judges and Jury: The Judges are the Ministers of the Lord: the Jury are the Sheep of his Flock: So I give myself up to the Judgment of Men, to be tried according to the Laws of God and Man. Now, if I am refused so just and fair a Trial, I must judge myself in a Land that Darkness hath overspread, and gross Darkness the Eyes of the People; where Justice is fallen in the Streets, and Equity cannot enter.[12]

Unlike Trosse, however, Southcott's guidance comes through the agency of a spirit voice, giving instructions, prophecies and explanations of dreams.

> Thus, by types, shadows, dreams, and visions, I have been led on, from 1792, to the present day; whereby the mysteries of the Bible, with the future destinies of nations have been revealed to me, which will all terminate in the Second Coming of Christ; and the Day of Judgment, when the seven thousand years are ended.[13]

The most strikingly characteristic feature of Joanna Southcott's writings is her absolute certainty of the truth of her undertaking. The biblical language lends her a rhetoric of conviction on a large scale, but equally significant is her own tone of personal confidence. Every little detail of her life and thoughts is explained and elevated into an element in God's plan. She is, for example, copying verses on God's impending judgment dictated to her by her spirit when a domestic accident occurs, which she mentions in a footnote:

> Just as I had written, 'these things to mock,' my meat kettle, which was on the fire, fell suddenly off, and in my stooping to take it up, I threw my writings before it, which involved them in smoke, ashes, and water; fortunately, however, on getting dry, I found no part of them obliterated.

The resourceful spirit immediately accommodates the incident:

> The blood of all that you have slain;
> They all were murder'd by such men,
> Who now appear these things to mock,
> And now on them I'll bring the stroke;
> As down the kettle then did fall,
> You shall perceive I'll bring on all.[14]

Similarly, each one of an apparently endless series of vivid dreams has been sent in order to reinforce, again and again, the message of God's purpose and his unique intentions for Southcott. Indeed, she is assured in *Sound An Alarm in My Holy Mountain*, 'Joanna, Joanna, the Angels rejoiced at thy birth'.[15]

Not that she does not also experience, like Trosse, interference from Satan. But Southcott has no difficulty in recognising the voice of the Devil, and deals with him in typically sturdy fashion.

> As I was meditating on the unbounded love of Christ to man, Satan's blasphemy broke in upon me, 'Christ's love was out of pride.' Here my passions grew high: 'Thou devil incarnate, (said I) thou hast lost thy honour, and thou enviest that Christ hath retained his. . . .' Here Satan came in, with dreadful blasphemy against God and Christ. This enraged my passions, as I could not bear to hear any thing spoke against God or Christ. I cried out 'Thou Devil, wherefrom didst thou come? Canst thou dare thus to trifle with God? Hast thou not sunk thyself low enough already? . . .'
> In this manner, I continued with Satan for ten days. His answer and blasphemy was too shocking to pen; till I was worn out with rage and malice aganst him, I could not bear myself.[16]

Similarly incontrovertible recognition of the presence and person of the Devil is shown by several of Haslam's patients in Bethlem:

> they all represented him as a big, black man, with a long tail, cloven feet, and sharp talons, such as is seen pictured in books. . . . One . . . solemnly declared, she heard him break the iron chain with which God had confined him, and saw him pass fleetly by her window, with a truss of straw upon his shoulder.[17]

What is distinctive about Southcott's account, apart from her own rage and invective, is that she cannot bring herself to include within

137

her text the words that constituted Satan's side of the dialogue. Other narratives involving confrontation with the Devil give a strong sense of the sinister nature of the encounter and of the subtlety of Satan in linguistic disguise. Southcott's Satan is neither subtle nor, apparently, particularly sinister. His tactic seems to be less the offering of temptation than the arousing of wrath. At the same time, Southcott, like Trosse, does find the necessity for action in order to enable her to deal with the emotions she is discovering within herself.

> I went out of the house, sometimes in the garden; but the garden was not large enough to contain me; so I went out in the open fields; and went from field to field to dispute with the Devil, till I had got rid of him, and wearied myself out with passion.[18]

Southcott's text, which has space for the many varieties of dream, verse and prose, letters from ministers and followers, is closed to the words of the Devil. Yet those words, as she heard them, necessitated the finding of space in order to accommodate the passions aroused. Within the system of her derangement, an emotional balancing affords textual space for that which she recognises as divine, while reducing to silence that mode of the inner voice that is heard as infernal. She shouts with rage, she seeks the open fields in order to find an arena large enough for a 'dispute' that is not to be recorded. The image itself, of Southcott's raging 'from field to field', is given the textual space to stand for that which has taken place out of earshot. Within her madness, a second madness threatens when the inner voice speaks of that which cannot be heard. The full force of divinely approved energy is brought to bear, corroborated by the dimensions of a familiar landscape, in the achievement of a massive act of linguistic censorship.

Joanna Southcott's writing is on a large scale: her prophecies involve the future of nations and of mankind, her visions are apocalyptic, the voices she hears are sent from Heaven. Her texts move between prose and verse, self and spirit with the confidence of absolute conviction. At the beginning of the second part of *The Strange Effects of Faith*, for example, she explains why so large a proportion of her writing is in verse, and then straight away moves into an undertaking of Miltonic dimensions.

I must beg to assign some reasons, why my writings are spoken so much in verse. Verse is an addition to words, and so is mine to the Bible: Verse gives an echo, and it is the voice of the Lord echoing back to man. Consider how many were the songs of Solomon – and mine is indited by a greater than Solomon.

I shall commence this part with the mystery of the Fall, and how it was explained.

> 'Over the earth the darkness it is gone,
> Nothing but darkness in the sons of men:
> And how my Bible will they all explain,
> For all dark sayings to be brought to light?
> I say the Bible's cover'd from men's sight,
> Left to men's wisdom simply to explain;
> And by men's wisdom simply it is done.'[19]

Southcott places herself defiantly in the tradition of Solomon, of David, and of Abraham and the prophets. In part one of *The Strange Effects of Faith* she recounts the first of her dialogues with God himself, an encounter that took place in 1792.

Then these words came to me: 'The Lord is awake, as one out of sleep. The voice of the Lord shall shake terribly the earth. Pestilence and famine shall go thro' the lands. Men's hearts shall fail them for very trouble; because they have not known the visitation of the Lord.' As soon as these words came to me I trembled, and was afraid of his majesty and greatness. Tears of humiliation ran down my eyes, and a holy fear seized my soul. I wept bitterly, and wondered at his divine goodness to such an unworthy creature as I was. But these words were answered me; 'I have seen all thy enquiries, to know my will and obey it; and now I will reward thee. Dost thou believe it?' – I cried out, 'Yea, Lord; if it be thy voice, I do believe it; for I know thou art not a man to lie, nor the son of man to be wavering. I have always found thee a God, like thyself, faithful to thy word, and faithful to thy promises.' – I was answered, 'Dost thou think I will now?' – I said, 'Yea, Lord; if it be thy word, I know thou wilt. Thou hast been faithful to thy word throughout the Bible, in every age of the world; a God, the same yesterday, today, and for ever.' I was answered, 'This thou believest, and this thou shalt find me;

faithful to my word, and faithful to my promises; and next
Sunday I will fulfil my promise at my table.'[20]

She is less imaginatively inventive than James Tilley Matthews,
though equally believing herself under the influence of a massively
powerful force. Southcott's framework is exclusively biblical, and
as such she can make claim to rights and traditions to which
Matthews has little access. He, generating the language that is to
validate his unique and dynamic system of explanations, wins no
converts. For Joanna Southcott, the Bible and its patterns is the
validating model for beliefs and expression that are fundamentally
as insane as Matthews's. Her behaviour, as she describes it, falls
within the traditional range of response to a visitation by God – she
trembles and is afraid, she weeps, she considers herself unworthy.
Her description is arranged in simple patterns of double main clauses
– '. . . I trembled, and was afraid', 'Tears . . . ran and . . . fear
seized', 'I wept . . . and wondered'. When the Lord speaks, he too
has has a tendency to echo her structures – 'I have seen . . . and I
will' – though he also shows a reassuringly human side in his need
to ask questions. Southcott, as in her dialogue with the Devil, has
quite enough confidence not only to recognise at once the source
of this voice but to supply answers at length and in appropriately
biblical phrasing – 'Yea, Lord', 'the same yesterday, today, and for
ever'. At the same time, the exchange is not without its down-to-
earth side, not least the assurance to God that he is, quite literally of
course, 'not a man to lie', and the Almighty's own precision as to
timing in the fulfilment of his promise. In a mechanically minded
age, the age of electric shock treatment and of the revolving chair,
Matthews's remorselessly mechanistic explanations were used as
evidence of his madness, and his own language cited as justification
for his continued confinement. Joanna Southcott, as outrageous in
her claims, and able to publish her beliefs to the world, remained
at liberty to multiply her followers and prophesy the future for
mankind.

With Joanna Southcott madness achieves a remarkable triumph: it
broadcasts itself, making ever more extraordinary claims, presenting increasing threats to public sanity and religious orthodoxy,
and, as if in obedience to Andrew Harper's recommendation in
1789 'to give full scope to . . . incipient Insanity', still goes free.
Richard Brothers, a contemporary and equally outrageous prophet,
was arrested on charges of 'treasonable activities' in March 1795

after the publication of his book, *A Revealed Knowledge of the Prophecies and Times*. Brothers announced himself as 'Nephew of the Almighty', and his language, like Southcott's, revels in the biblical, especially in the patterns and images of Revelation: 'The dead will increase so fast and be in such prodigious numbers . . . that the living will not be sufficient to bury them, but will leave the bodies exposed to the fowls of Heaven for meat.'[21] After his arrest he was quickly redefined as mad and transferred to a private asylum where he remained until 1806. Brothers's capacity for reaching to the centres of political power was demonstrated when he was vigorously defended in the House of Commons at the end of March 1795 by the Member for Lymington, Nathaniel Brassey Halhed, a supporter of Warren Hastings and close friend of Richard Brinsley Sheridan. Halhed declared that 'the man was very well apart from his pen and ink, but when he mounted on the Pegasus of Prophecy, he has galloped over all our heads'. He also solemnly stated, however, that he personally believed that all of Brothers's prophecies had either been fulfilled or were still capable of being proven correct.[22]

What unites Southcott, Brothers, Matthews and earlier mad writers like Alexander Cruden, is their single-minded conviction of mission. This represents a significant distinction from the double perspectives detectable in the writing of Trosse or Hannah Allen: they may believe firmly in the purpose of their suffering, but they also recognise that they were mad at the time they experienced it. For the religious or the political fanatic, suffering and persecution are not only a means to a higher end but also proof positive that their calling is not a delusion. Cruden began his pamphleteering career by protesting against wrongful confinement in a madhouse, but continued it through some fifteen years during which he developed his mission as 'Alexander the Corrector', 'Alexander the Conqueror' and a 'Joseph' about to be brought to greatness. His several spells of confinement added to his sense of injury, but also proved how desperately the values and morals of the time were in need of his 'correction'. For Cruden, the models that confirm his mission are biblical, but above all the accident of his native Scottish Christian name is the single feature that validates his vision of impending conquest. Where Hannah Allen 'much delighted' in her phrase *'the Monster of the Creation'*, Cruden revels in being and becoming an 'Alexander'.[23]

Religious inspiration is undoubtedly the most potent source of inner conviction, and Cruden, Brothers and Southcott would have been reduced to silence without the expressive opportunities afforded by patterns of biblical rhetoric. Political fervour, however, also presents a favourable climate for the nurturing of delusions, particularly when the element of secrecy is present. While religious inspiration obliges its devotees, like Christopher Smart, to pray in the streets, those of a political colouring are attracted more by plots, conspiracies and the certainty of being one of a chosen few with dangerous knowledge. The inner conviction, rather than broadcasting itself, seeks validation through the prospect of clandestine sharing in the face of a generally unperceived menace. In 1792, very near the beginning of his mission, Richard Brothers warned the English government about involvement in the wars with France, claiming that here were the beginnings of the fulfilment of the prophecies written of in the book of Daniel.[24] Very soon afterwards, James Tilley Matthews started his long career into insanity with a stay in revolutionary France.

Matthews detected conspiracies at every turn. His efforts to achieve a peace between England and France were frustrated, and he was imprisoned in Paris by the Jacobins in 1793. Disappointed, too, in his attempts to find support or vindication from leading members of the British government he developed, instead, the founding theory for his entire system. The disadvantage of his being the only person to acknowledge its validity is compensated for by the ambitiously far-reaching implications of the plot. Haslam quotes from documents 'written down' by Matthews himself, in which these early events are described.

While I was detained in Paris by the then existing French Government, during the years 1793–4–5, and the beginning of 1796, I had even in the early part thereof, sufficient information, to be certain that a regular plan existed, and was furthering by persons in France, connected with persons in England, as well for surrendering to the French every secret of the British Government, as for the repub-licanizing Great Britain and Ireland, and particularly for disorganizing the British navy; to create such a confusion therein, as to admit the French armaments to move without danger.[25]

Matthews, as the only person aware of the conspiracy and the only hope of saving his country, is therefore an immediate danger to the conspirators and a main target of their efforts to secure his silence.

The pressures upon written English are all too apparent, even in Matthews's recollection of the events:

> They have ever avowed also; that my having immediately on my return set about exposing the quoted infamies, occasioned a magnetic spy to be appointed from each gang of event-workers in London, specially to watch and circumvent me: for that the chiefs of such gangs were the real persons who were cloked under certain names and titles used in the information given me, and which I have for years found such vile spy-traitor-assassins called by among their fraternity.[26]

The explosion of anger in the phrase 'vile spy-traitor-assassins' represents a surfacing of the emotional undercurrent that has been frustrating the direction of this sentence, just as the 'spy-traitor-assassins' have frustrated the exposing of the 'infamies'. Matthews's obsession is itself the magnet to which every grammatical item clings as he struggles to express sensibly the reality of his conviction. Nothing quite fits together because the true subjects of the prose structures are hidden, 'cloked under certain names and titles': 'They' have 'avowed', but it is not 'their' infamies but 'the infamies' that are to be exposed; and it is not 'they' who have 'appointed' the 'magnetic spy', but rather that a nameless subject has 'occasioned' one 'to be' appointed. Events are put in train, of that Matthews is quite certain, but the responsibility for the working of those events belongs just out of sight: there is no clear line of command, no direct logic to the structuring of the prose. Even the 'chiefs of such gangs' are both 'real persons' and 'cloked under certain names and titles'. Wherever one looks there are conspiracies, fraternities, but nothing to be seen except the force of one's own anger, frustrated by the denial of its proper outlet.

> That the persons mentioned by me in my letters, narratives, &c, to each of the 1796 administration, and to the then Speaker of the House of Commons as spies, whom I could not discover, but found, as it were, before me, behind me, and on every side of me, every where, and in every thing (as was my expression) were magnetic spy-workers coming from Paris, at the time I was trudging it from thence, and having

the charge of circumventing me; and such were so appointed by each of the London gangs, event-working assassins: who having found my senses proof against their fluid and hand-working, as it is termed, were employed to actuate the proper persons to pretend I was insane, for the purpose of plunging me into a madhouse, to invalidate all I said.[27]

Matthews's dilemma is apparent: only he has the clear-sightedness to perceive the dangers that threaten, but what he has to say will be taken as insanity. The constraints upon mad language are doubly imposed upon him, for not only is he not listened to, but there are forces positively working to render him impotent. The linguistic consequence of these constraints is, in Matthews's case, a move towards ever more outrageous utterances couched in the most grandiloquent terms and forms. His assuming of titles:

James, Absolute, Sole, & Supreme Sacred Omni Imperious Arch Grand Arch Sovereign Omni Imperious Arch Grand Arch Proprietor Omni Imperious Arch-Grand-Arch-Emperor-Supreme etc. March the Twentieth One Thousand Eight hundred & four.[28]

His issuing of death warrants for all the ruling and governing heads of the world, as usurping his rightful authority, and his insistence that the criminals are proven dead for all to see:

But for the Executing the said Usurper fairly as by Me Commanded or Permitted of all which fair Modes I shall Prefer the Hanging them by the Neck till Dead and afterwards Publickly burning them or Severing their heads from their dead Bodies to assure that they are Dead to be proved.[29]

His offering of appropriate rewards for the tasks carried out:

The Executors shall Receive the Rewards hereafter against each Class specified, in those for each to be Executed; within Thirty days after My Absolute Possession of the said part of my OmniEmpire Territories &c Viz:

Denmark Norway &c ——	4	Three Hundred Thousand Pounds Sterling
Sweden &c————	4	Six Hundred Thousand Pounds Sterling
All the Russias————	4	One Million Pounds Sterling
China ————	4	One Million Pounds Sterling

All between China and Per-
sia ———————————————— One Years amount of their
Civil List for each –
Persia———————————— 4   One Million Pounds Sterling
Turkey———————————— 4   One Million Pounds Sterling
Africas one Years Amount of their Civil List for each; but if
the Civil List of Morocco does not amount to

> Three Hundred thousand pounds Sterling: Algiers to Two
> Hundred Thousand Pounds Sterling; and Tunis & Tripoli
> to One hundred thousand pounds Sterling each; Such shall
> be the Sums —[30]

His accusations of treachery against people in high places were equally extravagant, such as his letter to Lord Liverpool, in which his Lordship was pronounced 'to be in every sense of the word a most diabolical traitor'.[31]

The tendency in expressions of anger, resentment and frustration in mad writing is inevitably towards the large scale, with models of either divine or regal authority adopted as the basis for extensive prophecies, accusations and instructions. This is one extreme of a reaction against a general refusal of linguistic space by professional and public attitudes towards the mad throughout the eighteenth century. When no one is listening, you shout louder. Equally inevitably, the outrageous madman, fixed at one pole of the world of the insane, was recognised as a familiar face of insanity. Raving, as we have seen, was one of the most readily diagnosed signs of a person's being mad. For the melancholiac, or the voice of despair, an opposite orientation made for different linguistic dilemmas. The melancholy man or woman was as familiar a type, but his or her silence was usually considered to be symptomatic of a condition. It was not that what the melancholiac had to say could not be comprehended, but that such a patient had nothing to say at all. Expressions of extreme despair are therefore often matters of furtive confidence, of the confession of a madness that can hardly sigh out its own name.

Haslam describes the progress of 'Those under the influence of depressing passions'. They

> exhibit a train of symptoms. The countenance, wears an anxious and gloomy aspect. They retire from the company of those with whom they had formerly associated, seclude themselves in obscure places, or lie in bed the greatest part of their time. They next become fearful, and, when irregular

combinations of ideas have taken place, conceive a thousand fancies: often recur to some former immoral act which they have committed, or imagine themselves guilty of crimes which they never perpetrated; believe that God has abandoned them, and with trembling, await his punishment. Frequently they become desperate, and endeavour by their own hands to terminate an existence, which appears to be an afflicting and hateful incumbrance.[32]

James Boswell, as a young man newly arrived in Holland for the study of Scots law, wrote a confession of despair to his close friend William Johnson Temple from Rotterdam on 16 August 1763.

My Dearest Temple, – Expect not in this letter to hear of anything but the misery of your poor friend. I have been melancholy to the most shocking and most tormenting degree. You know the weakness and gloominess of my mind, and you dreaded that this would be the case. I have been at Leyden; from thence I went to Utrecht, which I found to be a most dismal place. I was there entirely by myself and had nobody to speak to. I lived in an inn. I sunk altogether. My mind was filled with the blackest ideas, and all my powers of reason forsook me. Would you believe it? I ran frantic up and down the streets, crying out, bursting into tears, and groaning from my innermost heart. O good GOD! what have I endured! O my friend, how much was I to be pitied! What could I do? I had no inclination for anything. All things appeared good for nothing, all dreary. I thought I should never recover, and that now the time was come when I should really go mad.[33]

There is none of the linguistic playfulness of Thomas Gray's letter to his friend West. Boswell's writing is marked, on the contrary, by its artlessness. Half of the sixteen sentences in this paragraph begin simply 'I'. Many of them consist of just one main clause, or of a series of main clauses, as Boswell gives the most direct expression to what he has felt and done. Syntactical subordination is almost completely absent, and with it the opportunity for systematic analysis of thought or behaviour. This kind of language is produced not in order to write about a mental state, but to be it, to stand for it. The effect of 'I lived in an inn. I sunk altogether' and 'I ran frantic up and down the streets, crying out . . .' is to communicate the immediacy of actual experience, rather than the experience of language itself. Significantly, Boswell has been suffering in a silence imposed not only by social factors but by his residing in a foreign country. His inarticulate 'crying out' and 'groaning' in the streets of Utrecht is the public voice of his private conviction that 'All things' are 'good for nothing' and that this is Boswell's 'really' going mad. At the same time, 'this letter' is an opportunity to enable a rational mind to 'hear' of this impending insanity, for some degree of recognisable linguistic order to be imposed on the incoherence of fact.

Boswell arrived in Utrecht on the evening of Saturday 13 August, and so was writing to Temple within two or three days of the emotions he had suffered. The immediacy of this confession is particularly striking when compared to the account given in a much longer and more varied letter to another close friend, John Johnston, over a month later on 23 September.

> I arrived at Utrecht on a Saturday evening. I went to the Nouveau Château d'Anvers. I was shown up to a high bedroom with old furniture, where I had to sit and be fed by myself. At every hour the bells of the great tower played a dreary psalm tune. A deep melancholy seized upon me. I groaned with the idea of living all winter in so shocking a place. I thought myself old and wretched and forlorn. I was worse and worse next day. All the horrid ideas that you can imagine, recurred upon me. I was quite unemployed and had not a soul to speak to but the clerk of the English meeting, who could do me no good. I sunk quite into despair. I thought that at length the time was come that I should grow mad. I actually believed myself so. I went out to the streets, and even in public could not refrain from groaning and weeping bitterly. I said always, 'Poor Boswell! is it come to this? Miserable wretch that I am! what shall I do?' – O my friend, pause here a little and figure to yourself what I endured. I took general speculative views of things; all seemed full of darkness and woe. Tortured in this manner, I determined to leave Utrecht, and next day returned to Rotterdam in a condition that I shudder to recollect.[34]

The basic story is the same, and much of the sentence structure is similar – in fact the proportion of 'I' sentences is far greater than in the letter to Temple. But there is a pronounced difference in the kind of information being given and in the picture that is being constructed from it. There is far more detail: the bedroom, the furniture, the eating alone, the relentless bells and their 'dreary' tune. Boswell is no longer the desperate, silent spirit whose fear of madness must find a linguistic outlet. He now has time to present a context, building up item after item before the dreadful climax, 'A deep melancholy seized upon me.' There had been, after all, someone to speak to, but his conversation apparently had no effect. (Later in his stay Boswell employed him as a teacher of French.) He still feels the imminence of madness, but the behaviour that in writing to Temple was most persuasively proof of it has now been moderated. Instead of running 'frantic up and down the streets' and 'crying out', Boswell's mature recollection is far more restrained: 'I went out to the streets, and even in public could not refrain from groaning . . .'. His words to himself, 'Poor Boswell!', have a coherence, even a posturing, quite different in effect from his silence in the Temple version. His asking Johnston to 'pause' shows the design behind this presentation of his suffering, and again the effect differs from the artless plea to Temple, 'O my friend, how much was I to be pitied!'

Recollection of despair produces an inevitable modifying of suffering as the leisure to work with the resources of language opens up opportunities that are absent when the impetus to communicate is all powerful. Boswell's entire stay in Holland was a period of desperate depression for him, broken by bouts of wild behaviour or by stoic resolutions to bear it heroically. The absence through loss of his Dutch journals is an eloquent comment on the pressures he experienced during this time, and the surviving letters, memoranda, notes, snatches of 'Ten lines a day' verses and the self-imposed 'French themes' give an appropriately broken sense of his unbalanced identity. The memoranda in particular show the tenuousness of his hold on a secure sense of sanity.

> Tuesday 20 March. Yesterday you lay abed purely to have a little present ease. You called on Brown; told him you was not well. Said he, 'You are melancholy.' . . . You was direfully melancholy and had the last and most dreadful thoughts. You came home and prayed. . . .

> Thursday 22 March. Yesterday you was better. Rose and you walked after dinner. He said he was very lazy. You owned

nothing. He drank coffee with you and talked of suicide. . . .
You grew well at night. . . .

Saturday 24 March. Yesterday you was very bad after dinner,
and shuddered with dire ideas. You was incertain and confused
and lazy, talked of going to bed, and could scarcely read
Greek. . . .

Sunday 25 March. Yesterday you awaked in great disorder,
thinking that you was dying, and exclaiming, 'There's no
more of it! 'Tis all over.' Horrid idea! . . .[35]

What Haslam observes of his patients in Bethlem, and writes
out at length as a coherent set of symptoms marking a steady
decline towards self-destruction, Boswell jots down in a series of
reminders, euphemisms ('the last and most dreadful thoughts') and
silences (the ellipsis after 'suicide', for example, is Boswell's own)
that forms the broken record of his living through his own case
history.

Boswell's despair is expressed in terms of uncertainty, change-
ability, his language a struggle between the tones and syntax of
opposing inner voices. One speaks of what is 'good for nothing'.
The other asserts identity, 'Poor Boswell', demands an audience,
requires his friend to 'figure' his suffering, and constructs the
language of posture for its effective communication. For William
Cowper, on the other hand, his identity was completely inscribed
within the parameters of his despair.

Writing and silence are in a constantly renewed relation in
Cowper's letters, and together represent opposite edges of the
despair that was the uncontestable feature of his existence. To
Lady Hesketh, 30 August 1787: 'My dearest Cousin – Though it
costs me something to write, it would cost me more to be silent.'
To William Hayley, 2 October 1792:

My dear Hayley,
A bad night succeeded by an East wind and a sky all in sables
have such an effect on my spirits, that if I did not consult
my own comfort more than yours I should not write to-day,
for I shall not entertain you much. Yet your letter, though
containing no very pleasant tidings, has afforded me some
relief. . . . I will endeavour not to repay you in notes of
sorrow and despondence, though all my sprightly chords
seem broken.[36]

In particular, there is the significant silence that lasted from 14 November 1772 until 18 May 1776, a period that included Cowper's mental breakdown of over a year following the dream in February 1773 that convinced him of his damnation.

The words of the dream, 'Actum est de te, periisti', 'It is all over with thee, thou hast perished',[37] were the linguistic paradigm of which Cowper's subsequent silence, and the despair that his later writing expresses, were endlessly repeated versions. After his earlier experience of madness, and the hard struggle with language that characterised his restoration and the recognition of his own sanity, the visitation allowed of no misinterpretation and no escape. Under the burden of such certainty, despair became the only sane response. In despair, silence and writing are two sides of an acceptance that nothing can possibly make any difference. No communication can be truly effective, for no one can possibly enter into the reality of such a despair from such a cause. There is no help, such as Boswell sought, and no alleviation in expression. There is only the knowledge that can never be better expressed than in the words that 'were not of my own production'.[38] Cowper puts it with characteristic baldness in a letter to John Newton, written on 10 May 1780.

All that is Ænigmatical in my case would Vanish, if you and Mrs U. were able to avail Yourselves of the Solution I have so often given You. That a Calvinist in principle, should know himself to have been Elected, and yet believe that he is lost, is indeed a Riddle, and so obscure that it Sounds like a Solecism in terms, and may well bring the assertor of it under the Suspicion of Insanity. But it is not so, and it will not be found so.

I am trusted with the terrible Secret Myself but not with the power to Communicate it to any purpose. In order to gain credit to such a Relation, it would be necessary that I should be able to produce proof that I received it from above, but that power will never be given Me. In what Manner or by whom the denoüment will be made hereafter, I know not. But that it will be made is certain. In the mean time I carry a load no Shoulders Could Sustain, unless underpropped as mine are, by a heart Singularly & preternaturally hardened.[39]

For Cowper, language has been stripped of any power to express or communicate the dimensions of his despair. The 'terrible Secret' is in his possession, and the very possession of it ensures that it will remain a secret. Language, thus prevented from fulfilling the single most important function of Cowper's mental life, is liberated to address anything and everything else with coherence and without passion. To Mrs Maria Cowper he writes on the occasion of her brother's death:

> My dear Cousin,
> I do not write to Comfort you; that Office is not likely to be well performed by One who has no Comfort for Himself. Nor to comply with an impertinent Ceremony, which in general, might well be spared upon such occasions. But because I would not seem indifferent to the Concerns of those I have so much reason to Esteem and Love. If I did not Sorrow for your Brother's Death, I should expect that nobody would for mine.[40]

To John Newton, in contrast, he writes of his own obsession with the month of January, a dread particularly associated with the dream of 1773:

> When January returns you have your feelings concerning me, and such as prove the faithfulness of your friendship. I have mine also concerning myself but they are of a different cast from yours. Yours have a mixture of sympathy and tender solicitude which makes them perhaps not altogether unpleasant. Mine on the contrary are of an unmix'd nature and consist simply and merely of the most alarming apprehensions. Twice has that month returned upon me accompanied by such horrors as I have no reason to suppose ever made part of the experience of any other man. I accordingly look forward to it and meet it with a dread not to be imagined. I number the nights as they pass, and in the morning bless myself that another night is gone and no harm has happened. This may argue perhaps some imbecillity of mind and no small degree of it, but it is natural I believe, and so natural as to be necessary and unavoidable. I know that God is not governed by secondary causes in any of his operations, and that, on the contrary, they are all so many agents in his hand which strike only when he bids them. I know consequently

that one month is as dangerous to me as another, and that in the middle of summer, at noon-day, and in the clear sunshine, I am in reality, unless guarded by him, as much exposed as when fast asleep at midnight and in mid-winter. But we are not always the wiser for our knowledge, and I can no more avail myself of mine than if it were in the head of another man and not in my own.[41]

Like John Hunter's patient of a few years earlier, described in Chapter 3, who when in want of food himself 'would tell his nurse or the bystanders that they were hungry or thirsty', Cowper's suggestion of a displacement of his own 'knowledge' is indicative of an emotional removal from personal identity. Here, in the rational detailing of an obsession, there is the kind of analysis of which Boswell was incapable when confessing his despair. Cowper's hold on language is more than adequate for writing about his state of mind, even though his experiences of 'that month' are spoken of as quite unique to himself, and his 'dread' is 'not to be imagined'. Boswell was writing to Temple as an emotional outlet, and his letter therefore is a confession of the heart of his experience, expressed in the language of the moment. Cowper's emotions are so well in hand that his prose is at times hardly in touch with them at all. The balance and propriety of grammar and expression (the understatement of 'alarming apprehensions', the unostentatious verbal and syntactic patterns of the sentence 'I know consequently . . . at midnight and in mid-winter') suggest not an engulfment by feelings of despair but rather a linguistic endeavour that is at a remove from the reality of the obsession and of the terrible knowledge that lies behind it. When language cannot touch the truth, when there is simply no possible means of expression for the horror within, then detail and analysis become marginal activities and Cowper's written self is allowed to exist at the periphery of his mental and spiritual life. What we read when we read Cowper's letter is the capacity of the English language to be formed into coherent sentences. The inner voice, meanwhile, is saying something quite different, and something that can never be put into words.

One final piece of prose that has a significant bearing on the language that has expressed varying kinds and degrees of madness is in fact a sane work, or at least the production of a mind that was medically regarded as cured. Urbane Metcalf was a patient in Bethlem on a number of occasions during the first two decades of the nineteenth century, and was released for what seems to have been the last time in November 1818. His pamphlet *The Interior of Bethlehem Hospital* was published in the same year, and is a detailing of the abuses and maltreatments he witnessed as an inmate. Metcalf, according to the case notes of his last stay between 1817 and 1818, was a 'Hawker and Pedlar' who thought himself 'heir to the Throne of Denmark' by virtue of his being the 'Son of Matilda', sister of the then king. He was placed in the incurable gallery on admission in October 1817. As a patient, it seems that he was considered 'extreamly orderly', took 'medicine' regularly, and had good appetite, digestion and sleep. He gradually came to abandon his delusion, but was observed to be still subject to depression, and on 1 August 1818 it was remarked that 'there is still something peculiar in his manner'. The note for the day concluded: 'as there is abundance of evidence of his having been frequently deranged I cannot help thinking that there is some latent disorder existing'. He became increasingly 'irritable', made frequent complaints about the treatment of other patients, and was finally discharged after 'a months leave of absence'.[42]

Metcalf's pamphlet is of immense interest as an early record of what life in Bethlem was like from the inmate's point of view, but what is particularly intriguing is precisely the 'point of view', the perspective taken on the experience of having been confined in the 'interior' of England's most famous hospital for the insane. Typically, Metcalf describes not his own experience, but the experiences of others of which he has been an observer.

> I well remember on Saturday, the day after Good Friday, a patient of the name of Lloyd, Dr Munro's patient, was in the green yard, no other patient being there, during two or three hours excessive rain, Dr Munro going through the upper gallery with a friend with him, came to the window of the keeper's room, I was standing by, he observed to his friend that that was the airing ground, I opened the window hoping that he would see Lloyd in the green yard, but he took no notice of him, though he, Lloyd, appeared to me to stand in full view.
>
> . . . another patient, Charles Saunders, had in the old house, though as inoffensive as a child, had been kept chained for

years, that the keeper might have his clothes to sell. On the sixteenth of October, when I went in, his age was nearly 70 years, he appeared dropping into the grave through the decays of nature, and gradually got worse; I three distinct times remember him asking Dr Munro his physician, to put him on the sick mess, as his appetite was so bad he could not eat the regular provisions, but his request was disregarded, he was not put on the sick mess till two days before he died: he died on the last day of the year.[43]

Metcalf, even more than Cowper, writes as a man at the periphery of his own identity, or rather he has been obliged, by the circumstances of his confinement, to experience his identity through observation and not through participation in action and dialogue with others. His act of having 'opened the window' goes unnoticed, as if the power involved in the performance ends with the act itself, having no other effect than the moving of an object. Similarly, Lloyd stands unnoticed in the rain, and Saunders's request to be 'put on the sick mess' is three times 'disregarded'. There is, consequently, a sense of detachment in all that Metcalf describes: the brutality of the keepers is always directed at others, reported language is the speech of others, requests and punishments are instigated and suffered by others. Other patients find release in violence: 'in a short time Kendal and Freeman got again to fighting, Freeman with a broom cut Kendal's head'.[44] In *The Interior of Bethlehem Hospital* it is just reported. Others suffering like Metcalf from delusions of grandeur insist vigorously on their rightful titles: James Tilley Matthews with his string of offices, or John Haslam's patient who constantly wrote 'directions for his release from confinement' and 'never omitted his high titles of God's King, Holy Ghost, Admiral and Physician'.[45] Metcalf, however, simply contents himself with the most restrained of judgements: 'O what cruelty!', 'O what a scoundrel!', 'These honest men still hold their situations!'[46]

Metcalf's language is not, like Cowper's, at a remove from the true focus of his identity, but expresses an identity that has no basis in agency. The strings of clauses no doubt reflect a rudimentary grasp of English prose, but they also convey a mentality that can exert little authority over the structures of the language of its own expression. Metcalf's curious absence from the experience of life in Bethlem is consolidated by the writing that describes the 'interior' not of a personality but of an institutional system. This is language as a state of shock, language from which the power to shape and regulate has been usurped. The capacity of the former inmate to control his own experience from within has been so severely curtailed that in looking at *The Interior of Bethlehem Hospital* we find only the lobotomised English of a man who no longer believes himself to be heir to the throne of Denmark.

7

RHYME AND REASON

One of the main issues so far discussed has been the linguistic relationship between suppression and endorsement within writing about madness. Medical and psychiatric authorities with few exceptions were found ultimately to allow little real space for the expression of madness, and writers working within sane forms of English unavoidably sanitised the insanity they tried to address. The features of mad writing, looked at over the last two chapters, have shown an uneasy balance in terms of this relationship, from the self-contained visions of Cruden, Matthews and Southcott, each of them sustained by a potent and self-validating rhetoric, through the dual perspectives of Trosse and Allen and the shifting uncertainty of Boswell, to the writing at a distance of Cowper and Metcalf. The poetry of the mad, as suggested earlier, brings into particularly sharp focus the issues that are involved when mad individuals attempt to negotiate between their language and their madness. Some of the more distinctive features of mad prose, such as repetition, images, rhythmic patterns and obsession with sound, are inevitably going to be more strikingly pronounced in poetry. A more fundamental question, however, is the extent to which modes of mental existence are consolidated by their capacity for coherent and mellifluous expression. If a single word or phrase, as in the case of Allen, or a sentence from a dream, as with Cowper, could validate a month, a year, a lifetime of madness, and the linguistic strategies and evasions that involved, how much more completely might a poem be capable of performing an act of validation that both encapsulates and regenerates the reality of a mad mind.

As with mad prose, there is a problem of identification. Few of the poets who are known to have suffered periods of madness – Swift, for example, William Collins, or, at the end of the century, Matilda Betham – wrote poetry while mad, and the verses reportedly written or spoken by the patients of professionals such as William Perfect and John Haslam have, not surprisingly, failed to survive. Moreover, if the medical authorities in general tended to devalue attempts made by their patients to express the individuality of their mental states, there is a quite different devaluation of the distinctive creative potential of mad poetry by the availability of popular substitutes. Mad verses, or mock-mad, as Roy Porter points out, exercised a fascination for readers from the sixteenth century onwards that led to publication of various collections of nonsense and semi-nonsense puporting to derive from 'Bedlam'.[1] On another front, Dryden, Swift, Pope and the satirists stigmatised as mad the productions of those largely sane poets and dramatists they attacked. Even those poets who specialised in the expression of melancholy – Young, Akenside, the Wartons, Blair – did so for an audience whose expectations included stock attitudes and icons of a depressive temperament. Indulgence in graveyards, ruins, the hootings of owls and the heaviness of time was the melancholy of the market-place, and, while depressive temperaments could and did choose at times to think of themselves in terms of these available features, had little to do with the reality of chronic depression.

In William Cowper's case that reality, following his dream of 24 January 1773, imposed a silence that lasted for over a year, and was scarcely broken until 1779. The first poetry, dated 8 February 1774, is in Latin – the language most favoured by Samuel Johnson in his prayers composed against depression, and the language of the doom pronounced on Cowper himself – and comprises two four-line verses written into a copy of a book by John Gill, *An Exposition of the Book of Solomon's Song, Commonly Called Canticles*. By a poignant irony, the copy had been presented by Cowper to John Newton, and inscribed 'to his dear Friend and Brother in Christ'. The first verse is 'Tales Et Nostri Viguissent, Jesus, Amores' ('Such also, O Jesus, would our loves have flourished'), and the second 'Caesa Est Nostra Columba, Et Nostro Crimine, Cujus' ('My dove is slain, and by my own crime'). Both are to do with the book itself, but equally both have marked personal aptness. In particular, the final word of the second, 'monstrum' (from the phrase 'so accursed a wretch'), carries the meaning of 'something against the course of nature'.[2] If this is a reminder of Hannah Allen's 'monster of creation', it is also quite literally what Cowper now believed of himself, a man who was one of God's elect who was instead inexplicably and inexorably to be damned.

To write in Latin is to lend to one's words a permanence and validity that is not automatically imparted by English. The starkness of the sentiments finds an apt expression in the language of epitaphs and inscriptions. Cowper gradually turned again to poetry after the crisis of 1773 as he turned to gardening, carpentry, drawing and keeping pets: anything that could possibly act as a distraction from his terrible despair. True despair not only finds no expression through groves and graveyards. Its tendency is to remain wholly unexpressed. Its medium is silence, not creativity. The forms of language bespeak a self-containment that is wholly alien to the depressive personality, and poetry asserts an integrity absent from the introverted existence of the melancholiac. In writing poetry, Cowper was returning to a mode of expression that obliged him to look out into the world that was not part of the circle of his damnation and to address a variety of subjects that were not implicated in the awful knowledge.

Cowper's poetic distractions take many forms: natural objects, like 'Yardley Oak', 'The Poplar-Field', 'The Shrubbery'; human qualitites, like 'Hope' and 'Retirement'; events of national interest, such as 'On the Burning of Lord Mansfield's Library', or of local, like 'To Mr Newton On His Return From Ramsgate'; and other people, such as John Gilpin or Alexander Selkirk. Yet if this is poetry as displacement therapy, there is also and inevitably a firm pattern of self-reference within the topics treated. Alexander Selkirk, for example, who in his fictional reincarnation as Robinson Crusoe served too as a model for Alexander Cruden,[3] shares several crucial features of Cowper's own mental condition, not least the solitariness that his spiritual isolation imposes upon him:

> I am monarch of all I survey,
>   My right there is none to dispute,
> From the center all round to the sea,
>   I am lord of the fowl and the brute.
> Oh solitude! where are the charms
>   That sages have seen in they face?
> Better dwell in the midst of alarms,
>   Than reign in this horrible place.

I am out of humanity's reach,
I must finish my journey alone,
Never hear the sweet music of speech,
I start at the sound of my own.
The beasts that roam over the plain,
My form with indifference see,
They are so unacquainted with man,
Their tameness is shocking to me.

Society, friendship, and love,
Divinely bestow'd upon man,
Oh had I the wings of a dove,
How soon wou'd I taste you again![4]

Cowper, who could never directly express the reality of his imagined fate, is able to give shape to some of his feelings about his own experience through the vehicle of Selkirk. If the substance of these verses belongs to Selkirk's story, the metaphorical shadows are Cowper's. Selkirk is literally 'out of humanity's reach', but Cowper is beyond the sympathetic touch of even his closest friends. For Selkirk, marooned on an island, a 'journey' is not especially appropriate, while Cowper's freedom of physical movement mocks his spiritual imprisonment. Selkirk's language startles in an alien silence, but Cowper's capacity for 'sweet music' is such a sham that he is shocked to find that he still possesses the capacity for language. In particular, the 'dove' for which Selkirk yearns has already been 'slain' by Cowper, 'and by my own crime'.

The fundamental dilemma for depressive writing is the impossibility of giving form to the formless. Cowper's Latin verses stand in for silence, inarticulacy, personal collapse. Selkirk's fate is the template on which Cowper can lay his own. Other depressive poets found support in poetic form itself, for example in the strength of the sonnet. John Codrington Bampfylde, who wrote during the latter half of the eighteenth century and spent time towards the end of his life in a private madhouse, published a collection of *Sixteen Sonnets* in 1778, many of them on melancholy subjects. Charlotte Smith, who suffered from low spirits for most of her life, published her *Elegiac Sonnets* in 1784, with expanded editions in 1789 and 1792, and a second volume in 1797. One poem from 1797 offers a useful perspective on depressive writing.

*Sonnet. On being Cautioned against Walking on an Headland Over-
looking the Sea, because it was Frequented by a Lunatic*

Is there a solitary wretch who hies
　　To the tall cliff with starting pace or slow,
And, measuring, views with wild and hollow eyes
　　Its distance from the waves that chide below;
Who, as the sea-born gale with frequent sighs
　　Chills his cold bed upon the mountain turf,
With hoarse, half-uttered lamentation, lies
　　Murmuring responses to the dashing surf?
In moody sadness, on the giddy brink,
　　I see him more with envy than with fear;
He has no *nice felicities* that shrink
　　From giant horrors; wildly wandering here,
He seems (uncursed with reason) not to know
The depth or the duration of his woe.[5]

Madness, in the person of the 'lunatic', is both captured within this
poem and at the same time evades it. It is captured because a figure
is described through vivid detail – the walk, the eyes, his habits, his
inarticulate 'half-uttered lamentation', his surroundings. Madness,
however, as so often with writing that is fundamentally sane, also
evades the poem because, after all, the lunatic is only imagined
by the poet, and none of the details necessarily correspond to
the real man or woman who was believed to be frequenting the
headland. In fact, the interrogative form of the octet ('Is there
. . .?') lays open the question of whether this person exists at
all. The subject of the poem is a possible absence rendered as
a presence by the force of imaginative involvement, but it is an
absence that is necessarily negated, for the lunatic enables the
poet to focus on the shortcomings of her own mental existence.
Madness is envied for its security, its self-containment, its speaking
the language of 'the dashing surf' rather than the '*nice felicities*' of
the poet whose own 'response' to 'the dashing surf' has been the
felicitous rhyme word 'turf'. Above all the lunatic is envied for
his lack of self-consciousness, his not knowing. The parenthetical
'(uncursed with reason)' exactly captures the poet's dilemma: this
characteristic feature of the lunatic is held apart from the flow of
the poem, placed in a frame of its own, yet the terms from which
that frame is constructed derive wholly from the world of the poet.

Lunacy is defined not in its own terms but in terms of sanity, terms from which the lunatic himself is necessarily absent. It could not be otherwise, for the man is imagined as unconscious of his 'woe': he is unable to frame terms of his own. Consciousness belongs to the poet, she dictates from her own case the terms that will define the lunatic, and that is her curse. The lunatic's absence has brought into focus her overwhelmingly burdensome presence, from which she would gladly withdraw, but language holds her back, and poetic form requires that even a parenthetical aside must be incorporated into the wholeness of a linguistic construct.

The linguistic strength of the sonnet and the strength beyond language of the lunatic have combined to give form to the disabling self-consciousness of the poet. Yet the expression of the depressive self is fraught with contradictions. To take one final illustration, this time from a later period, when John Clare wrote in the Northampton County Asylum in the 1840s one of his best-known poems 'I Am' – 'I am – yet what I am, none cares or knows' – he could assert his own identity only in terms of its opposite. The poem itself enforces the acknowledgement that the existence of the poet only finds definition through the expression of non-existence – 'My friends forsake me like a memory lost', 'Into the nothingness of scorn and noise'. By the last verse,

> I long for scenes, where man hath never trod
>   A place where woman never smiled or wept
> There to abide with my Creator, God;
>   And sleep as I in childhood, sweetly slept,
> Untroubling, and untroubled where I lie,
> The grass below – above the vaulted sky.[6]

he is yearning for the kind of annihilation from the world that Charlotte Smith imagined for her lunatic. Accordingly, in the final line Clare's presence within his own poem has been reduced to a typographical gap ('–') for which space has been found between two overwhelmingly enduring features of nature, the self-renewing grass, the endless sky. The poem that purported to inscribe the self of the poet has concluded by expressing only his absence.

Smith's assumption that the truly mad are unconsciously secure in their 'woe' may be written more in fulfilment of her own needs than theirs, yet it seems to be true that the poetry of the manically insane displays a lack of self-consciousness quite distinct from the writing of depressives. In poems such as Smith's, the questioning and judging of the poet herself is always taking place alongside and through the ostensible subject of the writing. In the poetry of James Carkesse, on the other hand, there is an absolute conviction of the poet's own sense of self and, in spite of the manifold contradictions and inconsistencies within his poems, of his own sanity. Thus secure in his own inconsistency, the poet is released from the burden of self-consciousness to play with words, forms, ideas – especially ideas about madness – in an energetic and innocent mastery of his unique poetic medium.

Carkesse, having been to Westminster School and Christ Church, Oxford, worked under Samuel Pepys in the Navy Office during the 1660s but was discharged in 1667 for alleged financial corruption. He eventually came to the conclusion that he had a divinely ordained mission to reduce the meeting houses of Dissenters and bring their adherents to the true church. He began this work with such violence that he was committed to Dr Thomas Allen's private madhouse in Finsbury in the spring of 1678; from here he was transferred to Bethlem where he remained until being discharged as 'not now distracted' in November of the same year. His poems, audaciously titled *Lucida Intervalla: Containing divers Miscellaneous Poems, Written at Finsbury and Bethlem By The Doctors Patient Extraordinary*, were published in 1679.[7]

Carkesse's appetite for poetic expression was itself 'extraordinary'. Everything and anything is indiscriminately seized upon as sustenance for poetry. John Haslam, in describing the progress of sufferers from mania over a century later, picks up many of the features of Carkesse's writing:

> they are loquacious, and disposed to harangue, and decide promptly, and positively upon any subject that may be started. Soon after, they are divested of all restraint in the declaration of their opinions of those, with whom they are acquainted. Their friendships are expressed with fervency and extravagance; their enmities with intolerance and disgust. They now become impatient of contradiction, and scorn reproof. For supposed injuries, they are inclined to quarrel, and fight with those about them. They have all the appearance of persons inebriated, and people unacquainted with the symptoms of approaching mania, generally suppose them to be in a state of intoxication.[8]

So Carkesse declares his love for James, Duke of York:

> Why, I am down-right such a stark
>   Staring Lover of Royal *JAMES*, . . .
> The Passion's great I discover,
>   My affection it such is,
> That you will forgive the *Mad-Lover*,
>   If he Rival the very *Dutchess*[9]

and his equally extravagant hatred for his physician Dr Allen:

> While I 'gainst Keepers *Tyranny* Rebel,
> And with the *thought* of *Mad-quacks Poison* swell;
> He gives it out, that he my *head* can *Cure*,
> But my proud *heart* from *Physick* is secure:
> Pray then take heed, *Sir Tinker Chirurgion Quack*,
> Lest mending one, you may another *Crack*.[10]

The Duke of Grafton visits (or Carkesse says he does), and a poem promptly ensues, 'The Duke of Grafton, Looking into his Cloyster, And kindly asking him; How he did'. Another celebrates gifts of sixpence from each of two visitors, Lady Jane Levison Gower and Mrs Catherine Newport, while 'On his mistaking the Name Of Sir Gabriel Silvius' arises from Carkesse's having referred to Sir Gabriel as Sir George, 'And of an *Angel*, thus a *Saint* do forge'.[11] Nell Gwyn, Titus Oates and the Popish Plot are all addressed in separate poems.

Not surprisingly, Carkesse's main topics for poetry are his own confinement, his treatment and his opinion of it, and his interpretation of why he is there in the first place. These, the bulk of the poems, involve him in a variety of strategies, including '*Mascarade*' – he has only been feigning madness – the relation between poetry and madness, and justification of his mission. In 'On his being Seiz'd on for a Madman, only for having endeavoured to reduce Dissenters unto the Church', the problem of social recognition of madness is at once confronted.

> When *Zeal for God* inspires the *Breast*,
> Says the *Blind world*, the Man's *possest*;
> And flattering their own cold desire,
> Call *Lunacy*, the *Heavenly Fire*:
> But though their *Eyes* are by the *Flame*
> So Dasled, they mistake the *Name*;
> Know, that 'twas born with Christ at first
> In *Bethlehem*, and at *Bedlam* Nurst.[12]

Like Cruden, Southcott and Brothers, Carkesse has been mistaken as mad for performing God's work with an unusual degree of zeal and, like them, argues that he is truly sane, and that the name of 'lunatic' is simply a label attached by the world to something it cannot comprehend, in this case the *'Flame'* of the true *'Heavenly Fire'*. The mad, it seems, are the genuine Christians, and the *'Name'* that has been mistaken by 'the *Blind world*' is revealed for those who have the inspiration to see in the Bethlehem/Bedlam parallel. Christ, who was nursed in Bethlehem, lives on in those who are incarcerated in Bedlam.

Even Dr Allen, in spite of himself, has acknowledged Carkesse's prophetic status, although only in order to attempt to suppress it. In 'The Poetical History of Finnesbury Mad-house' he is made to describe the treatments he has administered to his patient, and their consequences:

> Moreover I him in the *Hole*,
>   As under a Bushel, confined;
> Lest God's Word, the Light of the Soul,
>   In my Mad–house should have Shin'd:
> Ne're the less into the *Dungeon*,
>   He let in the Rayes of the *Sun*,
> And i' th' Pit, where him I did plunge in,
>   Made Night and Day meet in one.[13]

The physical disadvantages of being placed in a dungeon appear to have presented no problems to Carkesse, any more than the necessity to find a rhyme for it has daunted his poetic progress. His energy and mission carry him over both medical and linguistic hurdles, to the confusion of the profession:

> Doctor, this Pusling *Riddle* pray explain;
> Others your *Physick* cures, but I complain
> It works with me the clean contrary way,
> And makes me *Poet*, who are *Mad* they say.
> The truth on't is, my *Brains* well fixt *condition*
> *Apollo* better knows, than his *Physitian*:
> 'Tis *Quacks* disease, not mine, my *Poetry*
> By the blind *Moon-Calf*, took for *Lunacy*.[14]

The relationship in the poet's mind, however, between poetry and madness is not entirely clear. If, as above, Carkesse's poetry is not

164

lunacy at all, but sanity so inspired that it is taken as mad by a mere doctor, he speaks elsewhere in more ambiguous terms. Poets and prophets, for example, in a poem called 'Poet no Lunatick', are admitted to be 'in a sense' mad, and poetry itself is recognised as a means of cure:

> Prophets and Poets Mad are (in a sense)
> And Sober grow, as they their gift dispense:
> One vents his Rage by words in open Air,
> By Ink on Paper He drops his with care.
> Physitian, *heal thy self*, we say; but know it,
> In earnest said to the Self-curing Poet.[15]

Carkesse himself seems to have turned poet upon his being confined at Finsbury, and left off after his discharge from Bethlem, yet in those poems that enter into dialogue with Allen the medical view that his poetry is now the major symptom of his madness is generally treated with scorn – 'Nay, to the *Governors* this *Fool* declares, Him fit for *Bedlam*, 'till he *Wit* forswears'.[16] Significantly, in two of the poems that petition for his release, Carkesse, as if anxious lest his poetic style create the wrong impression, explicitly curtails his addresses – 'Muse, sound a *Retreat*'; 'Muse, now *furl* your Sail'.[17] In the poem '*On the* Doctors *letting him Blood*' he distinguishes between two interpretations of his mad rhyming:

> *Doctor*, my *Rhythmes* on you which do reflect,
> Know, of *Poetick fury* are th'effect;
> To let me *Blood* then, you're but *Fool* in *grain*,
> Unless your *Lance* prick my *Poetick Vein*:
> No longer now, for shame, pretend the *Moon*,
> For *Phoebus* rules my *Madness* and *Lampoon*.[18]

Allen's art may cure conventional lunatics. Carkesse's madness is of a higher kind, but it is madness, albeit owing allegiance to Phoebus rather than the moon.

Like James Tilley Matthews, nothing appears that can daunt Carkesse's capacity to assimilate. Madness has claimed the absolute freedom to annex every event, remark, accident, not only from within its own walls but from the world of the sane and to make them inextricably part of its own 'witty' vision. This is particularly striking with regard to the medical world, for Dr Allen's is an important presence within these poems, but in a daring reversal of the normal relationship between doctor and patient his part is strictly controlled by Carkesse. The suppression and manipulation of patient symptoms and language evident in medical writing about madness is turned on its head as Carkesse allows his mad-doctor a series of feed-lines to his patient's crazily triumphant sense of humour. Thomas Allen is given entry into these poems that are a version of his own madhouse only on Carkesse's terms, and in order for the professional view of madness, its treatments and the theories behind them, to be seen not from the perspective of cure but of scorn.

> Beyond all *darkness*, *chains*, and *keepers* blows,
> *Sir Madquack*, is the *Physick* you impose;
> Threatning, because my *Satyres* frisk & dance,
> With *Purge* and *Vomit* them to tame and Lance.[19]

This dialogue is a rewriting of the terms of engagement in which, if the professional is armed with medicines, chains and keepers, madness has adopted as its own the more flexible and enduring weapons of language and poetic form.

The most engaging aspect of Carkesse's madhouse work is its exuberant playfulness. Madness has taken full advantage of its outlawed position to create havoc among the norms of social, political and linguistic forms. Carkesse, like Southcott's spirit, has the capacity to generate couplets upon the slightest occasion (though he is by no means confined to the couplet), and the energetic renewal of this most repetitious of poetic forms is itself a factor in the regeneration of the vision he is expressing. Poetry allows him the space both for pointed debate with the world of sanity and for the liberties he takes with the language of the sane. Name-calling, for example, is one extravagant kind of inversion of the forms and addresses of sane society: '*Doctor Mad-Quack*', '*Abigail*' (his own wife), 'second *Cerburus*', '*Bishop Proserpine*' (Sir William Turner, president of Bethlem Hospital), '*Sir Tinker Chirurgion Quack*', and '*Jackstraw*' (himself).[20] Puns and wordplay, too, are expressions of the madman's complete mastery over the potential normally kept submerged under less adventurous forms of language: Mrs Moniment 'From *Charing-Cross*', who visits him, is not 'her own *Moniment* of *Stone*' and has proved herself neither '*Marble* she, or *Cross*'.[21] Mr Stackhouse, 'Presenting me with a Periwig', is addressed as '*Thatch-house*' who visits '*Jackstraws* Tenement', and is thanked 'for furnishing *Hair-brain* with *Huffing-Wigg*'.[22] Forced rhymes and tortured grammatical sense equally form part of Carkesse's '*Huffing*' over the English

language: 'such is . . . *Dutchess*'; and '*Religion* . . . *Pidgeon* . . .
Enchiridion . . . *Widgeon*'; and

> Let all the Birds, pair by pair,
>   As well the *crane*, as the *Stork*,
> Sing and Chatter in the Air,
>   God Bless the DUKE OF *YORK*:

and

> *Doctor*, I am (no ways, as worth *Remarque* is,
> Your *Patient*, but) *Your humble Servant*, Carkesse.[23]

Carkesse's poetry is an exhilarating triumph of unfettered madness
finding a wholly irresponsible expression of its own integrity.
Its internal contradictions and the need to force language into
ungainly feats of gymnastry fail to make any impression on the mad
personality. Carkesse's energy and humour suffer no contradiction,
not from the world at large and certainly not from within his own
poetic walls. His is a madness that looks at the world about it and,
like James Tilley Matthews, sees nothing that will not fit his vision
of the way things are, not even the forms and practices of English
poetry.

What in Carkesse was an opportunistic and piecemeal view of
the world, making itself up from the events, visitors and news
that reached his Bethlem confinement, becomes in the work of
Christopher Smart, and especially in his remarkable *Jubilate Agno*,
a vision large enough to incorporate a universe. What in Carkesse
was a no-holds-barred engagement with the English language is
in Smart an elaborate and learned construction based on models
of form and knowledge that stretch from the canticles and the
sacred verse of the Hebrews, as recently described by Smart's friend
Bishop Robert Lowth in his lectures *De sacra poesi Hebraeorum*,
through Pliny's *Natural History* and Robert Ainsworth's adaptation
of it in his *Thesaurus Linguae Latinae compendiarius*, and on to
contemporary obituary lists in periodicals. If Carkesse has left
from his period of madness a brief example of insanity's capacity
to turn the tables on sane modes of existence, Smart's poem is
a sustained effusion on the endlessly renewing wonder of God's
creation in which everything fits and nothing is excluded.[24]

Smart, after an education in Durham and at Pembroke College,
Cambridge, and an early career as a writer, became ill around 1756,

at which time he was in his mid-thirties, and in May 1757 he was admitted to St Luke's Hospital, newly founded by William Battie. He was discharged a year later, uncured and, in Battie's opinion, apparently incurable:

> Christopher Smart continues disordered in his Senses notwith-
> standing he has been admitted into this Hospital above 12
> Calendar Months. And from the present Circumstances of
> his Case there not being sufficient reason to expect his speedy
> Recovery.[25]

Smart entered a private madhouse in Bethnal Green where he remained until January 1763. *Jubilate Agno* was written between 1758 or 1759 and 1763, with the bulk of it probably composed during his confinement in Mr Potter's house at Bethnal Green. (Smart is also believed to have written his *Hymns and Spiritual Songs* during the same period, and possibly some of the *Song to David*.) The exact nature of Smart's illness, as with most eighteenth-century mad patients, is not known, though he did suffer from alternating periods of depression and elation, and during the latter, according to Samuel Johnson, he 'shewed the disturbance of his mind, by falling upon his knees, and saying his prayers in the street, or in any other unusual place'.[26] In *Jubilate Agno* Smart declares that '*to worship naked in the Rain is the bravest thing for the refreshing and purifying the body*' (B384).[27] He certainly saw himself as being entrusted with a divine and evangelical mission – '*I am the Lord's News-Writer – the scribe-evangelist*' (B327) – and his poem was '*my MAGNIFICAT*' (A43). Whatever the reason for his confinement, and whatever the cause of his illness, *Jubilate Agno* remains the most extraordinary poem known to have been written during the eighteenth century, and the most eloquent of testaments to the creative potential of madness.

The structural basis for Smart's poem is deceptively straight-forward. Each standard verse comprises a 'Let' statement, on the model of the Benedicite of the canticles ('O ye Stars of Heaven, bless ye the Lord: praise him and magnify him for ever./O ye Showers and dew, bless ye the Lord: praise him, and magnify him for ever'), followed by an antiphonal '*For*' statement, after the structure of the sacred poetry of the Hebrews (Psalm 95, for example – 'Let us come before his presence with thanksgiving . . . For the Lord is a great God' – or Psalm 136 – 'O give thanks unto the God of all gods: for his mercy endureth for ever./O thank the

Lord of all Lords: for his mercy endureth for ever'). So, in Smart's poem:

> Let Elizur rejoice with the Partridge, who is a prisoner of state and is proud of his keepers. *For I am not without authority in my jeopardy, which I derive inevitably from the glory of the name of the Lord.* (B1)

If each '*For*' statement provides in some sense an answer, or comment, on each 'Let' statement, there is also a strong pattern of identity between the items in a sequence of 'Let' statements, and also between the items in a series of '*For*' statements. Smart thereby develops a cumulative effect as the verses progress, as well as an effect of counterpointing within the structure of each verse. The standard pattern is found for the first 297 verses of what is known as Fragment B and the 162 of Fragment C. The 113 verses of Fragment A consist only of 'Let' statements, as do the 237 verses of Fragment D, while verses 298 to 768 of Fragment B consist of '*For*' statements.

This structure, while impressive and certainly unusual, is in itself hardly evidence of insanity. To begin reading *Jubilate Agno* is to be in the presence of unfamiliar patterns of thought and expression, but the consistency of these patterns very quickly educates a reader into a degree of receptiveness that for a while becomes an expectational norm. Moreover, most of the items in Smart's lists, developed sometimes over several dozen verses, are themselves open to rational explanation, with names systematically drawn from a single source such as the Old Testament. These, for example, are verses on the four sons of Mahol from the first book of Kings:

> Let Ethan praise with the Flea, his coat of mail, his piercer, and his vigour, which wisdom and providence have contrived to attract observation and to escape it.

> Let Heman bless with the Spider, his warp and his woof, his subtlety and industry, which are good.

> Let Chalcol praise with the Beetle, whose life is precious in the sight of God, tho his appearance is against him.

> Let Darda with a Leech bless the name of the Physician of body and soul. (A36–40)

Where Carkesse called by name upon the crane and the stork to 'Bless the DUKE of *YORK*', Smart summons each and every known bird, animal, fish and insect, as well as most of the named figures from the Old Testament, to associate with him in his praise of God Almighty.

What does bespeak a mind wholly enrapt within a dimension of its own is the sheer remorselessness of the scope of Smart's vision, a vision that can look across the whole of creation and revel in the accumulation of species, names, knowledge, sound and language.

One of the features of Carkesse's mad poetry was his exuberant obliviousness to contradictions within his own arguments and to the damage done to poetic language. In Smart, the corresponding feature is not contradiction or linguistic infelicity but incongruity, a capacity to look upon the biblical and classical and the contemporary and personal as part of one continuous frame of vision.

> Let Achsah rejoice with the Pigeon who is an antidote to malignity and will carry a letter.
> *For I bless God for the Postmaster general and all conveyancers of letters under his care especially Allen and Shelvock.* (B22)

> Let Arodi rejoice with the Royston Crow, there is a society of them at Trumpington and Cambridge.
> *For I bless the Lord Jesus from the bottom of Royston Cave to the top of King's Chapel.* (B44)

> Let Ram rejoice with the Fieldfare, who is a good gift from God in the season of scarcity.
> *For my Angel is always ready at a pinch to help me out and to keep me up.* (B57)

> Let Joram rejoice with the Water-Rail, who takes his delight in the river.
> *For I pray God bless the CAM – Mr HIGGS and Mr and Mrs WASHBOURNE as the drops of the dew.* (B66)

Having firmly established rank and scale as essential to the structuring both of his lists and of his expression, Smart then proceeds to move suddenly between categories in a manner that defies not only reader expectation but also conventional means of laying mental hold upon systems of knowledge. This kind of cross-lateralism is a stock feature of English comic writing, but not of a species of poetry that purports to emulate the Psalms. Similarly, the degree of personal reference and punning that supports Smart's rapid shifts across categories is what we should now associate with a self-consciously Modernist work such as *Finnegans Wake*. Where Carkesse's flow of anger, humour, invective and self-assurance triumphed over the shortcomings of his material, Smart's incongruities are the very essence of his adoration. The assimilation of Mr and Mrs Washbourne with Joram and the Water-Rail is a measure of the breadth and particularity of his vision, a dynamic and all-embracing joy in which everything is implicated within everything else irrespective of time, place or species – the kinds of classification on which human understanding normally relies.

The breadth of Smart's particularity also extends to the structure of the English language itself. Already writing a poem in English that depends upon non-English poetic forms for the nature of its existence, Smart moves during its composition closer and closer towards a rapturous dissolution of the fabric of words. 'For in the education of children', says Smart, 'it is necessary to watch the words, which they pronounce with difficulty, for such are against them in their consequences' (B537). The latter part of Fragment B in particular makes a great deal of play with the forms of words and with the letters of the alphabet, not only offering several versions of both the English and the Hebrew, but thereby requiring that each of his own words be watched in terms of their composition, their sounds and appearances, and their relations with other words.

> *For God has given us a language of monosyllables to prevent our clipping.* (B579)

> *For the spiritual musick is as follows.* (B582)

> *For there is the thunder-stop, which is the voice of God direct.* (B583)

> *For the rest of the stops are by their rhimes.* (B584)

> *For the trumpet rhimes are sound bound, soar more and the like.* (B585)

> *For the flute rhimes are tooth youth suit mute and the like.* (B589)

> *For every word has its marrow in the English tongue for order and for delight.* (B595)

> *For the relations of words are in pairs first.* (B598)

171

For the relations of words are sometimes in opposition. (B599)

For the relations of words are according to their distance from the pair. (B600)

Languages also resemble animals, '*For the power of some animal is predominant in every language*' (B625). In Greek it is the cat, in Latin the mouse; the dog and the bull in English because '*English is concise and strong*' (B647). Language, for Smart, is neither inert nor simply a tool for everyday communication but is as full of vigour and distinctive vitality as any of the items it is used to name, to enlist, or to relate one to another. As such, the languages given by God to each and every people are themselves microcosms of his gift of creation, and display in their structures, in the shifting patterns of words and letters, in their lively adaptability, a reflection of the glory of interrelatedness.

At the peak of linguistic glory, language is capable at the same time both of withholding itself and of incorporating within itself the ultimate knowledge.

For the vowell is the female spirit in the Hebrew consonant. (C39)

For there are more letters in all languages not communicated. (C40)

For there are some that have the power of sentences. O rare thirteenth of march 1761. (C41)

Smart refers first here to the unwritten vowels of the Hebrews, which grammarians regarded as the soul of the word within the body of male consonants, and then to the Cabbalistic 'notaricon' which gives 'power of sentences' in that each letter of a word denotes the initial of another word, thus allowing an adept to form a series of sentences from the single words of an original sentence.[28] The ultimate in hidden knowledge, and that which language can never be framed to express, is the name of God himself. St Paul, says Smart, '*heard certain words which it was not possible for him to understand./For they were constructed by uncommunicated letters./For they are signs of speech too precious to be communicated for ever.*' (C43–5). The whole structure of *Jubilate Agno*, therefore, is a massive substitute for what cannot be otherwise spoken, written or understood: the name of God Almighty. It is a stand-in for silence, not a silence that betokens absence, but a silence more pregnant and resonant than any linguistic construct of which the human mind is capable.

Smart's sensitivity to the nature of language is so acute that it includes its silences and its hiddenness, as well as the infinite series of correspondences that enable words endlessly to relate to each other and to all other features of creation. It includes, too, the magical capacity of letters to dissolve and resolve between the forms of words, sentences and spaces in a dance of adoration and renewal. The madness of his rapture is intricated within the language he writes and the language that has been written and spoken since the beginnings of biblical history. His confinement within Mr Potter's madhouse in Bethnal Green, while regretted and resented by Smart, was apparently neither brutal nor restrictive. The visionary energy of the poet, moreover, enabled him to inhabit in his madness a universe of past and present in which an unhampered creativity gave full expression to the perpetual self-justification of the word.

> For in the divine Idea this Eternity is compleat and the
> Word is a making many more. (B329)

Smart was writing *Jubilate Agno* and *Song to David* at a significant period in the history of madness. The model asylum, St Luke's, had challenged in the public arena the traditional principles and practices of Bethlem, and that challenge had just made its way into print with the Battie–Monro debate of 1758, while the moral management movement that followed Battie's influence during the latter half of the century had not yet gathered force. A quarter of a century earlier, Smart might have been led by Patrick Blair 'whistling singing dancing and merrily leaping along' to receive '15 Ton' of water upon him. Some twenty-five or thirty years later, he would have been managed into silence, either through some elaborate theatrical hoax, contrived by Joseph Mason Cox, and involving angelic visitations, or through the power of William Pargeter's or Francis Willis's eye. As it was, he was left relatively unhampered to deal as he thought fit with the scope of his own madness. The compulsion to worship, if it was indeed the factor that led to his confinement, brought about a remarkable flowering of the mad mind. Only a few years after the long labours of Samuel Johnson to catalogue with precision in his *Dictionary* the definitions of English ('Let Johnson, house of Johnson rejoice with Omphalocarpa a kind of bur. God be gracious to Samuel Johnson.' D74), Smart achieved a dramatic dissolution of the capacity of words to be and mean through the linguistic resources of insanity.

★

Two years before Smart entered St Luke's, William Blake was born. Blake, as a canonised writer, is too vast a figure to be assimilated within the context of mad writing, or to be usefully located only in terms of the relation between madness and language. While he was regarded by many of his contemporaries as mad – Robert Southey, for example, and William Wordsworth – and experienced many of the characteristic features of insanity, including visions, voices, a belief in angelic messengers and a conviction that he composed from spiritual dictation, Blake never, as far as is known, received any form of psychiatric treatment. On the contrary, for Blake madness, particularly creative madness, was itself treatment for the world of sanity, of reason, Locke and Newton, and his work, both poetic and pictorial, represents the crusading spirit of true genius with a mission to convert as zealously pursued as Carkesse, Cruden, Matthews or Southcott pursued theirs. The small scale of Blake's operations undoubtedly saved him from the attention of medical authority, as it certainly did from the political repercussions of his views and activities. There is an irony here, in that the vastness of the scale of his vision and the extraordinary dynamism of his treatment of language, form and colour, were in the starkest of contrasts with the obscurity of his life in the less fashionable parts of London, and wholly outranked the beliefs that took Smart and Matthews to St Luke's and Bethlem Hospitals.

Wordsworth feared for his own sanity: 'We Poets in our youth begin in gladness;/But thereof come in the end despondency and madness.'[29] So did Blake, but he was coming from the opposite direction: 'Now God us keep/From single vision and Newton's sleep.'[30] Blake's work represents madness canonised, alternative arrangements that are no longer regarded as alternative. It is a fitting epitaph on the frustrations and oppressions experienced by the mad in the course of endlessly renewed engagements with conventional perceptions of insanity and conventional forms of the English language.

NOTES

Place of publication is London, unless otherwise stated

1 INTRODUCTION: TO BUILD A HOUSE FOR FOOLS AND MAD

1 See Fanny Burney, *Diary and Letters of Madame D'Arblay*, ed. C.F. Barrett, 1842, IV, 299–300, cited in Ida Macalpine and Richard Hunter, *George III and the Mad Business*, 1969, p. 28.
2 P.H. Stanhope, Earl Stanhope, *Life of the Right Honourable William Pitt*, 3rd edn, 1867, I, 391, cited in Macalpine and Hunter, *George III*, p. 28.
3 W.W. Grenville to the Marquis of Buckingham in *Memoirs of the Court and Cabinets of George the Third*, ed. Duke of Buckingham and Chandos, 1853, I, 438–40, cited in Macalpine and Hunter, *George III*, p. 29.
4 Burney, *Diary and Letters*, IV, 276, cited in Macalpine and Hunter, *George III*, p. 22.
5 Sir George Baker, *Diary*, 17 October – 7 November, cited in Macalpine and Hunter, *George III*, p. 19.
6 Burney, *Diary and Letters*, IV, 272, cited in Macalpine and Hunter, *George III*, p. 18.
7 *The Diaries of Colonel the Hon. Robert Fulke Greville*, ed. F.M. Bladon, 1930, p. 77, cited in Macalpine and Hunter, *George III*, p. 34.
8 Burney, *Diary and Letters*, IV, 290, cited in Macalpine and Hunter, *George III*, p. 26.
9 'The manuscripts of Earl Spencer', *Historical Monuments Commission*, 1871, 2nd Report, p. 14, cited in Macalpine and Hunter, *George III*, p. 36.
10 *The Letters of Richard Brinsley Sheridan*, ed. Cecil Price, Oxford, 1966, I, 191.
11 *Morning Post*, 14 November 1788, cited in Price, *Letters of Sheridan*, I, 188 n. 1.
12 *Willis Papers*, 16 December 1788, British Library Add. Mss 41690–1, cited in Macalpine and Hunter, *George III*, p. 65.
13 ibid., p. 64.
14 From *Détails sur l'établissement du docteur Willis, pour la guérison des*

Aliénés in *Bibliothèque Britannique, Littérature,* 1796, in Richard Hunter and Ida Macalpine, *Three Hundred Years of Psychiatry, 1535–1860,* 1963, pp. 538–9. (The report is of a visit to Willis's house in Lincolnshire in 1795 or 1796.)

15 *Diaries of Robert Fulke Greville,* p. 199, cited in Macalpine and Hunter, *George III,* p. 79.

16 See, for example, William Llewellyn Parry-Jones, *The Trade in Lunacy, A Study of Private Madhouses in England in the Eighteenth and Nineteenth Centuries,* 1971; also Roy Porter, *Mind-Forg'd Manacles: A History of Madness in England from the Restoration to the Regency,* 1987, pp. 136–47.

17 See Michel Foucault, *Madness and Civilization: A History of Insanity in the Age of Reason,* 1961; trans. Richard Howard, 1967, especially p. 78ff.

18 See Roy Porter, *A Social History of Madness: Stories of the Insane,,* 1987, p. 20; and *The Anatomy of Madness: Essays in the History of Psychiatry,* 1985, I, *People and Ideas,* ed. W.F. Bynum, Roy Porter and Michael Shepherd, p. 7. See also Peter Rushton, 'Lunatics and idiots: mental disability, the community, and the Poor Law in North-East England, 1600–1800', *Medical History* 32 (1988): 34–50.

19 See especially Michel Foucault, *The Archaeology of Knowledge,* 1967.

20 George Rosen, 'People, disease and emotion: some newer problems for research in medical history', *Bulletin of the History of Medicine* 41 (1967): 10.

21 Bynum *et al., Anatomy of Madness,* I, 4.

22 W.F. Bynum, 'The nervous patient in eighteenth- and nineteenth-century Britain: the psychiatric origins of British neurology', in Bynum *et al., Anatomy of Madness,* I, 90.

23 See, for example, Porter, *Mind-Forg'd Manacles,* pp. 176–84.

24 *Boswell: the Ominous Years, 1774–1776,* ed. Charles Ryskamp and F.A. Pottle, New York, 1963, p. 252; *Boswell's Column (The Hypochondriack, 1777–1783),* ed. Margery Bailey, 1951, p. 208. See also Allan Ingram, *Boswell's Creative Gloom: A Study of Imagery and Melancholy in the Writings of James Boswell,* 1982, pp. 16–18.

25 Foucault, *Madness and Civilization,* p. 100.

26 John Locke, *An Essay Concerning Human Understanding,* 1690, Book II, ch. 11, paras 12 & 13; ed. John W. Yolton, 1961, I, 127–8. See also Rushton 'Lunatics and idiots', 37–40 for practical distinctions that were made between lunatics and idiots in North-East England.

27 B. Bernstein, *Theoretical Studies Towards a Sociology of Language,* 1970, in *Language and Social Context,* ed. Pier Paolo Giglioli, Harmondsworth, 1972, pp. 161–2.

28 See John Haslam, *Illustrations of Madness,* 1810, London and New York, 1988, ed. Roy Porter; also Porter, *Mind-Forg'd Manacles,* pp. 236–40.

29 Locke, *An Essay,* Book II, ch. 27, 9 & 18 (I, 280, 287).

30 ibid., ch. 11, 11 & 13 (I, 126, 127).

31 Foucault, *Madness and Civilization,* p. 100.

32 ibid., pp. 94–101.

33 See Porter, *Mind-Forg'd Manacles,* pp. 247–60; also Roy Porter, 'The diary of a madman, 17th century style: Goodwin Wharton, M.P. and communer with the fairy world', *Psychological Medicine* 16 (1986):

503–18, and Goodwin Wharton, 'The autobiography of Goodwin Wharton', 2 vols, British Library Add. Mss, 20,006–7.

34 Fredric Jameson, *The Prison-House of Language*, Princeton and London, 1972.

35 Queen Charlotte to Lord Chancellor Thurlow, 3 January 1789, British Library Egerton Mss 2232 folio 71, cited in Macalpine and Hunter, *George III*, p. 73.

36 Foucault, *Madness and Civilization*, p. 107.

37 Quoted in Porter, *Social History*, p. 232.

38 Hunter and Macalpine, *Three Hundred Years*, p. 567.

39 Public Record Office, *Privy Council Minutes*, PC 2–131 folios 357–88, cited in Macalpine and Hunter, *George III*, p. 311.

40 'Verses on the death of Dr Swift', ll. 483–6, in *Swift: Poetical Works*, ed. Herbert Davis, Oxford, 1967, pp. 512–13.

41 ibid., ll. 1–10 (p. 496).

42 Quoted in Porter, *Mind-Forg'd Manacles*, p. 43, from Max Byrd, *Visits to Bedlam*, Columbia, South Carolina, 1974, p. 63.

2 THE HISTORY OF SILENCE

1 Michel Foucault, *Madness and Civilization: A History of Insanity in the Age of Reason*, 1961; trans. Richard Howard, 1967, pp. xii–xiii.

2 See, for example, David G. Schappert, 'Selected bibliography of primary materials', in *Psychology and Literature in the Eighteenth Century*, ed. Christopher Fox, New York, 1987, pp. 303–45.

3 Richard Hunter and Ida Macalpine, *Three Hundred Years of Psychiatry, 1535–1860*, 1963, p. 330.

4 Thomas Willis, *Dr Willis's practice of physick, being all the medical works of that renowned and famous physician: . . . Done into English by S[amuel] P[ordage]*, 1681, p. 126, Pybus Collection of the University Library, Newcastle upon Tyne, PYB M.i.14; see also Hunter and Macalpine, *Three Hundred Years*, pp. 187–9.

5 Willis, *Dr Willis's practice*, pp. 78–9.

6 ibid., p. 129.

7 Thomas Willis, *De anima brutorum*, 1672; trans. as *Two Discourses Concerning the Soul of Brutes*, S. Pordage, 1683, in Hunter and Macalpine, *Three Hundred Years*, pp. 190, 192.

8 ibid., pp. 191–2.

9 Thomas Sydenham, *The entire works of Dr Thomas Sydenham, newly made English from the originals. . . . By John Swan*, 1742, p. 609, Pybus Collection, PYB F.ii.

10 ibid., pp. 384–6.

11 ibid., pp. 368–71.

12 Nicholas Robinson, *A New System of the Spleen, Vapours, and Hypochondriack Melancholy*, 1729, in Hunter and Macalpine, *Three Hundred Years*, pp. 343–7.

13 John Monro, *Remarks on Dr Battie's Treatise on Madness*, 1758, ed. Richard Hunter and Ida Macalpine, 1962, pp. 50–2.

14 William Cullen, *First Lines of the Practice of Physic*, III, Edinburgh, 1783

and IV Edinburgh, 1784, in Hunter and Macalpine, *Three Hundred Years*, pp. 473–8.

15 John Haslam, *Observations on Insanity*, 1798, p. 105, Pybus Collection, PYB G.ii.15.

16 ibid., pp. 122–30.

17 ibid., pp. 132–47; see also Hunter and Macalpine, *Three Hundred Years*, p. 632.

18 Haslam, *Observations*, pp. 132, 122.

19 ibid., pp. 105–6.

20 See Hunter and Macalpine, *Three Hundred Years*, pp. 254–5.

21 Patrick Blair, *Some Observations on the Cure of Mad Persons by the Fall of Water*, 1725, in Hunter and Macalpine, *Three Hundred Years*, pp. 326–7.

22 Robinson, in Hunter and Macalpine, *Three Hundred Years*, p. 344.

23 Hunter and Macalpine, *Three Hundred Years*, p. 596.

24 Joseph Mason Cox, *Practical Observations on Insanity*, 1806, in Hunter and Macalpine, *Three Hundred Years*, pp. 596–7.

25 See Hunter and Macalpine, *Three Hundred Years*, pp. 534–5.

26 John Wesley, *The Desideratum: or, Electricity Made Plain and Useful. By a Lover of Mankind, and of Common Sense*, 1760, in Hunter and Macalpine, *Three Hundred Years*, p. 422.

27 John Wesley, *The Journal of the Rev. John Wesley*, ed. N. Curnock, 1906–16, in Hunter and Macalpine, *Three Hundred Years*, p. 424. This remark is also discussed in Klaus Doerner, *Madmen and the Bourgeoisie: A Social History of Insanity and Psychiatry*, 1969; trans. Joachim Neugroschel and Jean Steinberg, Oxford, 1981, pp. 38–9.

28 Roy Porter, *Mind-Forg'd Manacles: A History of Madness in England from the Restoration to the Regency*, 1987, p. 12.

29 John Birch, 'A Letter to the Author, from Mr John Birch, on the Subject of Medical Electricity', in George Adams, *An Essay on Electricity*, 1792, in Hunter and Macalpine, *Three Hundred Years*, pp. 534–7.

30 David Macbride, *A Methodical Introduction to the Theory and Practice of Physick*, 1772, in Hunter and Macalpine, *Three Hundred Years*, p. 449.

31 Hunter and Macalpine, *Three Hundred Years*, p. 449.

32 Thomas Tryon, *A Treatise of Dreams & Visions*, 1689, in Hunter and Macalpine, *Three Hundred Years*, p. 234.

33 Monro, *Remarks*, p. 6.

34 David Bayne Kinneir, 'A copy of a letter from Dr David Kinneir . . . to Dr Campbell . . . touching the efficacy of camphire in maniacal disorders', in *Philosophical Transactions* 35 (1727): 347–51, in Hunter and Macalpine, *Three Hundred Years*, p. 333.

35 George Young, *A Treatise on Opium, Founded upon Practical Observation*, 1753, in Hunter and Macalpine, *Three Hundred Years*, p. 397.

36 Robinson, in Hunter and Macalpine, *Three Hundred Years*, p. 346; Haslam, *Observations*, p. 56.

37 Haslam, *Observations*, pp. 27–9.

38 ibid., pp. 37, 47–8.

39 ibid., pp. 67–8.

40 ibid., pp. 63–4.

41 ibid., pp. 49–50.
42 ibid., pp. 40–1.
43 ibid., pp. 19–20.
44 ibid., p. 21.
45 Blair, in Hunter and Macalpine, *Three Hundred Years*, pp. 327–9.
46 On the subject of gender in science and medicine, see Ludmilla Jordanova, *Sexual Visions: Images of Gender in Science and Medicine between the 18th and 20th Centuries*, Hemel Hempstead, 1988.

3 CRACKS IN THE WALLS

1 See Richard Hunter and Ida Macalpine, *Three Hundred Years of Psychiatry, 1535–1860*, 1963, pp. 402–3.
2 ibid., p. 404.
3 William Battie, *A Treatise on Madness*, 1758, ed. Richard Hunter and Ida Macalpine, 1962, pp. 93–4.
4 ibid., pp. 98–9.
5 ibid., p. 1.
6 ibid., pp. 59–67.
7 ibid., pp. 5–6.
8 Klaus Doerner, *Madmen and the Bourgeoisie: A Social History of Insanity and Psychiatry*, 1969; trans. Joachim Neugroschel and Jean Steinberg, Oxford, 1981, p. 41.
9 ibid., p. 42.
10 Battie, *Treatise*, pp. 93, 68.
11 John Monro, *Remarks on Dr Battie's Treatise on Madness*, 1758, ed. Richard Hunter and Ida Macalpine, 1962, 'Advertisement'.
12 ibid., pp. 3–4.
13 Richard Baxter, *The Signs and Causes of Melancholy . . . Collected . . . By Samuel Clifford, Minister of the Gospel*, 1716, in Hunter and Macalpine, *Three Hundred Years*, p. 242.
14 Timothy Rogers, *A Discourse Concerning Trouble of Mind, and the Disease of Melancholy . . . By Timothy Rogers, M.A. who was long afflicted with both*, 1691, in Hunter and Macalpine, *Three Hundred Years*, pp. 248–51.
15 See for example Nigel Smith, *Perfection Proclaimed: Language and Literature in English Radical Religion, 1640–1660*, Oxford, 1988.
16 Sir Richard Blackmore, *A Treatise of the Spleen and Vapours: or, Hypochondriacal and Hysterical Affections*, 1725, in Hunter and Macalpine, *Three Hundred Years*, p. 320.
17 Peter Shaw, *The Reflector, Representing Human Affairs, as they are; and may be improved*, 1750, in Hunter and Macalpine, *Three Hundred Years*, p. 313.
18 Sir George Baker, *De Affectibus Animi et Morbis Inde Oriundis*, Cambridge, 1755; translated version in Hunter and Macalpine, *Three Hundred Years*, p. 400.
19 Peter Shaw, *The Juice of the Grape: or, Wine Preferable to Water*, 1724, in Hunter and Macalpine, *Three Hundred Years*, p. 313.
20 ibid., pp. 311–13.
21 George Cheyne, *The English Malady: or, a Treatise of Nervous Diseases*

of all Kinds, . . . With the Author's own Case at Large, 1733, p. 24, Pybus Collection, University Library, Newcastle upon Tyne, PYB G.ii.8.

22 ibid., pp. 54–5.
23 ibid., p. 26.
24 ibid., p. 112.
25 ibid., pp. 125, 134, 136.
26 ibid., p. 113.
27 ibid., pp. 139–42.
28 ibid., p. 114.
29 ibid., p. 144.
30 ibid., p. 361.
31 ibid., p. 327.
32 ibid., p. 331.
33 ibid., p. 199.
34 Francis Hutcheson, An Essay on the Nature and Conduct of the Passions and Affections, 1728, in Hunter and Macalpine, Three Hundred Years, pp. 335–7.
35 Thomas Reid, An Inquiry into the Human Mind, on the Principles of Common Sense, Edinburgh, 1764, in Hunter and Macalpine, Three Hundred Years, pp. 431–3.
36 John Gregory, A Comparative View of the State and Faculties of Man with those of the Animal World, 1765, in Hunter and Macalpine, Three Hundred Years, pp. 439–40.
37 Reid, in Hunter and Macalpine, Three Hundred Years, p. 432.
38 Kinneir, ibid., p. 333.
39 John Haslam, Observations on Insanity, 1798, pp. 95–6.
40 ibid., pp. 78–9.
41 ibid., p. 67.
42 John Woodward, Select Cases, and Consultations, in Physick. By the late Eminent John Woodward . . . Now First Published by Dr Peter Templeman, 1757, in Hunter and Macalpine, Three Hundred Years, pp. 338–41.
43 Erasmus Darwin, Zoonomia: or, the Laws of Organic Life, 1794–6, II, 361–2, Pybus Collection, PYB N.v.17–18.
44 William Perfect, Select Cases in the Different Species of Insanity, Lunacy, or Madness, Rochester, 1787, in Hunter and Macalpine, Three Hundred Years, p. 504.
45 Hunter and Macalpine, Three Hundred Years, pp. 491–2.
46 John Hunter, The Works of John Hunter, F.R.S. with Notes. Edited by James F. Palmer, 1835–7, in Hunter and Macalpine, Three Hundred Years, pp. 494–5.
47 Andrew Harper, A Treatise on the Real Cause and Cure of Insanity, 1789, in Hunter and Macalpine, Three Hundred Years, p. 524.
48 Battie, Treatise, pp. 73–6.
49 Hunter and Macalpine, Three Hundred Years, p. 405 and Porter, Mind-Forg'd Manacles: A History of Madness in England from the Restoration to the Regency, 1987, pp. 131–4.
50 Porter, Mind-Forg'd Manacles, p. 209.
51 Joseph Mason Cox, Practical Observations on Insanity, 1806, p. 88, quoted in Porter, Mind-Forg'd Manacles, p. 217.

52 Samuel Tuke, *Description of the Retreat, an Institution Near York*, York, 1813, ed. Richard Hunter and Ida Macalpine, 1964, p. 1.
53 See Anne Digby, 'Moral treatment at the Retreat, 1796–1846', in W.F. Bynum, Roy Porter and Michael Shepherd (eds) *The Anatomy of Madness: Essays in the History of Psychiatry*, 1985, II, *Institutions and Society*, p. 58; also Tuke, *Description*, p. 110ff.
54 Tuke, *Description*, p. 141ff.
55 Cited in Digby, 'Moral treatment', p. 60.
56 Tuke, *Description*, p. 151.
57 ibid., p. 157.
58 See also Michel Foucault, *Madness and Civilization: A History of Insanity in the Age of Reason*, 1961; trans. Richard Howard, 1967, pp. 243–54; Doerner, *Madmen and the Bourgeoisie*, pp. 77–82; Fiona Godlee, 'Aspects of non-conformity: Quakers and the lunatic fringe', in Bynum *et al.*, *Anatomy of Madness*, II, 73ff.
59 Samuel Johnson, *Rasselas*, 1759, ed. J.P. Hardy, Oxford, 1968, p. 104.
60 Cited in Doerner, *Madmen and the Bourgeoisie*, p. 72. See also Michel Foucault, *Discipline and Punish: The Birth of the Prison*, 1975; Part Three, ch. 3.

4 BORROWED ROBES

1 Gilbert White, *The Natural History of Selborne*, 1789, ed. W.S. Scott, 1962, pp. 143–4.
2 See *The Correspondence of Edward Young, 1683–1765*, ed. Henry Pettit, Oxford, 1971, p. 241, n. 1.
3 Somerset House, Prerogative Court of Canterbury, Glazier 824, pr. 11 August 1756, cited in Young, *Correspondence*, p. 241, n. 1.
4 Young, *Correspondence*, p. 242.
5 ibid., p. 242–3.
6 ibid., p. 243.
7 ibid., p. 246.
8 *The Piozzi Letters: Correspondence of Hester Lynch Piozzi, 1784–1821 (formerly Mrs Thrale)*, I, 1784–1791, ed. Edward A. and Lillian D. Bloom, 1989, p. 291.
9 ibid., I, 292, n. 6.
10 *The Letters of Thomas Gray*, ed. D.C. Tovey, 3 vols, 1900–12, I, 102. This passage is cited and discussed by William B. Ober, 'Eighteenth-century spleen', in *Psychology and Literature in the Eighteenth Century*, ed. Christopher Fox, New York, 1987, p. 250.
11 Michel Foucault, *Madness and Civilization: A History of Insanity in the Age of Reason*, 1961; trans. Richard Howard, 1967, p. 107.
12 Between 1747 and 1776, performances of tragedies at the patent theatres indicate that *Jane Shore* was third in popularity after *Romeo and Juliet* and *Hamlet*. (See Cecil Price, *Theatre in the Age of Garrick*, Oxford, 1973, p. 143.)
13 Nicholas Rowe, *Jane Shore*, 1714, V. i.
14 Charles Churchill, *The Rosciad*, ll. 787–92, in *The Poems of Charles Churchill*, ed. James Laver, New York and London, 1970 edn, p. 36. See

also Price's account of Garrick's performance as Hastings, pp. 7–14.

15 Alexander Pope, 'Epistle to Dr Arbuthnot', ll. 83–8, in *Poems*, Twicken-ham edn, 1954–67, III ii, *Epistles to Several Persons*, ed. F.W. Bateson, 2nd edn, 1961.

16 See Allan Ingram, *Intricate Laughter in the Satire of Swift and Pope*, 1986, especially ch. 2, 'Acts of exclusion: laughter and the satiric victim'.

17 Sir William Blackstone, *Commentaries on the Laws of England*, Oxford, 1765–9, in Richard Hunter and Ida Macalpine, *Three Hundred Years of Psychiatry, 1535–1860*, 1963, pp. 434–5.

18 Anon., *The Case of Henry Roberts, Esq; a Gentleman, who, by Unparalleled Cruelty was Deprived of his Estate, under Pretence of Idiocy*, 1747, in Hunter and Macalpine, *Three Hundred Years*, pp. 374–5.

19 Joel Peter Eigen, 'Intentionality and insanity: what the eighteenth-century juror heard', in W.F. Bynum, Roy Porter and Michael Shepherd (eds), *The Anatomy of Madness: Essays in the History of Psychiatry*, 1985, II, *Institutions and Society*, pp. 34–51.

20 ibid., p. 38.

21 Thomas Erskine, *Speech for the Defence*, in *Proceedings on the Trial of James Hadfield*, 1820, in Hunter and Macalpine, *Three Hundred Years*, pp. 569–70, 571.

22 'Deposition of John Haslam before King's Bench November 1809', in John Haslam, *Illustrations of Madness*, 1810, ed. Roy Porter, London and New York, 1988, pp. l–li.

23 William Godwin, *Caleb Williams, or Things as They Are*, 1794, 'Author's Latest Preface', 1832, ed. David McCracken, 1970, p. 339.

24 ibid., p. 4.

25 ibid., pp. 135–6.

26 ibid., p. 136.

27 ibid., p. 326.

28 Tobias Smollett, *The Life and Adventures of Sir Launcelot Greaves*, 1760–1, ed. David Evans, 1973, pp. 185–6.

29 ibid., pp. 191, 192. David Evans, citing Hunter and Macalpine, 'Smollett's reading in psychiatry' (*Modern Language Review* 51, 1956: 409–11) points out that part of the doctor's remarks are reproduced 'almost verbatim' from Battie's *Treatise on Madness*, 1758.

30 Smollett, *Launcelot Greaves*, p. 193.

31 Like very many other eighteenth-century writers, of course: see, for example, Henry Mackenzie, *The Man of Feeling*, 1771, ed. Brian Vickers, Oxford, 1970, ch. 20.

32 George Crabbe, 'Sir Eustace Gray', l. 1; all quotations from *The Poetical Works of George Crabbe*, ed. A.J. and R.M. Carlyle, 1932, pp. 88–93.

5 THE STRUGGLE FOR LANGUAGE

1 Erasmus Darwin, *Zoonomia: or, The Laws of Organic Life*, 1794–6, II, 356–8.

2 William Turner, *A Compleat History of the Most Remarkable Providences, both of Judgement and of Mercy which have Happened in this Present Age*,

1697, in Hunter and Macalpine, *Three Hundred Years of Psychiatry, 1535–1860*, 1963, p. 272.

3 William Salmon, *Iatrica: Seu Praxis Medendi. The Practice of Curing Diseases*, 1681, 3rd edn 1694, in Hunter and Macalpine, *Three Hundred Years*, pp. 259–60.

4 William Perfect, *Select Cases in the Different Species of Insanity*, Rochester, 1787, in Hunter and Macalpine, *Three Hundred Years*, p. 502.

5 John Ferriar, *Medical Histories and Reflections*, 1795, in Hunter and Macalpine, *Three Hundred Years*, p. 544.

6 Perfect, in Hunter and Macalpine, *Three Hundred Years*, p. 503.

7 ibid., pp. 504–5.

8 John Haslam, *Illustrations of Madness*, 1810, ed. Roy Porter, London and New York, 1988, p. 45.

9 ibid., pp. 47–8.

10 ibid., pp. 49–50.

11 ibid., p. 73.

12 ibid., p. 75.

13 ibid., pp. 19–20.

14 ibid., pp. 30–6.

15 ibid., pp. 31–6.

16 ibid., p. 33.

17 ibid., p. 35.

18 ibid., pp. 43–4.

19 ibid., p. 58.

20 ibid., pp. 57–8. The language here is quite clearly Haslam's.

21 Alexander Cruden, *The London-Citizen Exceedingly Injured*, 1739, p. 1.

22 ibid., p. 3.

23 See here *The Life of the Reverend Mr George Trosse . . . Written by Himself, and Published Posthumously According to his Order in 1714*, Exeter, 1714, ed. A.W. Brink, Montreal and London, 1974, 'Introduction', pp. 32–8.

24 Hannah Allen, *A Narrative of God's Gracious Dealings With That Choice Christian Mrs Hannah Allen*, 1683, pp. 72–3.

25 Trosse, *Life*, p. 132.

26 *The Letters and Prose Writings of William Cowper*, I, *1750–1781*, ed. James King and Charles Ryskamp, Oxford, 1979, p. 46.

27 Allen, *A Narrative*, pp. 40, 42, 43.

28 ibid., pp. 42–3.

29 Trosse, *Life*, pp. 106–7.

30 Allen, *A Narrative*, pp. 69–70.

31 Cowper, *Letters and Prose*, I, 10.

32 ibid., p. 26.

33 ibid., pp. 26–7.

34 ibid., p. 28.

35 ibid., pp. 28–9.

36 ibid., p. 31.

37 ibid.

38 ibid., p. 32.

39 ibid., p. 35.

40 ibid., p. 38.
41 ibid., p. 39.
42 ibid., p. 40.
43 ibid., p. 44.

6 THE INNER VOICE

1 *The Life of the Reverend Mr George Trosse . . . Written by Himself, and Published Posthumously According to his Order in 1714*, Exeter, 1714, ed. A.W. Brink, Montreal and London, 1974, p. 85.
2 ibid., pp. 86–7.
3 ibid., p. 87.
4 Hannah Allen, *A Narrative of God's Gracious Dealings With That Choice Christian Mrs Hannah Allen*, 1683, pp. 40–1.
5 Jeremiah, 20: 3–4.
6 Allen, *A Narrative*, pp. 64–5.
7 John Haslam, *Observations on Insanity*, 1798, p. 23.
8 ibid., p. 24.
9 See, for example, Roy Porter, *A Social History of Madness: Stories of the Insane*, 1987, p. 31.
10 See James K. Hopkins, *A Woman To Deliver Her People: Joanna Southcott and English Millenarianism in an Era of Revolution*, Austin, 1982, pp. 27, 29.
11 ibid., pp. 76–7.
12 Joanna Southcott, *The Strange Effects of Faith; With Remarkable Prophecies (Made in 1792, &c.) Of Things Which Are To Come: Also, some Account of my Life* [First Part], Exeter, 1801, p. i.
13 ibid., p. 16.
14 ibid. [Sixth Part], 1802, p. 275.
15 Joanna Southcott, *Sound an Alarm in My Holy Mountain*, Leeds, 1804, p. 10.
16 Southcott, *Strange Effects* [First Part], pp. 32–4.
17 Haslam, *Observations*, p. 6.
18 Southcott, *Strange Effects* [First Part], p. 34.
19 ibid. [Second Part], 1801, p. 49.
20 ibid. [First Part], pp. 27–8.
21 Richard Brothers, *A Revealed Knowledge of the Prophecies and Times*, 1794, p. 48, cited in Hopkins, *Joanna Southcott*, p. 171.
22 *Mr Halhed's Speech in the House of Commons*, 1795, pp. 4–8, cited in Hopkins, *Joanna Southcott*, pp. 175–6.
23 See, for example, Alexander Cruden, *The Adventures of Alexander the Corrector*, 1754; also Porter, *Social History*, pp. 126–35.
24 Hopkins, *Joanna Southcott*, p. 171.
25 John Haslam, *Illustrations of Madness*, 1810, ed. Roy Porter, London and New York, 1988, pp. 61–2.
26 ibid., pp. 62–3.
27 ibid., pp. 63–4.
28 ibid., p. lvii.
29 ibid., p. lix.

30 ibid.
31 Cited in Roy Porter, *Mind-Forg'd Manacles: A History of Madness in England from the Restoration to the Regency*, 1987, p. 239, from British Library Add. Ms 38231.
32 Haslam, *Observations*, pp. 17–18.
33 James Boswell, *Boswell in Holland, 1763–1764*, ed. F.A. Pottle, New York, 1952, p. 7. See also Allan Ingram, *Boswell's Creative Gloom: A Study of Imagery and Melancholy in the Writings of James Boswell*, 1982, p. 18ff for Boswell's melancholy.
34 *Boswell in Holland*, p. 6. See also Boswell, *Correspondence of James Boswell and John Johnston of Grange*, ed. Ralph S. Walker, 1966.
35 *Boswell in Holland*, pp. 184–91.
36 William Cowper, *The Letters and Prose Writings of William Cowper*, ed. James King and Charles Ryskamp, 1979–84, III, *1787–1791*, Oxford, 1982, p. 19; IV, *1792–1799*, Oxford, 1984, pp. 205–7.
37 ibid., I, 259.
38 ibid., p. 46.
39 ibid., pp. 341–2.
40 ibid., p. 344.
41 ibid., III, 342–3.
42 Cited by Dale Peterson (ed.), *A Mad People's History of Madness*, Pittsburgh, 1982, pp. 75–6.
43 Urbane Metcalf, *The Interior of Bethlehem Hospital*, 1818, in Peterson, *Mad People's History*, pp. 80, 81.
44 ibid., p. 82.
45 Haslam, *Observations*, p. 81.
46 Metcalf, in Peterson, *Mad People's History*, pp. 82, 84, 89.

7 RHYME AND REASON

1 Roy Porter, 'Bedlam and Parnassus: mad people's writing in Georgian England', in *One Culture: Essays in Science and Literature*, ed. George Levine, Madison, 1987, pp. 263–4 and n. 15.
2 *The Poems of William Cowper*, ed. John D. Baird and Charles Ryskamp, I, *1748–82*, Oxford, 1980, p. 209 and 'Commentary', p. 488.
3 See also Roy Porter, *A Social History of Madness: Stories of the Insane*, 1987, pp. 134–5.
4 Cowper, 'Verses, Supposed To Be Written By Alexander Selkirk, During His Solitary Abode In The Island Of Juan Fernandez', in *Poems*, I, 403.
5 Charlotte Smith, *Elegiac Sonnets*, II (1797), 11. Text from Roger Lonsdale (ed.) *Eighteenth-Century Women Poets: An Oxford Anthology*, Oxford, 1989, p. 372.
6 *John Clare: Selected Poetry and Prose*, ed. Raymond and Merryn Williams, 1986, pp. 193–4.
7 Details from *James Carkesse: Lucida Intervalla: Containing Divers Miscellaneous Poems*, 1679, ed. Michael V. De Porte, Los Angeles, 1979, pp. iii–xi.

8 John Haslam, *Observations on Insanity*, 1798, pp. 16–17.

9 Carkesse, 'Presented to the Duke On New Years-Day', in *Lucida Intervalla*, p. 8.

10 Carkesse, 'Mr Dr Mr D-', ibid., p. 62.

11 ibid., p. 60.

12 ibid., p. 17.

13 ibid., pp. 12–13.

14 Carkesse, 'The Riddle', ibid., p. 32.

15 ibid., p. 36.

16 Carkesse, 'Poets are Mad', ibid., p. 50.

17 Carkesse, 'To The Duke, General Of The Artillery Ground, Overlookt by Finnes-burrough Mad-house, Where I was Confin'd' and '*To His Royal Highness*', ibid., pp. 4, 5.

18 ibid., p. 52.

19 Carkesse, 'The Patients Advice To The Doctor', ibid., pp. 39–40.

20 ibid., pp. 42, 19, 23, 38, 62 and *passim*.

21 Carkesse, 'On Mrs Moniments Giving him a Visit at *Bedlam*', ibid., p. 65.

22 ibid., p. 49.

23 ibid., pp. 8, 47, 7, 61.

24 Details, and those that follow, from *The Poetical Works of Christopher Smart*, I: *Jubilate Agno*, ed. Karina Williamson, Oxford, 1980, pp. xxv–xxxi. See also Arthur Sherbo, *Christopher Smart: Scholar of the University*, East Lansing, 1967.

25 Quoted in Richard Hunter and Ida Macalpine, *Three Hundred Years of Psychiatry, 1535–1860*, 1963, p. 403.

26 James Boswell, *The Life of Samuel Johnson, LL.D.*, ed G.B. Hill, 1934–50; revised edn ed. L.F. Powell, Oxford, 1964, I, 397.

27 All quotations from *Jubilate Agno* are from the Williamson edition.

28 ibid., p. 94 nn 39, 41.

29 William Wordsworth, 'Resolution and Independence', in *William Wordsworth: The Poems*, ed. John O. Hayden, Harmondsworth, 1977, I, 553.

30 William Blake, 'To Thomas Butts, 22 November 1802', in *William Blake, The Complete Poems*, ed. Alicia Ostriker, Harmondsworth, 1977, p. 487.

BIBLIOGRAPHY

PRIMARY SOURCES

Allen, Hannah, *A Narrative of God's Gracious Dealings With That Choice Christian Mrs Hannah Allen,* . . . London, 1683.

Anon., *The Case of Henry Roberts, Esq; a Gentleman, who, by Unparalleled Cruelty was deprived of his Estate under Pretence of Idiocy,* London, 1747.

—— *Détails sur l'établissement du docteur Willis, pour la guérison des Aliénés,* Bibliothèque Britannique, Littérature, Geneva, 1796.

—— *Loving Mad Tom. Bedlamite Verses of the Seventeenth and Eighteenth Centuries,* ed. Jack Lindsay, Welwyn Garden City, 1969.

Arnold, Thomas, *Observations on the Nature, Kinds, Causes and Prevention of Insanity,* 2 vols, Leicester, 1782–6.

Baker, Sir George, *Diary,* Baker Mss, Rode Hall, Cheshire.

—— *De Affectibus Animi et Morbis Inde Oriundis,* Cambridge, 1755.

Battie, William, *A Treatise on Madness,* London, 1758, ed. Richard Hunter and Ida Macalpine, London, 1962.

Baxter, Richard, *Reliquiae Baxterianae,* London, 1696.

—— *The Signs and Causes of Melancholy . . . Collected . . . By Samuel Clifford, Minister of the Gospel,* London, 1716.

Belcher, William, *Address to Humanity, Containing a Letter to Dr Munro, a Receipt to Make a Lunatic, and Seize his Estates and a Sketch of a True Smiling Hyena,* London, 1796.

—— *Intellectual Electricity,* London, 1798.

Bentham, Jeremy, *Panopticon; or, the Inspection-House,* London, 1791.

Birch, John, 'A Letter to the Author, from Mr John Birch, on the Subject of Medical Electricity', in George Adams, *An Essay on Electricity,* London, 1792.

Black, William, *Dissertation on Insanity,* London, 1810.

Blackmore, Sir Richard, *A Treatise of the Spleen and Vapours: or, Hypochondriacal and Hysterical Affections,* London, 1725.

Blackstone, Sir William, *Commentaries on the Laws of England,* 4 vols, Oxford, 1765–9.

Blair, Patrick, *Some Observations on the Cure of Mad Persons by the Fall of Water,* 1725; quoted in Richard Hunter and Ida Macalpine, *Three Hundred Years of Psychiatry, 1535–1860,* London, 1963.

Blake, William, *William Blake, The Complete Poems*, ed. Alicia Ostriker, Harmondsworth, 1977.

Boswell, James, *Boswell in Holland, 1763–1764*, ed. F.A. Pottle, New York, 1952.

—— *Boswell: the Ominous Years, 1774–1776*, ed. Charles Ryskamp and F.A. Pottle, New York, 1963.

—— *Boswell's Column (The Hypochondriack, 1777–1783)*, ed. Margery Bailey, London, 1951.

—— *Correspondence of James Boswell and John Johnston of Grange*, ed. Ralph S. Walker, London, 1966.

—— *The Life of Samuel Johnson, LL.D., together with Boswell's Journal of a Tour to the Hebrides and Johnson's Diary of a Journey into North Wales*, 6 vols, ed. G.B. Hill, 1934–50; revised edn. ed. L.F. Powell, Oxford, 1964.

Brothers, Richard, *A Revealed Knowledge of the Prophecies and Times, Book the First*, London, 1794.

—— *A Revealed Knowledge of the Prophecies and Times, Book the Second*, London, 1794.

Bruckshaw, Samuel, *The Case, Petition and Address of Samuel Bruckshaw, who Suffered a Most Severe Imprisonment for Very Near the Whole Year*, London, 1774.

—— *One More Proof of the Iniquitous Abuse of Private Madhouses*, London, 1774.

Brydall, John, *Non Compos Mentis: or the Law Relating to Natural Fools, Mad-Folks and Lunatick Persons*, London, 1700.

Burney, Fanny, *Diary and Letters of Madame D'Arblay*, 7 vols, ed. C.F. Barrett, London, 1842–6.

—— *The Letters and Journals of Fanny Burney (Madame d'Arblay)*, 12 vols, ed. Joyce Hemlow *et al.*, Oxford, 1972–84.

Carkesse, James, *Lucida Intervalla: Containing Divers Miscellaneous Poems*, 1679, ed. Michael V. DePorte, Los Angeles, 1979.

Cheyne, George, *An Essay of Health and Long Life*, London, 1724.

—— *The English Malady; or, a Treatise of Nervous Diseases of all Kinds, . . . With the Author's own Case at Large*, London, 1733.

—— *An Essay on Regimen*, London, 1740.

Churchill, Charles, *The Poems of Charles Churchill*, ed. James Laver, New York and London, 1970 edn.

Clare, John, *John Clare: Selected Poetry and Prose*, ed. Raymond and Merryn Williams, London, 1986.

Cowper, William, *The Letters and Prose Writings of William Cowper*, 4 vols, ed. James King and Charles Ryskamp, Oxford, 1979–84.

—— *Memoir of the Early Life of William Cowper, Esq*, in *The Letters and Prose Writings of William Cowper*, I, *1750–1781*, ed. James King and Charles Ryskamp, Oxford, 1979.

—— *The Poems of William Cowper*, ed. John D. Baird and Charles Ryskamp, I, *1748–1782*, Oxford, 1980.

—— *The Poetical Works of William Cowper*, ed. H.S. Milford, 4th edn, Oxford, 1967.

Cox, Joseph Mason, *Practical Observations on Insanity*, London, 1806.

Crabbe, George, *The Poetical Works of George Crabbe*, ed. A.J. and

R.M. Carlyle, London, 1932.

Crichton, Sir Alexander, *An Inquiry into the Nature and Origin of Mental Derangement*, . . . 2 vols, London, 1798.

Cruden, Alexander, *The London Citizen Exceedingly Injured*, London, 1739.

—— *Mr Cruden Greatly Injured*, London, 1739.

—— *The Adventures of Alexander the Corrector*, London, 1754.

Cullen, William, *First Lines of the Practice of Physic*, 4 vols, Edinburgh, 1778–84.

Darwin, Erasmus, *Zoonomia: or, the Laws of Organic Life*, 2 vols, London, 1794–6.

Erskine, Thomas, 'Speech for the Defence,' in *Proceedings on the Trial of James Hadfield*, London, 1820.

Fallowes, Thomas, *The Best Method for the Cure of Lunaticks*, London, 1705.

Faulkner, Benjamin, *Observations on the General and Improper Treatment of Insanity*, London, 1789.

Fawcet, Benjamin, *Observations of the Causes and Cure of Melancholy, especially of that which is called Religious Melancholy*, Shrewsbury, 1780.

Ferriar, John, *Medical Histories and Reflections*, 3 vols, London, 1795.

Fox, Edward Long, *Brislington House, an Asylum for Lunatics, Situated Near Bristol*, Bristol, 1806.

Godwin, William, *Caleb Williams, or Things as They Are*, London, 1794, ed. David McCracken, London, 1970.

Gray, Thomas, *The Correspondence of Thomas Gray*, 3 vols, ed. Paget Toynbee and Leonard Whibley, Oxford, 1935.

—— *The Letters of Thomas Gray*, 3 vols, ed. D.C. Tovey, London, 1900–12.

Gregory, John, *A Comparative View of the State and Faculties of Man with those of the Animal World*, London, 1765.

Greville, Robert Fulke, *The Diaries of Colonel the Hon. Robert Fulke Greville*, ed. F.M. Bladon, London, 1930.

Halhed, Nathaniel Brassey, *Mr Halhed's Speech in the House of Commons*, London, 1795.

—— *The Second Speech of Nathaniel Brassey Halhed Esq.*, London, 1795

Hall, John, *A Narrative of the Proceedings Relative to the Establishment etc. of St Luke's House*, Newcastle upon Tyne, 1767.

Harper, Andrew, *A Treatise on the Real Cause and Cure of Insanity*, London, 1789.

Hartley, David, *Observations on Man*, London, 1749.

Haslam, John, *Observations on Insanity*, London 1798.

—— *Illustrations of Madness*, London, 1810, ed. Roy Porter, London and New York, 1988.

Heberden, William, *Medical Commentaries on the History and Cure of Diseases*, London, 1802.

Hill, Sir John, *Hypochondriasis, A Practical treatise on the Nature and Cure of That Disorder Commonly Called the Hyp or Hypo*, London, 1766, ed. G.S. Rousseau, Los Angeles, 1966.

Hunter, John, *The Works of John Hunter, F.R.S. with Notes. Edited by James F. Palmer, 1835–7*, 4 vols, London, 1835–7.

Hutcheson, Francis, *An Essay on the Nature and Conduct of the Passions and Affections*, London, 1728.

James, Robert, *Medicinal Dictionary*, 3 vols, London, 1743.

Johnson, Samuel, *Rasselas*, London, 1759, ed. J.P. Hardy, Oxford, 1968.

Jones, John, *The Mysteries of Opium Reveal'd*, London 1700.

Kinneir, David Bayne, 'A copy of a letter from Dr David Kinneir . . . to Dr Campbell . . . touching the efficacy of camphire in maniacal disorders', *Philosophical Transactions* 35 (1727): 347–51.

Locke, John, *An Essay Concerning Human Understanding*, London, 1690; ed. John W. Yolton, 2 vols, London, 1961.

Macbride, David, *A Methodical Introduction to the Theory and Practice of Physick*, London, 1772.

Mackenzie, Henry, *The Man of Feeling*, 1771, ed. Brian Vickers, Oxford, 1970.

Mandeville, Bernard, *A Treatise of Hypochondriack and Hysterick Passions*, London, 1711.

Mead, Richard, *Medical Precepts and Cautions*, trans. Thomas Stack, London, 1751.

Metcalf, Urbane, *The Interior of Bethlehem Hospital*, London, 1818.

Monro, John, *Remarks on Dr Battie's Treatise on Madness*, London, 1758; ed. Richard Hunter and Ida Macalpine, London, 1962.

Montagu, Lady Mary Wortley, *Letters from Lady Mary Wortley Montagu*, ed. R. Brimley Johnson, London, 1925.

Moore, John, *Religious Melancholy*, London, 1692.

Pargeter, William, *Observations on Maniacal Disorders*, Reading, 1792.

Parliamentary Papers, 'Report from the Committee appointed to enquire into the state of private madhouses', *House of Commons Journal* 29 (1763): 486–9.

—— *Report from the Committee appointed to Examine the Physicians who have attended His Majesty, During His Illness, Touching the State of His Majesty's Health*, House of Commons, 1788.

—— *Reports from the Committee on Madhouses in Emgland*, House of Commons, 1815.

—— *Reports from the Committee on Madhouses in England*, House of Commons, 1816.

Pepys, Samuel, *The Diary of Samuel Pepys*, 11 vols, ed. R. Latham and W. Matthews, London, 1970–83.

Perfect, William, *Select Cases in the Different Species of Insanity*, Rochester, 1787.

—— *A Remarkable Case of Madness, with the Diet and Medicine used in the Cure*, Rochester, 1791.

Pinel, Philippe, *Traité Medico-philosophique sur l'aliénation mentale*, Paris, 1809; repr. New York, 1976.

Piozzi, Hester Lynch, *The Piozzi Letters: Correspondence of Hester Lynch Piozzi, 1784–1821 (formerly Mrs Thrale)*, ed. Edward A. and Lillian D. Bloom, London, 1989.

Pope, Alexander, *Poems*, 10 vols, Twickenham edn., ed. J. Butt *et al.*, London, 1954–67.

Privy Council Minutes, Public Record Office, PC 2–131.

Reid, John, *Essays on Hypochondriacal and Other Nervous Affections*, London, 1816.

Reid, Thomas, *An Inquiry into the Human Mind, on the Principles of Common Sense*, Edinburgh, 1764.

Robinson, Nicholas, *A New System of the Spleen, Vapours, and Hypochondriack Melancholy*, . . . London, 1729.

Rogers, Timothy, *A Discourse Concerning Trouble of Mind and the Disease of Melancholy*, . . . *By Timothy Rogers, M.A. who was long afflicted with both*, London, 1691.

Rowe, Nicholas, *Jane Shore*, London, 1714.

Rowley, William, *A Treatise of Female Nervous, Hysterical, Hypochondriachal, Bilious, Convulsive Diseases*, London, 1788.

Salmon, William, *Iatrica: Seu Praxis Medendi. The Practice of Curing Diseases*, London, 1681; 3rd edn 1694.

Shaw, Peter, *The Juice of the Grape; or, Wine Preferable to Water. A Treatise Wherein Wine is Shewn to be a Grand Preserver of Health, with a Word of Advice to the Vintners*, London, 1724.

—— *The Reflector, Representing Human Affairs, as they are: and may be Improved*, London, 1750.

Sheridan, R.B., *The Letters of Richard Brinsley Sheridan*, 3 vols, ed. Cecil Price, Oxford, 1966.

Smart, Christopher, *Jubilate Agno* in *The Poetical Works of Christopher Smart*, I, ed. Karina Williamson, Oxford, 1980.

—— *The Poetical Works of Christopher Smart*, 2 vols, ed. Marcus Walsh and Karina Williamson, Oxford, 1980–3.

Smith, Charlotte, *Elegiac Sonnets*, London, 1797.

Smith, Sydney, 'An account of the York Retreat', *Edinburgh Review* 23 (1814): 189–98.

Smollett, Tobias, *The Life and Adventures of Sir Launcelot Greaves*, London, 1760–1, ed. David Evans, London, 1973.

Southcott, Joanna, *The Strange Effects of Faith; With Remarkable Prophecies (Made in 1792, &c.) of Things Which Are to Come: Also Some Account of my Life*, Exeter, 1801–2.

—— *A Continuation of Prophecies, by Joanna Southcott, from the Year 1792, to the Present Time*, Exeter, 1802.

—— *The Continuation of the Prophecies of Joanna Southcott. A Word in Season to a Sinking Kingdom*, London, 1803.

—— *Sound an Alarm in My Holy Mountain*, Leeds, 1804.

Sterne, Laurence, *The Life and Opinions of Tristram Shandy*, London, 1760–7, ed. Christopher Ricks, Harmondsworth, 1970.

Stukeley, William, *Of the Spleen, its Description and History*, London, 1723.

Swift, Jonathan, *Poetical Works*, ed. Herbert Davis, Oxford, 1967.

—— *Prose Writings*, 14 vols, ed. Herbert Davis *et al.* Oxford, 1939–63.

Sydenham, Thomas, *The entire works of Dr Thomas Sydenham, newly made English from the originals*. . . . *By John Swan*, London, 1742.

Synge, Edward, *The Cure of Melancholy*, London, 1742.

Trosse, Thomas, *The Life of the Reverend Mr George Trosse, Late Minister of the Gospel in the City of Exon, Who Died January 11th, 1712/13. In the Eighty Second Year of His Age, Written by Himself and Publish'd According to his Order in 1714*, Exeter, 1714, ed. A.W. Brink, Montreal and London, 1974.

Tryon, Thomas, *A Treatise of Dreams and Visions*, London, 1689.

Tuke, Samuel, *Description of the Retreat, an Institution Near York*, York, 1813, ed. Richard Hunter and Ida Macalpine, London, 1964.

Turner, William, *A Compleat History of the Most Remarkable Providences, both of Judgement and of Mercy which have Happened in this Present Age*, London, 1697.

Ward, Ned, *The London Spy*, London, 1698–1709, ed. K. Fenwick, London, 1955.

Warton, Thomas, *The Pleasures of Melancholy*, London, 1747.

Wesley, John, *The Journal of the Rev. John Wesley*, ed. N. Curnock, London, 1909–16.

—— *Primitive Physick*, London, 1747; repr. Beverly Hills, 1973.

—— *The Desideratum: or, Electricity made Plain and Useful. By a Lover of Mankind, and of Common Sense*, London, 1760.

Wharton, Goodwin, *The Autobiography of Goodwin Wharton*, 2 vols, British Library Add. Mss. 20,006–7.

White, Gilbert, *The Natural History of Selborne*, 1789, ed. W.S. Scott, London, 1962.

Whytt, Robert, *Observations on the Nature, Causes and Cure of those Disorders which have been called Nervous, Hypochondriac, or Hysteric*, Edinburgh, 1765.

Willis, Francis, *Willis Papers*, British Library Add. Mss 41690–1.

Willis, Thomas, *De anima brutorum*, London, 1672; trans. as *Two Discourses Concerning the Soul of Brutes*, S. Pordage, London, 1683.

—— *Dr Willis's practice of physick, being all the medical works of that renowned and famous physician: . . . Done into English by S[amuel] P[ordage]*, London, 1681.

Wilson, Andrew, *Nature and Origin of Hysteria*, London, 1776.

Withers, Thomas, *Observations on Chronic Weakness*, York, 1777.

Woodward, John, *Select Cases, and Consultations, in Physick. By the late Eminent John Woodward . . . Now First Published by Dr Peter Templeman*, London, 1757.

Wordsworth, William, *William Wordsworth: The Poems*, ed. John O. Hayden, Harmondsworth, 1977.

Young, Edward, *The Correspondence of Edward Young, 1683–1765*, ed. Henry Pettit, Oxford, 1971.

Young, George, *A Treatise on Opium, Founded upon Practical Observation*, London, 1753.

SECONDARY SOURCES

Abrams, M.H., *The Mirror and the Lamp*, New York, 1953.

Alexander, Franz G. and Seleznick, Sheldon T., *The History of Psychiatry: an Evaluation of Psychiatric Thought and Practice from Prehistoric Times to the Present*, London, 1967.

Allderidge, Patricia H., 'Bedlam: fact or fantasy?', in W.F. Bynum, Roy Porter and Michael Shepherd (eds), *The Anatomy of Madness*, 2 vols,

London, 1985, II, 17–33.

Babb, L., *The Elizabethan Malady: A Study of Melancholia in English Literature from 1580–1640*, East Lansing, 1951.

Baker, F., '"Mad Grimshaw" and his covenants with God: a study in eighteenth-century psychology', *London Quarterly and Holborn Review* 182 (1952): 202–15, 270–9.

Barnes, B. and Shapin, S. (eds), *Natural Order: Historical Studies of Scientific Culture*, London, 1979.

Bernstein, B., *Theoretical Studies Towards a Sociology of Language*, London, 1970.

Busfield, Joan, *Managing Madness. Changing Ideas and Practice*, London, 1986.

Bynum, W.F., 'Theory and practice in British psychiatry from J.C. Prichard (1786–1848) to Henry Maudsley (1835–1918)', in T. Ogawa (ed.), *History of Psychiatry*, Osaka, 1982, pp. 196–216.

—— 'The nervous patient in eighteenth- and nineteenth-century England: the psychiatric origins of British neurology', in W.F. Bynum, Roy Porter and Michael Shepherd (eds), *The Anatomy of Madness*, 2 vols, London, 1985, I, 89–102.

Bynum, W.F., Porter, Roy and Shepherd, Michael (eds), *The Anatomy of Madness: Essays in the History of Psychiatry*, 2 vols, London, 1985.

Byrd, Max, *Visits to Bedlam*, Columbia, South Carolina, 1974.

Carlson, Eric T. and Dain, N. 'The psychotherapy which was moral treatment', *American Journal of Psychiatry* 117 (1960): 519–24.

—— 'The meaning of moral insanity', *Bulletin of the History of Medicine* 36 (1962): 130–40.

Carlson, Eric T. and Simpson, Meredith, 'Madness of the nervous system in eighteenth century psychiatry', *Bulletin of the History of Psychiatry* 43 (1969): 101–15.

Clark, J.K., *Goodwin Wharton*, Oxford, 1984.

Clark, J.R., *Form and Frenzy in Swift's 'Tale of a Tub'*, Ithaca and London, 1970.

Cox, S.D., *'The Stranger Within Thee': The Concept of the Self in Late Eighteenth Century Literature*, Pittsburgh, 1980.

Craig, M., *The Legacy of Swift, A Bicentenary Record of St Patrick's Hospital, Dublin*, Dublin, 1948.

Cunningham, S., 'Bedlam and Parnassus: eighteenth century reflections', in *Eighteenth Century Studies* 24 (1971): 36–55.

Dain, N., *Concepts of Insanity, 1789–1865*, New Brunswick, 1964.

DePorte, Michael V., *Nightmares and Hobby Horses. Swift, Sterne and Augustan Ideas of Madness*, San Marino, California, 1974.

Dewhurst, K., *Dr Thomas Sydenham (1624–1689): His Life and Original Writings*, London, 1966.

Digby, Anne, 'Changes in the asylum: the case of York, 1777–1815', *Economic History Review*, 2nd series 37 (1983): 218–39.

—— 'The changing profile of a nineteenth century asylum: the York Retreat', *Psychological Medicine* 14 (1984): 739–48.

—— *Madness, Morality and Medicine*, Cambridge, 1985.

—— 'Moral treatment at the Retreat, 1796–1846', in W.F. Bynum, Roy

Porter and Michael Shepherd (eds), *The Anatomy of Madness*, 2 vols, London, 1985, II, 52–72.

Doerner, Klaus, *Madmen and the Bourgeoisie: A Social History of Insanity and Psychiatry*, 1969; trans. Joachim Neugroschel and Jean Steinberg, Oxford, 1981.

Donnelly, M., *Managing the Mind*, London, 1983.

Eigen, J.P., 'Intentionality and insanity: what the eighteenth century juror heard', in W.F. Bynum, Roy Porter and Michael Shepherd (eds), *The Anatomy of Madness*, 2 vols, London, 1985, II, 34–51.

Ellenberger, Henri F., *The Discovery of the Unconscious: The History and Evolution of Dynamic Psychiatry*, New York, 1971.

Engell, J., *The Creative Imagination*, Cambridge, Mass., 1981.

Feder, L., *Madness in Literature*, Princeton, 1980.

Finnane, Mark, *Insanity and the Insane in Post-Famine Ireland*, London, 1981.

Foucault, Michel, *Madness and Civilization, A History of Insanity in the Age of Reason*, 1961; trans. Richard Howard, London, 1967.

—— *The Archaeology of Knowledge*, 1967; trans. A.M. Sheridan Smith, London, 1974.

—— *Discipline and Punish: The Birth of the Prison*, 1975; trans. Alan Sheridan, London, 1977.

Fox, Christopher (ed.), *Psychology and Literature in the Eighteenth Century*, New York, 1987.

French, C.N., *The Story of St Luke's Hospital*, London, 1951.

French, R.K., *Robert Whytt, the Soul and Medicine*, London, 1969.

Fullinwider, S.P., 'Insanity and the loss of self: the moral insanity controversy revisited', *Bulletin of the History of Medicine* 49 (1975): 87–101.

Fussell, Paul, *The Rhetorical World of Augustan Humanism*, Oxford, 1965.

Giglioli, Pier Paolo (ed.), *Language and Social Context*, Harmondsworth, 1972.

Gilbert, Sandra and Gubar, Susan, *The Madwoman in the Attic: The Woman Writer and the Nineteenth-Century Literary Imagination*, New Haven, 1978.

Godlee, Fiona, 'Aspects of non-conformity: Quakers and the lunatic fringe', in W.F. Bynum, Roy Porter and Michael Shepherd (eds), *The Anatomy of Madness*, 2 vols, London, 1985, II, 73–85.

Grange, Kathleen, 'Pinel and eighteenth century psychiatry', *Bulletin of the History of Medicine* 35 (1961): 442–53.

—— 'Dr Samuel Johnson's account of a schizophrenic illness in *Rasselas* (1759)', *Medical History* 6 (1962): 162–8.

Hagstrum, Jean H., 'Towards a profile of the word *Conscious* in eighteenth-century literature', in Christopher Fox (ed.), *Psychology and Literature in the Eighteenth Century*, New York, 1987, pp. 23–50.

Hill, A.W., *John Wesley Among the Physicians: A Study of Eighteenth Century Medicine*, London, 1958.

Hill, Draper, *Mr Gillray, the Caricaturist*, London, 1966.

Holmes, Geoffrey, *Augustan England, Professions, State, and Society, 1680–1730*, London, 1982.

Hopkins, James K., *A Woman To Deliver Her People: Joanna Southcott and English Millenarianism in an Era of Revolution*, Austin, 1982.

Hunter, Michael, *Science and Society in Restoration England*, Cambridge, 1981.

Hunter, Richard and Macalpine, Ida, *Three Hundred Years of Psychiatry, 1535–1860*, London, 1963.

Ingram, Allan, *Boswell's Creative Gloom: A Study of Imagery and Melancholy in the Writings of James Boswell*, London, 1982.

—— *Intricate Laughter in the Satire of Swift and Pope*, London, 1986.

Irwin, G., *Samuel Johnson. A Personality in Conflict*, Auckland, 1971.

Isler, Hansruedi, *Thomas Willis, 1621–1675, Doctor and Scientist*, New York, 1968.

Jackson, Stanley W., *Melancholia and Depression from Hippocratic Times to Modern Times*, New Haven, 1986.

Jameson, Fredric, *The Prison-House of Language: A Critical Account of Structuralism and Russian Formalism*, Princeton and London, 1972.

Jones, W.L., *Ministering to Minds Diseased. A History of Psychiatric Treatment*, London, 1983.

Jordanova, Ludmilla, *Sexual Visions: Images of Gender in Science and Medicine between the 18th and 20th Centuries*, Hemel Hempstead, 1988.

King, Lester, S., *The Medical World of the Eighteenth Century*, Chicago, 1958.

—— *The Philosophy of Medicine. The Early Eighteenth Century*, Cambridge, Mass., 1978.

Kraepelin, E., *One Hundred Years of Psychiatry*, London, 1962.

Kramnick, I., *The Rage of Edmund Burke*, New York, 1977.

Lane, Joan, '"The doctor scolds me". The diaries and correspondence of patients in eighteenth century England', in Roy Porter (ed.), *Patients and Practitioners. Lay Perceptions of Medicine in Pre-Industrial Society*, Cambridge, 1985, pp. 204–48.

Lawrence, C.J., 'The nervous system and society in the Scottish Enlightenment', in B. Barnes and S. Shapin (eds) *Natural Order: Historical Studies of Scientific Culture*, London, 1979, pp. 19–40.

Levine, George (ed.), *One Culture: Essays in Science and Literature*, Madison, 1987.

Lonsdale, Roger (ed.), *Eighteenth-Century Women Poets: An Oxford Anthology*, Oxford, 1989.

Lyons, Bridget Gellert, *Voices of Melancholy, Studies in Literary Treatment of Melancholy in Renaissance England*, London, 1971.

Lyons, J.O., *The Invention of the Self*, Carbondale, 1978.

Macalpine, Ida and Hunter, Richard, *George III and the Mad Business*, London, 1969.

MacDonald, Michael, *Mystical Bedlam: Madness, Anxiety and Healing in Seventeenth Century England*, Cambridge, 1981.

Mackenzie, C., 'Women and psychiatric professionalization 1780–1914', in London Feminist Collective (ed.), *The Sexual Dynamics of History*, London, 1983, pp. 107–19.

Masters, A., *Bedlam*, London, 1972.

Mell, Donald C., Braun, Theodore E.D. and Palmer, Lucia M. (eds), *Man, God, and Nature in the Enlightenment*, East Lansing, 1988.

Mora, George, 'The history of psychiatry: a cultural and bibliographic survey', *The Psychoanalytic Review* 52 (1966): 335–56.

Musher, Daniel M., 'The medical views of Dr Tobias Smollett, 1721–71', *Bulletin of the History of Medicine* 41 (1967): 455–62.

Ober, William B., *Boswell's Clap and Other Essays*, Carbondale, 1979.

—— 'Eighteenth-century spleen,', in Christopher Fox (ed.), *Psychology and Literature in the Eighteenth Century*, New York, 1987, pp. 225–58.

Ogawa, T. (ed.), *History of Psychiatry*, Osaka, 1982.

Olivier, Edith, *The Eccentric Life of Alexander Cruden*, London, 1934.

Pagliaro, H.E. (ed.), *Irrationalism in the Eighteenth Century (Studies in Eighteenth Century Culture* vol. II), Cleveland, Ohio, 1972.

Parry-Jones, William Llewellyn, *The Trade in Lunacy, A Study of Private Madhouses in England in the Eighteenth and Nineteenth Centuries*, London, 1971.

Percival, W. Keith, 'Linguistic and biological classification in the eighteenth century', in Donald C. Mell, Theodore E.D. Braun and Lucia M. Palmer (eds), *Man, God, and Nature in the Enlightenment*, East Lansing, 1988, pp. 205–14.

Peterson, Dale (ed.), *A Mad People's History of Madness*, Pittsburgh, 1982.

Price, Cecil, *Theatre in the Age of Garrick*, Oxford, 1973.

Porter, Roy, 'Bedlam and Parnassus: mad people's writing in Georgian England', in George Levine (ed.), *One Culture: Essays in Science and Literature*, Madison, 1987, pp. 258–84.

—— 'Being mad in eighteenth century England', *History Today* Dec. 1981: 42–8.

—— 'The diary of a madman, 17th century style: Goodwin Wharton, M.P. and communer with the fairy world', *Psychological Medicine* 16 (1986): 503–18.

—— '"The Hunger of Imagination": approaching Samuel Johnson's melancholy', in W.F. Bynum, Roy Porter and Michael Shepherd (eds), *The Anatomy of Madness*, 2 vols, London, 1985, I, 63–88.

—— *Mind-Forg'd Manacles: A History of Madness in England from the Restoration to the Regency*, London, 1987.

—— (ed.), *Patients and Practitioners. Lay Perceptions of Medicine in Pre-Industrial Society*, Cambridge, 1985.

—— *A Social History of Madness: Stories of the Insane*, London, 1987.

Rabb, Melinda Alliker, 'Psychology and politics in William Godwin's *Caleb Williams*: double bond or double bind?', in Christopher Fox (ed.), *Psychology and Literature in the Eighteenth Century*, New York, 1987, pp. 51–67.

Rather, L.J., *Mind and Body in Eighteenth Century Medicine*, Berkeley, 1965.

Rosen, George, 'Forms of irrationality in the eighteenth century', in H.E. Pagliaro (ed.), *Irrationalism in the Eighteenth Century (Studies in Eighteenth Century Culture*, vol. II), Cleveland, Ohio, 1972, 255–88.

—— *Madness in Society. Chapters in the Historical Sociology of Mental Illness*, London, 1968.

—— 'People, disease and emotion: some new problems for research in medical history', *Bulletin of the History of Medicine* 41 (1967): 5–23.

—— 'Social attitudes to irrationality and madness in seventeenth and eighteenth century Europe', *Medical History* 18 (1963): 220–40.

Rousseau, G.S., 'Science and the discovery of the imagination in Enlightenment England', *Eighteenth Century Studies* 3 (1969): 108–35.

Rushton, P., 'Lunatics and idiots: mental disability, the community and the Poor Law in North-East England, 1600–1800', *Medical History* 32 (1988): 34–50.

Schappert, David G., 'Selected bibliography of primary materials', in Christopher Fox (ed.), *Psychology and Literature in the Eighteenth Century*, New York, 1987, pp. 303–45.

Scull, Andrew, 'From madness to mental illness: medical men as moral entrepreneurs', *European Journal of Sociology* 16 (1975): 219–61.

—— (ed.), *Madhouses, Mad-doctors, and Madmen: the Social History of Psychiatry in the Victorian Era*, London, 1981.

—— *Museums of Madness*, London, 1979.

Sells, A.L. Lytton, *Thomas Gray: His Life and Works*, London, 1980.

Sena, John F., *A Bibliography of Melancholy, 1600–1800*, London, 1970.

Sherbo, Arthur, *Christopher Smart: Scholar of the University*, East Lansing, 1967.

Showalter, Elaine, *The Female Malady: Women, Madness and English Culture, 1830–1980*, New York, 1985.

Skultans, Vieda, *English Madness: Ideas on Insanity, 1580–1890*, London, 1979.

Smith, Nigel, *Perfection Proclaimed: Language and Literature in English Radical Religion, 1640–1660*, Oxford, 1988.

Spacks, Patricia M., *Imagining a Self: Autobiography and Novel in Eighteenth-Century England*, Cambridge, Mass. and London, 1976.

Spillane, J., *The Doctrine of the Nerves*, London, 1981.

Szasz, Thomas S., *The Manufacture of Madness*, London, 1972.

—— *The Myth of Mental Illness*, London, 1972.

Tomalin, C., *The Life and Death of Mary Wollstonecraft*, Harmondsworth, 1977.

Wing, J.K., *Reasoning About Madness*, London, 1978.

Wright, John P., 'Association, madness, and the measures of probability in Locke and Hume', in Christopher Fox (ed.), *Psychology and Literature in the Eighteenth Century*, New York, 1987, pp. 103–27.

INDEX